WITHDRAWN
WESLEYAN UNIVERSITY
LIBRARY

OTTO BUTZ

Of Man and Politics

AN INTRODUCTION TO
POLITICAL SCIENCE

RINEHART & COMPANY, INC., New York

539551

Copyright © 1960 by Otto Butz
Printed in the United States of America
All rights reserved
Library of Congress Catalog Card Number: 60-8338

To the memory of
my teacher, friend, and colleague,

William Seal Carpenter

There are two things in which well-being always and everywhere exists. The first is to determine aright the aim and end of your actions. The second is to find out the actions which will best conduce to that end.

ARISTOTLE, *Politics*, Book VII.xiii,2.

The opposition of future to past or past to future is absurd. The future brings us nothing; it is we who in order to build it have to give it everything, our very life. But to be able to give, one has to possess; and we possess no other life, no other living sap, than the treasures stored up from the past and digested, assimilated, and created afresh by us. Of all the human soul's needs, none is more vital than this one of the past.

SIMONE WEIL, *The Need for Roots,* p. 51.

In the fabric of human events, one thing leads to another. Every mistake is in a sense the product of all the mistakes that have gone before it, from which fact it derives a sort of cosmic forgiveness; and at the same time every mistake is in a sense the determinant of all the mistakes of the future, from which it derives a sort of cosmic unforgiveableness.

GEORGE F. KENNAN, *American Diplomacy, 1900–1950,* p. 50.

Preface

THIS BOOK IS INTENDED to serve as an introduction to the principles, institutions, and practices of government and politics. Because the book is introductory, I have tried to make it comprehensible to the typical beginning student by defining all terms and presenting essential background information. Because the study of government and politics is one that a person may enter upon at various stages of his life, I have tried to present ideas and questions that any adult will find challenging.

The adage about not losing sight of the forest for the trees applies as much in the study of politics as elsewhere. For as basic to our discipline as facts about politics in themselves are, their ability to evoke wider interest and contribute to our political enlightenment depends always upon how relevant they can be made to our larger situation as human beings.

All too often, particularly at the introductory level of political study, we tend to neglect this imperative. While exposing the student to long and detailed chapters of information, we fail to provide sufficiently challenging perspectives to enable him to appropriate what he is learning as a living part of his own intellectual and moral experience. As a result, much of the potential value of the information presented is frequently lost to the student and he either becomes bored or turns away from political science altogether.

In the pages that follow I have attempted to guard against this danger. To do so I have sought to depict politics not only as a subject of scientific study but, at the same time, as a continuing human drama in which all of us—whether we know it or not —are inescapably involved. My purpose, that is, has been not only to introduce the reader to an array of political facts but, in so doing, to stimulate him to reflect upon those facts in their most meaningful possible philosophical, historical, and analytical contexts.

I am aware that this descriptive-interpretive approach is not without its price. I have had to be highly selective in my presentation of materials; and I have at many points felt it advisable to introduce my own views. Though I have taken care to explain and qualify these intrusions of subjectivity, I am certain to have left myself open to a good deal of justified criticism. Yet I trust that these disadvantages will not be found altogether prohibitive. After all, whatever biases in selection and interpretation there may be, there are always the instructor, the other readings, and the students' own common sense to set them straight.

After an introductory chapter defining and illustrating the meaning of politics, the book's organization follows the three major divisions in terms of which politics in the United States is usually studied. Part One traces the ideas, ideals, and objectives that philosophically and historically underlie our twentieth-century politics; Part Two describes how these ideas, ideals, and objectives are applied in the governmental structures and political processes of the United States, Great Britain, France, Germany, the Soviet Union, and the underdeveloped countries; and a concluding chapter examines some of the key aspects of present-day international politics, with particular reference to the problems of American foreign policy. A selected bibliography appears at the end of every chapter, and there are bibliographical notes at the back of the book.

It has been my personal conviction in this undertaking that what self-knowledge is to the individual as an individual, knowledge of politics is to the individual as a member of his society: the greater a man's command of such knowledge, the more intelligently he is able to participate in the management of his society's affairs, and the more fully he is likely to realize his dignity as a free and morally responsible citizen. To the extent that I may have succeeded in communicating this vital relevance of political knowledge, I will consider the book to have served its main purpose.

O.B.

Princeton, N.J.
January, 1960

Contents

« INTRODUCTION »

The Meaning
of Politics

« 1 »

The Challenge
of Man's Freedom

Man and Society

WHEREIN, AMONG ANIMALS, lies the human species' greatest uniqueness? It lies, above all, in the unique extent to which man is born with the need and ability to decide his own actions. In humanity's confrontation with this challenge of shaping its own destinies are rooted both its tragic vulnerabilities to anxiety and failure as well as its vast opportunities for hope and achievement.

Man's freedom to decide his own way of life is by no means absolute. On the one hand, he is confined in his actions to his given time and place. On the other, he must accept the nature with which his human heredity has endowed him: he must eat; he is driven to reproduce himself; and he must die. These facts place severe limits upon man's freedom. Yet what use he makes of his inherited faculties, how he provides for the satisfaction of his biological needs, and how he comes to grips with his earthly environment are matters in which man not only *can* reflect and choose, but *must* reflect and choose.

From his unique ability and need to direct his own development derive man's equally unique dimensions as a *social* animal. Among other species, survival and fulfillment result largely from the operation of more or less unwilled and unwitting instincts.[1] The distinguishing characteristic of *Homo sapiens* is that his way

3

of life is not as fully governed by his inherited impulses. Yet it is for that reason—as the price of his freedom of action, as it were —that man, unlike the other species, cannot chiefly rely on the dictates of his physical organism for his survival and fulfillment.

Of course, to make up for the much weaker direction of his innate drives, man possesses the incomparably richer gifts of his rationality and his capacity for moral character. But, at his birth, this human endowment is little more than a potential. For that potential to unfold, man must first learn how to use his rationality. He must be trained to develop his moral character. During the long years of infancy and childhood, while he is undergoing his crucial educational experience, he must be fed, clothed, and protected. And throughout his life the full exercise of his physical nature, his rationality, and his moral character is possible only in terms of constant and manifold relationships with his fellow man.

The most inclusive and continuous relationship in terms of which man pursues his fulfillment and survival—encompassing such more limited social arrangements as those of family, school, economic association, and club—is the relationship of *society*.[2] In the course of history man has lived and worked in a great many types of societies. Their guiding philosophies, organizational forms, and cultural symbols have varied widely. Even today they range from those of such highly developed industrial societies as the United States to those of such comparatively simple tribal communities as have been maintained by the aborigines of the Australian desert. Yet, however great the contrasts in the spirit and manner of these different societies, the ultimate purpose they have operated to serve has always and everywhere been the same. That purpose—a universal one because the need for it is rooted in human nature—has been to guide and organize the expression of man's inborn freedom in the interest of his survival and fulfillment.

Society and the Function of Politics

The carrying out of society's task of guiding and organizing the expression of man's freedom to reflect and choose is a highly complex matter. For purposes of analysis it may be said to in-

volve five major conditions.[3] Upon the extent to which these
conditions are successfully achieved depend a society's ability
to maintain itself and, in consequence, its effectiveness in further-
ing its members' survival and fulfillment.

First and most obviously, the individuals who make up a
society must so relate themselves to their environment that they
are able to reproduce, sustain, and protect themselves as physical
organisms. They must, for example, maintain some system of
economic production and distribution capable of providing their
minimum material needs. They must adjust to, or modify, such
circumstances as fertility of soil, climatic conditions, and the
actions of whatever neighbors they may have. And they must
maintain a ratio of births to deaths (and emigration to immigration) that will prevent them, on the one hand, from becoming extinct or too few to protect themselves, and, on the
other, from outrunning whatever food supplies their natural
resources and skills may be able to yield them.

Second, the members of a society must be joined in a
common basic way of looking at themselves and the world.
They must be able to understand, communicate, and work together as members of the same collectivity and in the name of
the same overriding collective interest. They must possess the
solidarity and unified direction that comes from commitment to
a common body of intellectual concepts, cultural symbols, and
emotional patterns. And they must share the belief that certain
ends, and the means of achieving those ends, are good, virtuous,
and desirable, while other ends and means are bad, immoral,
and to be avoided. They must, in short, be in agreement on
what usually are referred to as fundamentals.

Third, the members of a society must maintain an extensive
process of education. With each new generation, it has been
said, society is invaded by another wave of barbarians. Every
form of socially necessary behavior that they do not know by
instinct, these new recruits must be taught. They must have
instilled into them dedication to the ideals that hold the society
together and give it direction. They must be motivated and
taught to perform such socially essential roles as those of parents,
economic producers, teachers, administrators, doctors, and soldiers. And throughout their lives their adherence to what they

have learned as children and adolescents must be strengthened through constant testing against the standards and expectations of their fellows. For the more securely the disposition to socially constructive behavior is maintained as part of the individual's self-respect, the more stably society is able to function and the less it is compelled to achieve solidarity and co-operation through resort to coercion.

Fourth, a society must provide for the control of whatever forms of destructive behavior may threaten its harmonious functioning from within or without. Some antisocial conduct is likely to occur in all societies. It arises chiefly from the fact that the things people strive for are usually in scarce supply and, hence, tend to be the objects of more or less extreme competition and conflict. It is also caused by people's reactions to the disappointment of their material and social expectations. And it results, finally, from the fact that there are always in a society some individuals in whom the established values and behavior patterns are too weakly rooted to assure acceptable behavior. To protect the way of life of the collectivity against whoever would thus subvert it, a society must possess some type of police arrangements.

To the extent that any of these four conditions of a society's operation is not adequately performed, the collectivity in question becomes vulnerable to several types of danger. Its members may die out physically—the fate that in recent decades has all but eliminated the Bushmen of northern South Africa. It may internally disintegrate into anarchy or civil war, as occurred in pre-Communist China. Or it may be absorbed or destroyed from the outside by the actions of other societies, as happened to most of the native Indian communities of North America.

These destructive eventualities dramatize the fifth basic condition of a society's effective functioning: that it provide itself with some form of over-all management to assure the realization of the first four conditions. Those conditions, as we have seen, include economic and demographic balance, common goals and values, means of educating the young, and protection against internal or external threats. The process of overseeing and managing the various functions of a society is what in the broadest sense we mean by *politics*. The collective institutions, procedures, and policies by which this task is performed constitute what we call *government*. The term "state," finally, refers to a society whose members have come to feel a conscious need to manage their collective existence and who have equipped themselves with a government to carry out the task.

Politics and Government

The essential attribute of a state is the possession of the power and authority to enforce whatever rules for the life of the collectivity that may be decided upon. It is this supreme power and authority to make and enforce laws for and in the name of a political community that is called sovereignty. Yet, though sovereignty may if necessary be expressed through the use of force, it involves much more than merely the ability to compel. Its distinguishing characteristic, rather, is that it is an ultimate authority that the citizens of the state accept as legal and acknowledge themselves committed to abide by.

The political task of employing sovereign power for the management of a society's functioning must usually be performed through a complex process of accommodation of differences of interest and view among the individuals and groups concerned. Who is to have access to the legal power of making and enforcing decisions on behalf of the collectivity? On what conditions is such access to be allowed? By what procedures are political decisions to be arrived at and carried out? In the name of what philosophical principles and in pursuit of what political objectives is sovereign power to be operated? All of these questions must be decided through a constant process of bargaining and compromise in which everyone, usually alleging the best interests of the collectivity as a whole, tends to be striving for the most advantageous terms for himself.

The resulting drama is what in everyday parlance is quite correctly referred to as "politics." Yet this popular use of the term is justified only if one remembers always to look beyond the maneuverings of the process itself to the larger underlying purpose that it exists to serve. That purpose, of course, is to see to it that the conditions for the collectivity's sound functioning are constantly and adequately attended to.

The formal institutions through which a state attends to the conditions of its survival are customarily prescribed in a constitution, a philosophical and legal commitment regarding the political purposes and rules to be followed. A constitution usually provides for the performance of three distinct governmental functions. These are the making of laws, accomplished by some type of legislative institution; the administration and enforcement of laws, the responsibility of some form of executive; and the resolving of disputes between the law and individuals and groups who have come into conflict with it, the task of some kind of judiciary.

The allocation of responsibility among these three typical institutions, as well as the ways in which they are staffed and operated, varies widely from country to country. A legislature may come close to being all-powerful, as was the case in the French Fourth Republic; its chief function, as in Britain, may be to furnish the personnel for the executive branch and then either to support or to veto executive decisions; or, as in the Soviet Union, it may serve the quite different purpose of acting as an instrument of the executive for mobilizing public opinion and eliciting popular approval.

The role of the executive, for its part, may be supreme, as in the dictatorship of General Franco; it may be less than supreme though still dominant, as in the French Fifth Republic under General de Gaulle; or it may be required to share its responsibilities with an independent legislative and judicial branch, as in the United States. And a judiciary, finally, may be merely the dependent instrument of the executive, as in the Soviet Union; or it may function as freely and with as powerful an independent impact upon the course of public policy as does the American judicial system. The origins and implications of these and other features of governmental structure and operation are examined at some length in Part II below.

The Scope of Politics

Whenever government has functioned stably and securely, politics has tended to be understood rather narrowly as concerned with only a very few aspects of social life. The governmental ideal in such circumstances has generally been that of a more or less passive umpire, occupied with such minimal collective matters as the maintenance of a police force to watch over internal order and the collection of taxes to finance external defense. What has been assumed in situations of this kind has been that society progresses and remains secure almost automatically and as a matter of natural course.

Since this assumption represents an expression of confidence in man's inherent capacity for individual initiative and responsibility, it deserves to be deeply honored *as an ideal*. As much as we may thus honor it, however, we must face the fact that politics potentially extends to every aspect of social life. For, since there is no social action that under conceivable circumstances may not in some way affect a society's operation, the political process of managing society's over-all functioning may properly be concerned with all aspects of social life.

Exactly what aspects and how much of a society's life is actually subjected to active political management depends chiefly upon two kinds of circumstance. The one, as can be seen from the unprecedented growth of governmental intervention during World Wars I and II, is the condition of the state's external relations. The more threatened a country feels itself to be, and the greater the effort required to fend off such threats, the more extensively the various processes and relationships that constitute its life are likely to be governmentally supervised and, hence, brought within the domain of politics.

The other type of circumstance importantly affecting the extent to which a society's life is actively involved in politics hinges on this question: how well satisfied with the prevailing order of things are those who have effective access to the instruments of government? When, as happened in the United States during the depression of the 1930's, those who are politically dominant are discontented with the performance of society as traditionally constituted, the tendency is to extend the political management of the society so as to re-create a situation of general satisfaction. What happens when the sphere of active politics remains limited is simply the converse. That is, those who have the power to govern are satisfied with the operation of society as it is and believe that it will continue in that satisfactory condition without the extension of governmental intervention into any further aspects of its life.

To make these generalizations about the theoretical inclusiveness of politics is not to belittle the desirability of keeping politics and the role of government to a minimum in practice. The point is merely that, if politics be defined as a matter of over-all social management, it must be recognized to extend potentially to the entire realm of social relationships. If we want actual politics and the exercised role of government to be minimized, it does little good merely to say so or to look back nostalgically to the time when it was. The task, rather, is to work for the kind of conditions—including, above all, various types of *private* initiative and self-discipline—which will make it possible for people to live in harmony and according to their expectations without having to resort to a dominant role for government.

The Study of Politics

How should the subject matter of politics be intellectually organized for systematic study? If, as here suggested, politics be understood as concerned with the entire business of social management, what it involves may be analyzed most comprehensively in terms of four interrelated aspects. These are, first, the ends according to which society's functioning is to be ordered; second, the means society employs to implement its political ends; third, the physical and human environment in terms of which the chosen political ends and means must be made operative; and fourth, the historical traditions by which the choice of political ends and means is inevitably conditioned.

Politics as a matter of *ends* has to do with the ideas, ideals, and objectives according to which a society's relationships and processes are to be ordered. It is these ideas, ideals, and objectives that guide a society's individual and collective political behavior and become embodied in its political institutions. Without the unifying direction of such political ends, a society's collective life would be without purpose or cohesion. And without a knowledge of what in the case of a given society these ends are, the student of that society's politics could distinguish little more than seemingly meaningless action for action's sake. What sense, for example, could a stranger to American politics make of our system of separated executive and legislative powers, or of a law enacted by that system allocating a sum of public funds for foreign aid? Very little—unless he first understood the ideas and ideals of liberal democracy that are incorporated in the American governmental system and unless he was aware of the foreign policy objectives that the funds earmarked for foreign aid were designed to further.

Closely related to a society's political ideas, ideals, and objectives are the political *means* through which it hopes to implement its preferred way of life. These include most importantly the various governmental institutions and procedures already alluded to above. Where these political means are the product of uninterrupted historical evolution, as in Britain, they are accepted largely as a matter of custom. Where they originated as the outcome of successful revolutions—as in the United States—they are more or less precisely formulated in written constitutions.

The especial significance of these political means lies in the fact that in serving as a society's governmental instruments they also strongly affect the political objectives and policies that it is possible for government to pursue. In the now defunct French Fourth Republic, for example, the failure of two dozen cabinets to accomplish much more than to maintain the unstable *status quo* was a direct consequence of the constitutionally prescribed weakness of the French executive and the unchecked supremacy of the volatile French legislature. Comparable if less debilitating effects of governmental structure upon the determination and execution of policies can, of course, also be seen in the operation of American government. In the making of American foreign policy, for example, both the substance and the timing of decisions often seem as much dictated by the internal political bargaining necessitated by the separation of executive and legislative powers as by the known exigencies of America's international situation.

A third integral aspect of politics comprises the *environment* in terms of which the choice of political ends and means must be formulated and put into effect. What is a society's geographical location? How secure is it from its neighbors? How extensive and of what type are its natural resources? What is the level of its technology? What are the size and psychological condition of its population? What types of social stratification and power relationships prevail among its members?

A society's answers to these basic questions of environment represent the opportunities and limits, as it were, through and within which its political life may and must express itself. And though these environmental factors may be variously coped with —and so by no means fully *determine* the course of a society's political development—they are certain to leave upon it a most important conditioning imprint. It seems unlikely, for example, that the English would have achieved their unique successes as a nation-state, a world empire, and a parliamentary democracy, if Britain had not enjoyed the numerous environmental advantages deriving from its character and position as an island astride the sea lanes between the Old World and the New. Nor is it possible to understand the collapse of German Weimar democracy and the rise of Hitler without reference to Germany's weakened international situation, its grave social and economic crises, and the demoralization of its people following the German defeat in World War I.

What these and similar historical examples demonstrate, moreover, is that conditions of military security, cultural solidarity, social harmony, and economic stability tend to favor the successful development of liberal democratic government, whereas their absence tends strongly to discourage it. How telling such environmental discouragement may be is dramatically illustrated by the crises and failures that are currently besetting even the most dedicated efforts to implement liberal democratic political ends and means in the overpopulated, culturally fragmented, and economically underdeveloped new nations of Asia and Africa.

A fourth and final major focus upon which the study of politics must concentrate concerns the *historical traditions* by which a society's political ends, means, and environmental situation are always conditioned. To understand the politics of contemporary France, for example, one must constantly refer to that country's domestic and international experiences during and since the French people's glorious but politically disruptive

Revolution. Soviet totalitarianism, for its part, cannot be viewed as merely a matter of Communist ends, means, and environmental circumstances since 1917; its roots, rather, lie deep in five centuries of despotic centralization and submission to autocracy under the Russian czars. Nor is it possible to account in exclusively contemporary terms for many of the dominant characteristics of American politics. For here too, the legacies of such historical circumstances as the century of continental isolation, the frontier, and the successive waves of European immigration have left patterns of thought and action whose reality for present-day politics remains of the greatest significance. What can be said of the behavior of individuals must therefore be recognized as equally true of the behavior of societies as a whole: that our purposes, methods, and responses to our environment today are importantly (if most often unconsciously) affected by what we have been, done, and experienced in the past.

Because of these multiple and complex aspects of political reality, politics, as a subject of study, is necessarily both highly eclectic and unusually inclusive. Always, of course, from the point of view of its own proper focus on the function of society's over-all management, it must draw its information and insights from the humanities as well as from the whole body of the social sciences. In its concern with society's background and traditions, it must constantly look to the researches of historians and anthropologists. In its assessment of the role of environmental factors, it is heavily dependent upon the disciplines of geography, economics, demography, and psychology. In its analyses of the organizational aspects of politics, it must draw upon the work of constitutional lawyers, administrative experts, and sociologists. And for its understanding of political ideas, ideals, and objectives, it must turn to the writings of political ideologists, philosophers, and theologians.

In view of this many-sided and dynamic nature of its subject matter, the science of politics is at once the most challenging of the social sciences and, from the point of view of scientific systematization, the most trying. How can all that is involved in the various analytical aspects of politics be reduced to precisely formulated variables? How can the operation of such variables be properly treated and evaluated? Which of them, in

accounting for a specific political event, can be said to be
causes and which, effects? In terms of what concepts and theories
can different political events be most usefully compared? How
are political decisions and their consequences to be accurately
predicted?

Such problems of methodology have occupied researchers
and theorists in politics for more than two thousand years. Unfortunately, their final solution is far from agreed upon even
today.[4] Yet, difficult as is the extension and refinement of our
knowledge of politics, it is a task that demands our very best
intelligence and most determined effort. Particularly is this so
today, when a single political decision anywhere may vitally
affect the lives and fortunes of mankind the whole world over.

It is of course true that the mere possession of political
knowledge does not assure that it will be made use of, nor that
it will be used well. Though the political scientist may make his
suggestions, the uses of his work depend ultimately upon the
intelligence and moral sense of society as a whole.

Contemporary Politics in Historical Perspective

All human action, whether of individuals, societies, or the
groupings of kindred societies we call civilizations, is based upon
certain beliefs about man, history, and the universe. These beliefs, sometimes unspoken and sometimes elaborately formulated,
are incorporated in religion and literature, in social and economic custom, and in politics. What these beliefs chiefly accomplish is to provide man with ideas and ideals that will give
his life meaning and to suggest to him objectives in terms of
which life according to his ideas and ideals may successfully
be pursued.

The ideas, ideals, and objectives that have come to orient
the actions of more and more of the contemporary world are
rooted in twenty-five centuries of Western history. Throughout
their long evolution they have been based upon two fundamental
notions. The one has been the originally Greco-Roman belief
in the sovereignty of man's rational intellect. The other has been
the faith in man's spiritual relationship with an omnipotent,

loving God that first arose among the ancient Hebrews and early Christians. While these two basic notions have remained the very essence of Western civilization to the present day, each successive age, reflecting and responding to its own particular historical circumstances, has combined and applied them in its own characteristic way.

The dominant preoccupation of the feudal system of medieval Europe was with man's spirituality as inspired by the Scriptures and administered by the Catholic Church. Though the Greco-Roman valuation of man's speculative intellect was not repudiated altogether, it was assigned decidedly subordinate significance. At least as commanded by the pervasive voice of the universal Church, man was to seek his ultimate happiness in salvation in the world beyond and to exercise his rationality not for its own sake but as an instrument for the glorification of God.

During the five centuries since the end of the European Middle Ages this earlier subordination of rationality to other-worldly spirituality has been progressively reversed. The dominant Western view today urges man's fulfillment here and now. While it by no means denies man's spirituality, it sees it less as a matter of his relationship to God than as an ethical conscious-ness directing the use of his rationality in the service of his fellow man. The guiding inspiration of this modern Western world view is the ideal of maximized welfare here on earth. Its most insistent moral principle is the imperative that nature, human institutions, and even man himself be made to serve this ideal as efficiently and fully as possible.

It has been this philosophy of maximized secular welfare that has guided and disciplined modern man in all of his unique material and organizational achievements. By inspiring the interplay of scientific research, new forms of energy, in-creasingly productive technological means, and ever more rapid methods of communication, it has enabled even the masses of modern men to attain standards of wealth, health, leisure, and luxury undreamed of in all past ages. And, operating simultane-ously in the area of human relations, it has furnished the organizing principle which more than any other single factor has determined the structure of institutions and patterns of behavior in every phase of modern life. How else, for example, to understand the past century's experimentation with economic systems than as a sustained attempt to devise the most efficient possible mechanisms of production and distribution in the interest of the greatest achievable common good? How else to interpret the long and continuing struggle for government of, by, and for the people than as the effort of modern man to assure his maximized welfare (as he himself might see it) by making himself the master of his own political destiny? What has clearly been expressed in these and related developments has been the enthronement of the ideal and practice of the greatest possible secular well-being as the highest modern absolute.

In origin, this modern ethic was a wholly Western phenomenon. More and more, however, as can be seen from events throughout the non-Western world during the past quarter century, it has been adopted by the remainder of mankind as well. And to the extent that it has, its effect has been to orient men everywhere to the same welfare-minded way of life, to subject them to essentially the same processes of democratization and industrialization, and, in view of the growing mutuality of the pursuit of this-worldly betterment, to involve them in one and the same interdependent global community.

Because this development has proceeded so rapidly and occasioned such far-reaching disruptions of earlier and more traditional ways of life, it has frequently resulted in the most painful social, cultural, and psychological dislocations. Because its organizational achievements have lagged behind its technological potentialities, it has led to unprecedentedly destructive international conflicts and today threatens us with the possibility of a nuclear holocaust. And because it has occurred in very dissimilar historical situations and at very different tempos, it has been explained and urged in terms of very divergent and often warring ideologies. Yet none of these circumstances, however overwhelming for those immediately involved, can be understood or evaluated in and of themselves. Their larger significance, rather, has been as accompaniments of what has shown itself to be an irresistible universal striving: the determination of peoples everywhere—in greater or lesser disregard of whatever cultural and moral cost may be involved—to fashion for themselves the most fulfilling this-worldly utopia of which contemporary technological and organizational know-how may be capable.

The practical working out of this revolutionary dynamic has confronted modern man with two sets of fundamental problems. First and foremost, it has raised innumerable questions as to the *means* by which the ideal of maximized this-worldly welfare might most successfully be implemented. On what territorial scale should political units be established? By what principles of authority should they be regulated? Should they be operated on a unitary, federal, or confederative basis? In terms of what manner of decision-making arrangements should men under different conditions govern themselves? By what administrative techniques can the decisions of government be most efficiently carried out? What types of social relationships are the most conducive to harmony and welfare? What are the most efficient and equitable possible productive and distributive arrangements? Should major changes in society's way of life be carried out by evolutionary or revolutionary means? By what rules and procedures can politics be best conducted internationally?

Questions such as these have inspired the West's great classics of social, economic, and political literature and continue as the chief preoccupation of our social scientists to the present day. Until recently, indeed, it was widely held that this type of question represented the *only* problems raised by the unfolding of modern civilization's dominant ethic. Once these organizational problems were solved, it was assumed, want, disharmony, and oppression would once and for all be eliminated and utopia on earth be permanently secured.

In the past several decades, however, increasing attention has been drawn to a second set of modern problems. The concern of these is not with the *means* of man's maximization of his this-worldly welfare but, rather, with its possible consequences for his *ends*. What, for example, is likely to be the effect on a man's attitudes and behavior if—as our modern utopia envisages—he is guaranteed a satisfactory condition of social and economic well-being? Can he still be counted upon to give the high level of effort that the maintenance of the greatest possible economic productivity demands? Will he still engage in the

vigilant participation in public affairs that the sound functioning of a democratic political system is known to require? And,
in the face of industrial society's awesome technological achievements and growing social and economic pressures, can he still
be relied upon to maintain and exercise his own individual
conscience? If he cannot, by whom and by what standards is
democratic society's operation to be guided and its performance
judged? [5]

These more recently discovered psychological and cultural
problems and the previously mentioned more familiar organizational tasks are, of course, closely interrelated. For, on the one
hand, we are free to exercise our individual initiative and conscience only in so far as society's organized pursuit of this-
worldly welfare succeeds in liberating us from material and
physical insecurities. On the other, however, it is only to the
extent that the initiative and conscience of the individual are
preserved that we are collectively able to sustain our democratic and industrial processes and prevent them from being
used to enslave us in political totalitarianism or to destroy us in
nuclear war.

Taken together, that is to say, these problems pose contemporary civilization's most fundamental and universal challenge: *how to organize man's greatest possible welfare as a
member of society, while leaving him with the greatest possible
moral autonomy as an individual human being.* To find ways of
coping with the countless concrete issues in which this basic
contemporary challenge is expressed is the difficult and never-
ending business of twentieth-century politics. To understand its
origins, analyze its implications, and discover how it is being
variously confronted is the major task of present-day political
science.

SELECTED BIBLIOGRAPHY

CASSIRER, ERNST. *An Essay on Man,* New York, Doubleday Anchor Book A-3,
    1956.
DAVENPORT, RUSSELL W. *The Dignity of Man,* New York, Harper, 1955.
EASTON, DAVID. *The Political System,* New York, Knopf, 1953.
LEVY, MARION J., JR. *The Structure of Society,* Princeton, N.J., Princeton Uni-
    versity Press, 1952, Chap. 4, "The Functional Requisites of Any Society,"
    pp. 149–197.

MORISON, ELTING E., ed. *The American Style,* Essays in Value and Performance, New York, Harper, 1958, Pt. I, pp. 3–310.

ODEGARD, PETER H. "Politics: A New Look at *Leviathan,*" in Lynn White, Jr., *Frontiers of Knowledge,* New York, Harper, 1956, pp. 94–115.

TRUMAN, DAVID B. *The Governmental Process,* New York, Knopf, 1955, Pt. I, "Groups in the Political Process," pp. 3–110.

Max Weber: The Theory of Social and Economic Organization, Edited with an Introduction by Talcott Parsons, New York, Oxford University Press, 1947, Pt. III, "The Types of Authority and Imperative Co-ordination," pp. 324–429.

PART ONE

The Development of Liberal Democratic Political Ideas, Ideals, and Objectives

« 2 »

The Legacy
of the Greek City-State

The Historical Background

THE EARLIEST OF THE CULTURAL ANCESTORS to whom one must turn in tracing the development of Western political ideas, ideals, and objectives are the philosophers of ancient Greece. Such, indeed, were the way of life and collective experiences of these people that in a period of less than a century—from about 400 to 300 B.C.—they were able to think through the purposes and problems of politics with a penetration that has never since been surpassed.

The center of this ancient Greek probing into the life of man in society was the *polis,* or city-state, of Athens. The chief reason for Athens' pre-eminence in this field lay in the richness of the city's general cultural life, combined with the fact that the Athenians had evolved for themselves the most democratic system of citizen rule ever to exist up to that time. According to that system, every Athenian male over the age of twenty-five (with the exception of slaves and aliens) was eligible for jury duty; was entitled to participate in the meetings of the supreme political body, the Assembly or *Ecclesia;* and enjoyed the right to be elected to the Assembly's various executive councils. It was only natural, therefore, that these unusual opportunities for day-to-day political practice engendered in the Athenians an inquiring concern with the theory of politics as well, and that Athens, as the world's first democracy, also became the first community to develop a well-articulated political philosophy.

The proud self-awareness and confidence of Athenian democracy are nowhere better illustrated than in Pericles' famous Funeral Oration, commemorating Athenian soldiers who had fallen in a military campaign in the year 431 B.C. Speaking as the city's most popular democratic leader, at a time when Athens' fortunes were at their highest, Pericles interpreted Athenian political ideals and realities in ringing words:

> Our form of government does not enter into rivalry with the institutions of others. We do not copy our neighbors, but are an example to them. It is true that we are a democracy, for the administration is in the hands of the many and not of the few. But while the law secures equal justice to all alike in their private disputes, the claim of excellence is also recognized; and when a citizen is in any way distinguished, he is preferred to the public service, not as a matter of privilege, but as the reward of merit. Neither is poverty a bar, but a man may benefit his country whatever may be the obscurity of his station. There is no exclusiveness in our public life. . . . An Athenian does not neglect the state because he takes care of his own affairs; and even those of us who are engaged in business have a fair idea of politics. We alone regard a man who takes no interest in public affairs, not as a harmless, but as a useless character; and if few of us are originators, we are all sound judges of policy. . . . To sum up, I say that Athens is the school of Hellas, and that the individual Athenian in his own person seems to have the power of adapting himself to the most varied forms of action with the utmost versatility and grace. This is no passing and idle word, but truth and fact; and the assertion is verified by the position to which these qualities have raised the state. . . .[1]

If this Periclean ideal of democracy had proved realizable in actual practice, the Athenians would hardly have been moved to formulate the essentials of politics as searchingly as they did. What provided the final impetus to their introspection and analysis—as it so often does, whether in politics, economics, or love—was crisis and failure. In the history of Athens, indeed, this crisis and failure came so swiftly that—to judge from the recorded intellectual reactions to it—it was experienced as one of the most intensely felt shocks in the history of civilization.

The high point of Athenian political success, as reflected in this Periclean oration, had come between the years 500 and 431 B.C. It was at the beginning of this period that full Athenian democracy had finally been established, that the Athenians had become a major commercial and naval power, and that Athens had assumed leadership in the long struggle to block the Persians in their efforts to penetrate from Asia Minor into the mainland and islands of the Greeks. In exercising this leadership Athens had taken the initiative in establishing the great alliance of Greek city-states known as the Delian Confederacy, with its headquarters and treasury on the island of Delos. The alliance had served its purpose, the Persian threat had gradually subsided, and, in the course of time, many of Athens' former allies wished to terminate the confederate arrangement and reassert their full independence. But the Athenians refused to yield. Instead, in 454 B.C., they moved the treasury of the Delian Confederacy to Athens and converted the former alliance into a tribute-paying Athenian empire.

The Athenians succeeded in maintaining their rule over Greece and the area of the Aegean Sea for some twenty years. Finally, however, under the leadership of their traditional enemy, the authoritarian and agricultural state of Sparta, all of the Athenians' foes and former subjects banded together against them. The resulting conflict, the so-called Peloponnesian War, broke out in 431 B.C. and lasted twenty-seven years. When it was at last over and Athens had capitulated, Greek manpower had been decimated, dozens of Greek cities lay in ruins, and the Greeks' civic morality and political self-confidence were at a low from which they never again wholly recovered.

It was the experience of this collapse that prompted the reflection and theorizing that has come to be known as Greek political philosophy. And it was because the collapse was so far-reaching that the analyses it inspired dealt not merely with the particulars of Athenian politics but saw through to the more basic purposes and problems of human living together every-where and at all times.

On the Breakdown of Athenian Democracy

The very first precondition for being able to generalize from one's experiences is that one be able accurately to describe them and see them in some measure of historical perspective. The man who performed this task most outstandingly in regard to the political collapse of ancient Greece was the Athenian historian, Thucydides (455–400 B.C.). In his great work, *The Peloponnesian War,* Thucydides recorded the events of his time with a feeling for essentials that leaves his descriptions as interesting today as they were when first written more than two thousand years ago.

On the subject of the impact of the Peloponnesian War upon Athenian civic morale, for example, Thucydides penned such perceptive and hard-hitting passages as the following:

> With the growth of the revolutionary spirit stratagems became more ingenious and methods of revenge more extravagant. Words lost their familiar meaning. A new set of circumstances demanded a new use of terms. So now the reckless fanatic became the "loyal party man." Cautious statesmanship was "a cloak for cowardice"; moderation "the weakling's subterfuge," and intelligence was written off as "ineffective." Act like a maniac and you were styled "a real man." Walk warily and your fellow-conspirators set you down as a renegade. The hectoring bully never failed of a hearing, and any criticism of him was suspect. Claims of party took precedence over family ties; for the partisan knows no restraints of conscience or decency. And how should he, seeing that associations of this type are based on anti-social ambitions, and their strength springs not from the moral law but from partnership in crime. . . .
>
> The compelling motive behind all this was Power, pursued partly for notoriety's sake; partly for its material rewards; and the element of competition gave an added zest to the game. It mattered little what plausible slogans political leaders might adopt. One side might talk of "Aristocracy's genius for compromise"; the other of "Democracy's egalitarian principles." But such lip service could not disguise the truth. It was the control of the commonwealth that both sides coveted, and these rivals stuck at nothing in the struggle for power. In their lust for revenge all conventions of justice and patriotism were forgotten. It was enough if their party-

spite could be gratified by some savage sentence or violent *coup d'état*.²

And how had the war that led to this disastrous state of affairs come about? Thucydides answered this question from two points of view. Politically speaking, he found, "What made the war inevitable, though no one openly admitted it, was that Athens was becoming too powerful and her opponents were afraid of her." From a moral point of view, on the other hand, he interpreted what had happened in terms that were deeply rooted in Greek culture and religion: democratic Athens had abandoned the traditional Greek virtue of *sophrosune* (restraint and self-control), had indulged in the fatal sin of *hubris* (pride), and had inexorably harvested the retributive justice of *nemesis*.

A second type of Athenian intellectual reaction to the crisis of the times was that of the itinerant teachers known as Sophists (*Wise Men*). Though most of these were little more than instructors in what in our own day has become known as the art of "how to win friends and influence people," a few established themselves as serious-minded political critics. One of these, a man named Isocrates (436–338 B.C.), directed a number of letters to his fellow citizens in which he told them that unless they exercised greater political responsibility and abandoned their policy of imperialism, their city was certain to perish.

> You have no breadth of view [Isocrates warned]. You do not give equal attention to the men who address you, but really listen only to those who support your desires. If you truly wished to find out what is best for the country, you would listen more to those who oppose you than to those who try to please you. How can men decide wisely without giving an unbiased hearing to both sides? But you—you think those better friends of the people who dole out money to them than those who serve the state disinterestedly. . . . The masses like better a person who flatters them than one who really benefits them. They would rather lose with a man who smiles at everybody than profit with a man who is aloof. If they like someone they will forgive all faults and mistakes. . . . I know that it is dangerous to oppose you and although this is a free government there is no real freedom of speech, but none the less I am going to speak out. I tell you we should make peace with all mankind and stop setting our hearts upon ruling the sea. Once, we

recognized that it is not just for the stronger to rule over the weaker, as indeed we still recognize it in private life. But apart from that I say that such power is not to the advantage of the state. It depraves all who have it and all who seek it. They are led on until they even lay waste the land of those they conquer and rob them of part of it, even disperse them from their homes. . . . A rich and powerful democracy cannot endure. . . . The only sure foundation for a nation's prosperity is a religious regard for the rights of others. . . .[3]

A further type of reaction to the social and political disintegration of the Greek city-state was that of the Athenian moralist, Socrates (469–399 B.C.). Whereas Isocrates appealed to the citizenry of Athens in the mass, Socrates' formula for civic survival aimed at the self-improvement of the individual. His technique for such self-improvement was what has since become famous as "Socratic reasoning"—the frank questioning of one's basic assumptions and beliefs with a view to arriving at true wisdom. Such reasoning, Socrates was convinced, could accomplish two things. First, it could aid men to rise above the superficial and incidental to a knowledge of essentials, including an understanding of what Socrates called "the good." And second, in thus freeing men from enslavement to prejudice, ignorance, and vanity, it could make them more tolerant and co-operative members of the community.

In devoting himself to the person-to-person teaching of his message, Socrates' honesty and profundity won him the enthusiastic devotion of the best young minds of his day. Yet in pursuing his humble and independent course, Socrates successively alienated almost every important political faction of the times. Finally, a few years after the end of the Peloponnesian War, he was brought to trial and sentenced to death on trumped up charges of impiety and corrupting Athenian youth.

Although his friends urged him to flee into exile, Socrates insisted on staying in order to prove his loyalty as an Athenian even at the cost of his life. Yet before his poisoning by hemlock was carried out, he took the opportunity of subjecting the corrupt jury that had sentenced him to a speech that for its moral courage has remained a classic of Western civilization to the present day:

No, my friends, we must take a hopeful view about death; and you should bear one truth in mind. Alive or dead, no ill can touch a good man. His affairs are in the gods' keeping. So what has come to me is no accident. To be dead and quit of this troublous life is quite clearly for my good. That is why my conscience did not seek to divert me and why I have no serious quarrel either with those who brought this charge or with those who passed this verdict. Something different, of course, was in their minds. They thought to do me a mischief, and there they were wrong. But one favor, please. Some day my sons will grow up and they may well show signs of caring for money or suchlike more than they care for character. Then will be the time to have your revenge. Be as hard on them as I have been on you; and, if they fancy themselves when really they have nothing to fancy, you must abuse them just as I have abused you, for setting their hearts on the wrong things and misconceiving their own worth. We shall then have no cause to complain of our treatment, I and my sons. But enough. It is time to be going—I to death, you to your lives; and which of us goes to the better part, no one but God can tell.[4]

Plato's Republic

The example and tragic death of Socrates played an important part in inspiring the political ideas of another prominent Athenian, Socrates' friend and disciple, Plato (427–347 B.C.). But whereas Thucydides had responded to the crisis of the period as a historian, Isocrates as a critical commentator, and Socrates as a moralist, Plato, finally, advanced the diagnosis of Greek politics to the level of a truly systematic philosophy.

The son of a family of Athenian aristocrats, Plato as a youth had intended to follow in the footsteps of his fathers with a career in some branch of his city's public service. In the turbulent circumstances of the times, however, and especially after the execution of his revered teacher, Socrates, Plato had concluded that "now that Athens was no longer ruled by the manners and institutions of our forefathers" and "the whole fabric of law and custom [was] going from bad to worse at an alarming rate," a career in politics for an honest man was impossible. He therefore undertook instead—except for two brief forays into practical affairs as adviser to the rulers of the city-state of Syracuse—to devote his energies to studying "in what way this situation might be amended and, in particular, the whole organization of the state." It was in carrying out this purpose that he established his famous school of philosophical and political studies, the Academy, and, as textbooks for his students' training, wrote his great dialogues on society and the state.

The best known and most provocative of these works, written in Socratic conversational form, is Plato's *Republic*. *The Republic* begins as a discussion of the question, "What is justice?" and is carried out in the form of an exposition of an allegedly ideal state. In actual intention and content, however, it is less an outline of a utopia than a statement of Plato's views of the philosophical and technical foundations of politics in general. Contemporaries of his, working in the physical sciences, were attempting to formulate the basic concepts and relationships of space, time, and matter; Plato hoped to accomplish the same thing for the phenomena of ethics and government which, taken together, the Greeks called politics.

In launching *The Republic* as a consideration of the meaning of justice, Plato's first step is to reject as superficial and untenable all definitions that describe justice merely as the giving to every man what is due him or the obeying of laws. Plato's point in this initial discussion is that justice cannot be defined simply as the *doing* of any specific activity or the *refraining* from any activity. Rather, he maintains, justice— whether in individuals or in political systems—is always a matter of relationship, of the relationship to one another of the various elements of which individuals or political systems are composed.

After establishing this relational nature of justice, Plato shifts his analysis from the problem of defining the just individual to a consideration of the just state. His justification for this change of focus is that the state is in essence merely the individual on a larger scale and that if one understands the nature of the relationship that constitutes justice in the state, one also understands it in the individual. Indeed, he maintains, the precondition for an individual to be able to live a just life is the prior existence of a justly organized state in which he can play his proper role.

As does every political philosopher, Plato approached his undertaking with certain values in mind according to which he believed human relations should be organized. In Plato's case these were two in number. One was his conviction that the highest purpose of human life, to which all else should be subordinated, was the exercise of man's faculty for rational contemplation. The other was his belief that the essential precondition for the fullest possible exercise of man's contemplative intellect was his membership in a stably organized political community.

In proceeding with his blueprint for such a community, Plato found it necessary to make certain assumptions about society and human nature. Society he defined as a system of human interdependence in terms of a division of labor intended to make possible a fuller life for everyone concerned. More specifically, he suggested, there were three categories of essential tasks upon the performance of which society's operation depended and among which the activities of its members had therefore to be allocated: economic tasks involved in supplying the society's material wherewithal; military tasks required by the need for defense; and last and most important, the task of governing.

Human nature, in turn, Plato assumed to be characterized by what he called the three principles of appetite, spirit, and rationality. In some measure, at least, all three of these principles were operative in everyone. Yet in everyone, he maintained, one of the three tended to predominate. That is, there were people most inclined to material pursuits and pleasures; others who liked to do things in which they exercised their gift for spiritedness and physical courage; and still others who were happiest and performed best when using their rational faculties. From this fact, as Plato saw it, there followed two imperatives. The first was that every individual use whatever rationality he possessed to keep his predominating principle—whichever it might be—in harmony with the other two. And the second was that everyone engage in the category of occupation for which he was innately best endowed and in which he would therefore find greatest personal satisfaction and contribute most usefully to society's life as a whole.

With these imperatives, deduced from his values and his assumptions about society and human nature, Plato returns to his point of departure—the question of the meaning of justice. Justice, he asserts, is the condition achieved when people are selected, trained, and employed to perform society's necessary functions in such a way that everyone is doing the job for which nature has best fitted him. The just state, therefore, is the state that properly selects, trains, and maintains its citizens so as to implement this condition. And the just individual is the individual who is able to fit into such a system of interdependent common effort because the basic elements of his own personality are in a condition of similarly integrated harmony.

Plato's more specific suggestions for the organization of such a state follow closely from this definition of justice. His most fundamental provision is that the state's population be grouped into three classes, corresponding to the three types of human personality and the three types of work that must be done. The three classes he has in mind are the class of manual workers and merchants, the soldier class, and the class of philosopher-governors. Allocation to these three classes is to be based on successive examinations and is to be open to men and women alike. Those discovered to be best fitted for manual work and commerce (regardless of what class their parents belonged to) will be the first to be selected and will comprise the class whose natural and necessary job it is to provide society's economic needs. Those with a predominant aptitude for soldierly activities will be given longer training and, when their education has reached the limits of their natural ability, will join the class that Plato calls the state's auxiliaries, that is, those who aid the government in defending the state and maintaining internal order. Those, finally, with the richest inborn endowments of character and intellect will continue in the educational process into almost middle age and will then graduate into the third and most important class, that of the state's philosopher-governors.

To the education of the class of economic producers, Plato devotes little attention. The inference is that they may be left to the way of life that people concerned with manual labor and commerce have always engaged in everywhere. Since the most gifted members of this class have been taken out and absorbed into the two higher classes, the remainder may be safely permitted to do what comes natural to them. Helped in their adjustment to their humble position by a few imaginative propagandistic myths—"medicinal lies," as Plato calls them—they may be expected to play their part in the larger order of things happily and without protest.

Plato's chief concern in *The Republic* is with the two highest classes, and especially with the men and women who are to serve as the state's philosopher-governors. The problem in regard to these latter is to assure their continued moral integrity as rulers and to avoid conflicts between them and the remainder of the citizenry. The only dependable method of assuring that these preconditions for sound leadership of the state may prevail, Plato insists, is that the philosopher-governors, as well as their auxiliaries, be forbidden both private possessions as well as family ties. Their only fulfillment is to be in the pursuit of wisdom and in service to the state.

The one seeming inconsistency in the monastic, communal life prescribed for the members of Plato's elite is that they are to be permitted to beget children. Yet this is not intended by Plato as a concession to them as individuals. His reasoning, rather, is that since these people represent the most talented group in the state, it would be a grave loss to be deprived of their presumably gifted progeny. However, mating among the philosophers and auxiliaries is to be strictly impersonal and planned by the state. Once their children are born, they are to be taken from their mothers, raised in state-run nurseries, and considered offspring of the community as a whole.

Of equal concern to Plato as these precautions for maintaining his rulers' integrity is the planning of the educational process that is to cultivate their wisdom and public devotion in the first place. The main fare of their educational diet is to consist of mathematics and philosophy. For the rest, such literature, music, and art as they are exposed to is to be carefully supervised. Innovation, imagery, sensuality, or any other quality that might disturb the philosopher-governors' serenity are to be strictly deleted.

In the over-all plan of his work Plato presents two chief justifications for the special attention he devotes to the guardians of his state. The one, of course, is his conviction of their vital political necessity. For, as he says in Book V, "Until philosophers are kings, or the kings and princes of this world have the spirit and power of philosophy, and political greatness and wisdom meet in one, and those commoner natures who pursue either to the exclusion of the other are compelled to stand aside, cities will never have rest from their evils—no, nor the human race, as I believe. . . ." [5]

In their role as philosophers, on the other hand, Plato sees the activity of his guardians as nothing less than an end in itself. While he shows why and how they must earn their way, so to speak, by governing, he considers their ultimate justification to lie in their intellectual quest after knowledge of "the invariable, the immortal, and the true." For if, as he believes, man's greatest and unique gift is his faculty for rational contemplation, then clearly, those who are outstandingly endowed with this faculty should be given every opportunity to use and make the most of it.

Plato supports this philosophical self-justification of his guardians by resorting to the central feature of his metaphysics, his theory of the so-called hierarchy of forms. The foundation of this metaphysical theory is Plato's notion that all physical reality—whether a table, a plant, or a state—is only a particular and imperfect manifestation of a corresponding ideal essence, which Plato calls a form. The ordinary person, according to Plato, thinks and deals only in terms of visible reality's various outward manifestations; to penetrate to an understanding of the ideal forms behind them he has neither the ability, the training, nor the leisure. This abstract and pure type of knowledge is the domain, rather, of what we today call the scientific theorist, and what Plato thought of as the philosopher. And the highest type of such knowledge of the essentials behind visible reality, pursued by the most abstract thinkers of all—as in our own century by an Einstein—is the search for insights about the basic organizing principle underlying the operation of the whole universe. Knowledge concerning this ultimate challenge to man's intellect is what Plato conceived of as the highest possible type of human achievement. And the precondition for its being pursued, he insisted, was that those with the appropriate capabilities should be provided—as in his ideal state—with whatever special status, discipline, and leisure might be necessary.

In spite of the brilliance and profundity with which it is thus argued, *The Republic*'s blueprint for political utopia is generally rejected as highly unrealistic as well as undesirable. It has long been recognized, however, that in the course of expounding his ideas, Plato posed a number of fundamental political questions that have proven of recurring concern to men everywhere. How *does* a society assure itself of statesmanlike political leadership? How *does* it maintain harmony among its different classes of citizens? How *does* it prevent demagogues from whipping up mass support for policies that in the end are certain to prove disastrous for the public interest? And how *does* it recruit and support a sufficient number of its intellectually most gifted citizens for the important work of scientific theorizing?

In Plato's view, the only assurance of adequately solving these problems was through total, state-directed regimentation. At the root of this extreme pessimism was, of course, Plato's disappointment with the failures of democracy that he had witnessed in his own city. Generalizing from this experience, he branded the masses as hopelessly incapable of seeing to their own and the state's welfare and denounced as a villain or fool the man "who thinks that wisdom is the discernment of the tempers and tastes of the motley multitude, whether in painting or music, or, finally, in politics. . . . For when a man consorts with the many . . . necessity . . . will oblige him to produce whatever they praise. And yet the reasons are utterly ludicrous which they give in confirmation of their own notions about the honorable and the good." [6] Finally, Plato predicted, the masses' irresponsible obsession with freedom and equality must inevitably lead to civil strife, anarchy, and, sooner or later, the need to resort to some type of dictatorship: ". . . the excess of liberty, whether in states or individuals, seems only to pass into excess of slavery. . . . And so tyranny naturally arises out of democracy, and the most aggravated form of tyranny and slavery out of the most extreme form of liberty." [7]

Whether or not this pessimistic generalization of Plato's is correct has never been definitely established. Even today, twenty-four centuries later, the final word on the stable workability of democratic government has not yet been spoken. Nevertheless, a number of economic and social developments that have occurred since Plato's time would seem to justify several at least tentative qualifications of the conclusions expressed in *The Republic*.

Perhaps most important have been the vast improvements that have been achieved in our means of production and, hence, in our power to raise general standards of living. Throughout the ages, one of the chief reasons for the masses' seeming stupidity and political unreliability has been their abject poverty. It has been largely because of this that they have been involved in constant class conflicts; that they have shown little interest in political principle for principle's sake; and that they have so frequently been ready to support whatever leaders that would promise them the quickest material or emotional satisfaction.

At least in the present-day Western democracies, this former economic plight of the masses is at last in process of being eliminated. On the one hand, our modern industrialism yields us a measure of productivity incomparably greater than has been available to any previous age. On the other, our increasingly democratized systems of distribution afford even the poorest groups in the population a stake in the existing order of things that they have never known before. And to the extent that this has occurred, the masses' social bitterness has steadily lessened and their cultural and political self-respect grown.

Moreover, though it undoubtedly continues to be true that the public dedication and political wisdom of democratically elected leaders often leave much to be desired, there is at least some indication that even this aspect of democracy may be changing. For with the rise of general levels of education, the standards by which elective candidates are judged show signs of becoming considerably more discriminating and attuned to the political jobs to be done. Furthermore, more and more of the actual operations of government are no longer the work of elected officials at all but, rather, of professional administrators who have been selected and trained for their specific functions. And though this development raises difficult problems of political responsibility of its own, it does tend to approximate the ideal of government by experts subscribed to by Plato.

That these and other recent developments were not anticipated in Plato's analysis does not convict the author of *The
Republic* of error in the diagnosis of his own society. It does
mean, however, that Plato's ideas must be constantly rethought
in the light of changing realities. Indeed, it has been as a
uniquely provocative challenge to such political rethinking that
Plato's work has through the centuries had its most worth-while
and lasting impact.

Aristotle's Politics

No less important for the development of Western political
thought than the writings of Plato has been the work of that
other outstanding philosopher of the Greek city-state, Aristotle
(384–322 B.C.). Born in northern Greece and some forty years
Plato's junior, Aristotle was educated in Athens at Plato's
Academy and subsequently spent a number of years as tutor to
the future Alexander the Great, son of King Philip of Macedon.
Once Alexander had succeeded to his father's throne and embarked upon his conquests, Aristotle returned to Athens, founded
his own school there, called the Lyceum, and devoted most of
the remainder of his life to teaching and writing.

As he shows in his best-known treatise on government, *The
Politics,* Aristotle's approach to the problems of man in society
was in terms of essentially the same basic values as those held
by Plato. Life's highest purpose, he believed, was the achievement of virtue; by this he meant morality; and morality, in turn,
he understood as consisting chiefly of the possession and exercise
of rationality. The full realization of virtue, so defined, he
thought to be possible only through membership in a just
(that is, rationally and morally organized) political community.

Underlying his belief that "man is a being meant for
political association" was one of Aristotle's fundamental philosophical assumptions. That assumption was that every species
of creature has its own unique potentiality; that this potentiality
consists above all of the function that it is by nature meant to
play in the universal scheme of things; and that every creature's
highest virtue lies in its completest possible fulfillment of its
inherent potentiality and function. In Aristotle's words: "All

things derive their essential character from their function and
their capacity. . . . The 'nature' of things consists in their end
or consummation; for what each thing is when its growth is
completed we call the nature of that thing, whether it be a man
or a horse or a family." [8]

The unique potentiality of man, Aristotle continued, is
his inborn ability to think. Man's greatest virtue, therefore, consists in his fullest possible exercise of his rational faculty. But
since man as an individual is not self-sufficient, the precondition
for his being able to make the most of his rational faculty is
that he participate in the organized system of interdependence
and morality of a *polis:* "Man, when perfected, is the best of
animals; but if he be isolated from law and justice he is the
worst of all. Injustice is all the graver when it is armed injustice; and man is furnished from birth with arms which are
intended to serve the purpose of moral prudence and virtue,
but which may be used in preference for opposite ends. That is
why, if he be without virtue, he is a most unholy and savage
being, and worse than all others in the indulgence of lust and
gluttony. Justice belongs to the *polis;* for justice, which is the
determination of what is just, is an ordering of the political
association." [9]

The force that makes for justice—whether in individual
behavior, human relations, or the state—Aristotle called the
element of rule or command. As he put it: "The element which
is able, by virtue of its intelligence, to exercise forethought,
is naturally a ruling and master element; the element which is
able, by virtue of its bodily power, to do what the other element
plans, is a ruled element, which is naturally in a state of slavery.
. . . In all cases where there is a compound, constituted of more
than one part but forming one common entity . . . a ruling
element and a ruled can always be traced." [10] And since Aristotle
understood the chief component of this ruling element to be
deliberative rationality, the central problem of politics, he believed, was to see to it that all of society's decisions were made
by those most highly endowed with the faculty of deliberative
rationality.

Having reached this conclusion, Aristotle might well have
followed the example of Plato's *Republic* and proceeded to

expound his own version of an ideal state. But he did not. For though his basic values and assumptions in many ways paralleled Plato's, his primary intention was not to depict politics as it should be, but to describe and analyze it as it actually was. First and foremost, that is to say, Aristotle's *Politics* is the work of a political scientist rather than a political philosopher.

Typical of Aristotle's greater attention to empirical realities was his refusal to accept Plato's rigid and simplified classification of human nature. He recognized, for example, that it was not possible simply to divide men into the two categories of those who have virtue and governing ability, and those who do not. In actual fact, he found, there was some virtue and some ability to make decisions in every man. The essence of government, he therefore maintained, was not, as Plato had implied, simply a matter of a relationship between a superior ruling few and an inferior obedient mass. What it involved, rather, were such more complex matters as the nature and purposes of constitutions, the location of supreme or sovereign political power, the type of governmental organs through which this sovereign power was exercised, and the question of who should staff the organs of government.

To understand politics in terms of this more practical perspective, Aristotle collected and analyzed examples of no fewer than 158 actual city-state constitutions. He examined these from two points of view. First, in how many of the citizens was supreme governing power vested? And second, for whose benefit was this supreme political power employed—for the benefit of those making the decisions, or in the interest of the whole community?

On the basis of these two criteria—the one numerical, the other qualitative—Aristotle concluded that there were essentially six types of constitutions: *monarchy* and *tyranny, aristocracy* and *oligarchy,* and *polity* and *democracy.* Monarchy, aristocracy, and polity he defined as pure forms of government, that is, constitutions in which sovereign power was used for the general welfare; tyranny, oligarchy, and democracy, in contrast, he held to be the respective corruptions of the pure forms because in them government was not employed for the good of the whole state, but merely in the interest of those in political control.

Thus, according to Aristotle's classification, where highest power was vested in a single person and used for the benefit of·the whole state, the constitution represented the pure form of monarchy; where one person ruled only for his own benefit, the constitution was a tyranny. Where a minority enjoyed sovereign power, its constitution was aristocratic if that power was used for the common good, but oligarchic if it was employed only in the interest of the governing minority. And similarly, where supreme power resided in the majority, the constitution was what Aristotle called a polity if government was dedicated to the interest of the whole state, but a democracy if the masses ignored the welfare of the minority and governed only for the benefit of themselves.

In analyzing these constitutional forms, Aristotle noted that there appeared to be an almost universal evolution from the rule of one or a few to government by the many, and from the pure (that is, public-spirited) types of constitutions to their corrupt counterparts. The trend to the corruption of constitutions, he believed, was attributable to the inherent human inclination to use power selfishly. The progressive extension of supreme power to the masses, on the other hand, he found to have not only a political but also a philosophical aspect. For it seemed to him always to involve a conflict between two different definitions of equality. One was the notion of absolute equality advanced by the poor majority; the other was the concept of proportional equality subscribed to by the rich minority.

The claim to absolute equality, Aristotle pointed out, was based upon the belief that a man's political rights derived from and were completely justified by the mere fact of his existence as a human being. The concept of proportional equality, in contrast, argued that those who possessed superior ability, family background, or wealth were thereby entitled to a corresponding measure of superior privilege in the government of the state. And since it was, of course, the majority, claiming absolute equality, that in a revolutionary showdown could bring to bear the greater physical force, the sovereignty of one or a few was fated sooner or later to be turned into government by and for a greater and greater number.

Ideally, Aristotle argued, government should be by those with the greatest virtue and, preferably, by one man—a monarch —whose virtue exceeded that of all the other members of the community combined. However, since such an individual rarely exists, the immediate problem was to secure government by the most virtuous citizens possible. Practically speaking, Aristotle maintained, this solution could best be achieved in the pure form of constitution that he had called polity, that is, through government by a majority ruling for the benefit of the whole state.

It was the central characteristic of a polity, as Aristotle defined it, that it sought to balance the conflicting claims to absolute and proportional equality by dividing constitutional power between the rich and wellborn and the poor and common. The rich and wellborn, Aristotle pointed out, in many cases in fact did possess the superior knowledge and culture that tend to go with greater leisure, education, and privilege. On the other hand, it could safely be presumed that the poor majority represented the greater measure of common sense. Being more numerous, moreover, they tended to be less easily corruptible than might be a single or minority sovereign. What therefore had to be done was to secure the best possible contribution from both elements in the community and to develop government by compromise between them.

Government by compromise, Aristotle maintained in one of his most famous insights, could most easily be achieved in a state that possessed a large middle class:

> Men who are in this condition are the most ready to listen to reason. Those who belong to either extreme—the over-handsome, the over-strong, the over-noble, the over-wealthy; or at the opposite end the over-poor, the over-weak, the utterly ignoble— find it hard to follow the lead of reason. . . . It is a further merit of the middle class that its members suffer least from ambition, which in both the military and civil sphere is dangerous to states. . . . A state aims at being, as far as it can be, a society composed of equals and peers; and the middle class, more than any other, has this sort of composition. . . . The middle classes enjoy a greater security themselves than any other class. They do not, like the poor, covet the goods of others; nor do others covet their possessions, as

the poor covet those of the rich. Neither plotting against others, nor plotted against themselves, they live in freedom from danger. . . . It is therefore the greatest blessing for a state that its members should possess a moderate and adequate property. Where some have great possessions, and others have nothing at all, the result is either an extreme democracy or an unmixed oligarchy; or it may even be—indirectly, and as a reaction against both of these extremes—a tyranny. Tyranny is a form of government that may grow out of the headiest type of democracy, or out of oligarchy; but it is much less likely to grow out of constitutions of the middle order, or those which approximate them.[11]

Even a society that possesses a strong middle class, Aristotle added, should take at least three basic political precautions: it should be generous and kind to its poor; it should keep access to political office open to all—but without pay, so that many of the poor will be excluded indirectly; and it should use education to instill in its citizenry the profoundest possible reverence for its constitution. A state that pursued such policies, Aristotle was confident, would prove as resistant to revolutionary disruptions as human intelligence could make it.

Limitations of Plato and Aristotle

In spite of Plato's and Aristotle's uniquely rich contributions to the political language and self-understanding of the ages that followed, their impact upon the political life of their own times proved negligible. Since they had focused their thinking so exclusively upon the ideal of the traditional Greek city-state, and since this political form had in fact shown itself to be no longer effectively restorable, it was inevitable that from the point of view of their immediate situation their work should seem largely irrelevant.

As we know in retrospect, the most urgent needs of the period were twofold. One was to replace the small-scale city-state with political units of a size and nature that could again assure their inhabitants of internal harmony and external security. The other was the need to develop philosophies of life and government that would offer a sense of self-respect and political participation not only to an aristocratic Greek minority, but to every man—rich and poor, intelligent and ignorant, Greek and non-Greek alike.

To neither of these challenges were Plato and Aristotle prepared to address themselves. Their attachment was to an essentially aristocratic way of life that both believed to be achievable only within the intimate community of the city-state, and only by their Greek countrymen. In Aristotle's words, "The Greek stock . . . possesses both spirit and intelligence; the one quality makes it continue free; the other enables it to attain the highest political development, and to show a capacity for governing every other people." [12]

Both Plato and Aristotle, it is true, urged that the condition of slavery—which extended to at least 30 per cent of the Greek city-state populations—be limited to those who were intellectually inferior and mitigated by the most humane treatment possible. And both expressed the hope that all Greeks might at last cease their destructive interstate wars and recognize themselves as one people.[13] Yet neither felt it compatible with his highest cultural ideals either to consider all men as equal or to advocate the development of any larger and more inclusive type of political unit. In the last analysis, that is, Plato and Aristotle remain the great champions of the classical Greek city-state—committed to its values and prepared to accept its limitations. And though this fact in no way detracted from the intellectual validity of their writings, it meant that they could offer little inspiration and guidance for the long period of political disorganization that followed upon the city-state's final breakdown.

SELECTED BIBLIOGRAPHY

DE BURGH, W. G. The Legacy of the Ancient World, London, Pelican, 1955, Vol. I.
EBENSTEIN, WILLIAM. Political Thought in Perspective, New York, McGraw-Hill, 1957, Chap. 1, "Plato," pp. 1–50; and Chap. 2, "Aristotle," pp. 50–92.
HAMILTON, EDITH. The Echo of Greece, New York, Norton, 1957.
MULLER, HERBERT J. The Uses of the Past, New York, Mentor, 1956, Chap. 5, "The Romantic Glory of Classical Greece," pp. 102–143.
ROBINSON, C. E. Hellas: A Short History of Ancient Greece, Boston, Beacon, 1955.

« *3* »

The Western
Political Orientation

THE BASIC IDEAS by which Western civilization's historical evolution has been guided—and which, indeed, have philosophically constituted its very essence—derive from two principal
sources. The one is the rationalistic philosophy of ancient
Greece; the other, the revealed monotheism of the early Hebrews.
Yet neither of these components of the Western intellectual and
ethical orientation has had its greatest impact in its original
version. Both were given their historically most significant and
lasting formulations during the centuries of postclassical Greece
and imperial Rome—between approximately 200 B.C. and A.D.
400. The religion of the Hebrews came to play its historically
greatest role as universalized and elaborated in Christianity.
And classical Greek rationalism found its most influential expression in Stoicism and Roman law.

Neither the Judaic-Christian nor the Greco-Roman traditions, moreover, were originally concerned with politics as
such. The chief reason for this lay in the absence during this
period of any stable and satisfying form of political organization
to which political thinking could address itself. Plato and
Aristotle, that is, had believed that the ideal of the city-state
could still be salvaged. Their writings were therefore devoted
to the analysis of what this ideal involved and how it might
best be made to work. The philosophers of the later age, in

contrast, no longer considered the ideal of the city-state either desirable or attainable. Nor did they see any practically possible alternative formula for an effective political community. Their thinking, as a result, was not concerned with man as a citizen nor with the theory and practice of any type of state. Its purpose, rather, was to inspire man as an individual and to teach him how to live sanely and with dignity despite the absence of the opportunity for political participation and solidarity.

The prescriptions for life that were formulated during this period can thus hardly be called political in any narrow or immediate sense of the term. Yet in their more fundamental philosophical and ethical import they added up to the most universalistic and positive ideals for human conduct that have ever been evolved. Taken together, indeed, they have constituted the basic moral orientation that has guided Western civilization to the present day.

Stoicism

In its essentials, Stoicism was the rationalistic philosophy of Plato and Aristotle as reinterpreted in more universal terms and thereby made meaningful and accessible to men everywhere, regardless of their particular race, class, or personal endowments. It was founded about 308 B.C. by Zeno, a Greek-educated Phoenician, and took its name from the roofed colonnade (or "Stoa") in Athens in which Zeno taught. An indication of the breadth of its appeal may be seen in the fact that its two most eloquent spokesmen are considered to have been Epictetus (A.D. 50–120), a Phrygian slave who studied in Rome and later taught in Greece, and the Roman Emperor Marcus Aurelius (A.D. 121–180).

The central philosophical assumption of Stoicism was that all of nature was the manifestation of a universal rationality that could be considered synonymous with the concept of God. Man, as a thinking creature, shared in this rationality and was capable, through intellectual effort and self-discipline, of understanding and reconciling himself to the universe's and God's meaning. Moreover, such understanding and adjustment were potentially open to everyone. Since all men were endowed with the gift of rationality, all men were equal and all belonged to one natural, universal community.

Marcus Aurelius put this Stoic conviction in his personal journal, the *Meditations,* thus:

> If our intellectual part is common, the reason also, in respect of which we are rational beings, is common: if this is so, common also is the reason which commands us what to do, and what not to do; if this is so, there is a common law also; if this is so, we are fellow-citizens; if this is so, we are members of some political community; if this is so, the world is in a manner a state. For of what other common political community will any one say that the whole human race are members? And from thence, from this common political community comes also our very intellectual faculty and our capacity for law; or whence do they come? [1]

The ethics of this Stoic philosophy of universalism and egalitarianism were designed, above all, to enable man to accept life's imperfections and frustrations and to find comfort in the thought that in nature all things ultimately worked out for the best. The secret of happiness, Stoicism urged, lay in self-mastery and contemplation. In the words of the British historian, W. G. De Burgh,

> The Stoic taught that, impotent as man seemed to be in the face of hostile circumstances, of slavery, torture, disease, and death, in reality he was absolute master of his will, and that on this mastery of will alone depended all the value and good of life. . . . Therefore the wise man, the Stoic saint, recognizes willingly in whatever suffering may befall him the fulfillment of the providential purpose, and asserts his unconditional freedom in the face of it by willing it to be—what it is. [2]

The assumption of an ideal and universal Law of Nature against which all existing reality can be measured; an exhortation to selflessness and tolerance; a faith in the rationality and equality of men and women everywhere—these were the main principles of the Stoic creed. They introduced breadth and humanity into the world view of ancient Rome; they underlay the rationalistically utopian cry to battle of the French Revolution—liberty, equality, fraternity; and they inspired the conception of a "law above the law" which became the fundamental principle of the constitutional system of the United States. They have thus remained an integral part of our Western heritage from its earliest development. The best proof of this is the fact that we today consider them largely self-evident.

Cicero and the Law of Nature

Though the Roman Empire lasted for a thousand years, the Romans themselves produced almost no original political philosophy of their own. A major reason for this was that Rome, unlike the city-states of Greece, never developed into a truly stable and well-integrated political community. Though its power extended to most of the known world, the Roman Empire was in reality never more than the original Roman municipality plus an agglomeration of provinces, a network of roads and defenses, an efficient legal and administrative system, and a first-rate military machine. Impressive an achievement as this was organizationally, it could not inspire the intense identification with a traditional political ideal engendered by the Greek *polis* or, indeed, by the modern nation-state. Geographically as well as politically, that is to say, Rome proved too vast, complex, and dynamic to be definable and comprehensible in any systematic way.

Moreover, though involved in constant crises, Rome suffered no single shock such as was experienced by Athens during the Peloponnesian War and which occasioned the reflections of Plato and Aristotle. And even when the disintegration of the Roman Empire was finally past remedying, the men who contemplated its decline were not Romans or people concerned with the restoration of Rome. They were Roman imperial subjects whose greatest love was not Rome but the message and prospects of the Christian Church.

A second major reason for the Romans' failure to produce any substantial original political philosophy was the fact that they had so early in their history become intellectual disciples of the Greeks. On the one hand, this infusion of Roman culture with Greek learning proved an enriching and civilizing gain. On the other, however, it meant that in formulating their problems the Romans did not devise concepts and theories of

their own but attempted to apply the ideas they had taken over
from the Greeks. Yet the conditions and problems of the city-
state that had inspired this Greek theorizing had been very
different from those that confronted Rome. As a result, particularly in their descriptions and analyses of political developments, the Romans tended frequently to slip into intellectual
irrelevancy, imprecision, and rhetoric.

Most outstanding among the men who attempted to apply
Greek ideas to the Romans' situation was the lawyer, statesman,
and writer, Cicero. Born in 106 B.C., Cicero grew to adulthood
at a time when the long-gathering struggle between the Roman
aristocracy and the Roman masses was rapidly coming to a
climax. Throughout Rome's history, its citizens had never found
the common ground, either ideological or institutional, on which
this class antagonism might have been reconciled. By Cicero's
time, each side looked to and was in turn wooed by the great
Roman generals of the day, with the result that the Republic
seemed in imminent danger of destruction through dictatorship.

It was against this background that Cicero, in his book
On the Commonwealth, undertook his Aristotelian analysis of
Rome's governmental development. As he saw it, Rome had
begun as a monarchy and from that form had been passing
through Aristotle's entire constitutional sequence. Soon, he predicted, it would reach the final form of democracy. This, in
turn, was certain to give way to tyranny. The only way to prevent
such a development, he warned, was for Rome to return to what
he felt had been its governmental system when the Republic
had been at its healthiest and noblest: an Aristotelian type of
polity in which the majority was allowed some access to power
but in which there was also a strong admixture of tempering
aristocratic elements.

A second line of thought developed by Cicero concerned
the Stoic notion of the Law of Nature. Nature, rationality, and
morality, he asserted, could in effect be considered synonymous.
The functioning of nature reveals to man certain laws. These
laws, he held, indicate to man's intellect what is at once natural,
rational, and moral. They thus provide him with absolute standards of right and wrong by which all human conduct should
be guided and judged:

There is in fact a true law—namely, right reason—which is in accordance with nature, applies to all men, and is unchangeable and eternal. By its commands this law summons men to the performance of their duties; by its prohibitions it restrains them from doing wrong. Its commands and prohibitions always influence good men, but are without effect upon the bad. To invalidate this law by human legislation is never morally right, nor is it permissible ever to restrict its operation, and to annul it wholly is impossible. Neither the senate nor the people can absolve us from our obligation to this law. . . . It will not lay down one rule at Rome and another at Athens, nor will it be one rule today and another tomorrow. But there will be one law, eternal and unchangeable, binding at all times upon all peoples. . . .[3]

Roman Law

The most important impact of this Stoic notion of Natural Law upon the Roman world occurred through its incorporation into the later Roman legal system. From the beginning, law had occupied a highly honored place in the Roman scheme of things. During the early monarchical era, until about 450 B.C., Roman law had been in the hands of an aristocratic council of "pontiffs" or priests, who pronounced the law with an almost religious ritual. Later, in the time of the Republic, the system of declaring and applying law was taken from the priests and transferred to an annually elected official called the *praetor*. Since the politicians who occupied this office knew very little of the law, there developed the institution of the *jurisprudent*, or legal expert, who wrote the legal opinions upon which the praetors' decisions came to be based. By about 100 B.C. these jurisprudents, who had become a class of recognized and specially trained professionals, began writing compilations and textbooks of their own and others' opinions. It was through the efforts of these jurisprudents, particularly during the first three centuries after the Republic had given way to the Empire, that Roman law acquired its remarkable logical and precise definition.

In their development of Roman law these legal experts recognized three basic types of law. The oldest type they referred to as *jus civile,* or Roman municipal law. This was the native Roman customary law on the basis of which the jurisprudents

formulated their opinions for the praetors. A second category
of law they called *jus gentium,* or "the law of peoples." Whereas
jus civile pertained to the legal relations among Roman citizens,
jus gentium was law in the Roman Empire for cases in which
one or both parties were non-Romans. In recognizing and incorporating much of the law of Rome's subject peoples, *jus
gentium* soon came to be a much more elastic and complete
system of legal provisions than was the older *jus civile.*

Side by side with *jus civile* and *jus gentium,* the Roman
lawyers recognized a third, more philosophical type of law.
This was the body of ideal standards which, following the
Stoics and Cicero, they called *jus naturale.* Since *jus gentium*
was a synthesis of the law of many states and was therefore
characterized by a considerable universalism, the tendency at
first was to think of *jus gentium* as incorporating the dictates
of natural law. Gradually, however, many of the Roman lawyers
began to make a distinction. While they continued to believe that
jus gentium approximated universal standards more closely
than did the municipal civil law, they noted that in one respect
at least *jus gentium* and *jus naturale* were clearly not the same
thing. This was in regard to the institution of slavery. Because
slavery was recognized in the law of most of the peoples of the
times, it was also accepted in *jus gentium.* Yet according to the
teachings of Stoicism, slavery was merely an enforced and un-
natural convention: in nature all human beings were equal.
It therefore had to be concluded that the final word on absolute
and universal justice was not *jus gentium* but a still higher order
of standards that *jus gentium* in some respects merely approximated. Subsequent efforts of the imperial Roman lawyers went
into formulating these higher standards of natural law and
introducing them where possible into their opinions and judgments within the existing *jus civile* and *jus gentium.*

Some of the lasting principles that this Stoic-inspired human-
izing process introduced into Roman and later European law
have been summarized by one authority as follows:

> Natural law meant interpretation in the light of such con-
> ceptions as equality before the law, faithfulness to engagements,
> fair dealing or equity, the superior importance of intent to mere
> words and formularies, the protection of dependents, and the recog-

nition of claims based on blood relationships. Procedure was more and more freed from mere formality; contracts were made to rest on agreement rather than on words of stipulation; the father's absolute control over the property and persons of his children was broken; married women became the full legal equals of their husbands in the control of their property and children; and finally great progress was made in throwing legal safeguards about slaves, partly by way of protecting them against cruelty, partly by making their manumission as easy as possible.[4]

Enriched by the incorporation of Stoic concepts such as these, Roman law received its final systematization in the *Corpus Juris Civilis,* the vast codification of the opinions of the leading Roman jurists that was carried out between A.D. 529 and 534 at the behest of the Emperor Justinian. It was upon this code of Justinian that later lawyers drew very heavily in the development of the political ideas and legal systems of medieval and modern Europe.

The Judaic-Christian Tradition

While one of the two main stems of our Western political heritage is thus rooted in the philosophy of classical and post-classical Greece, the other and even more central one reaches back to the theology of the ancient Hebrews. Most fortunate, moreover, has been the fact that though the Greek and Judaic traditions differed markedly in their emphases and details, their intent and spirit were in many respects quite similar and complementary. Both developed as a response to conditions of cultural and political turmoil. Both advanced an ethic of restraint and humaneness. And both centered about the conception of men everywhere as equal and capable of individual moral self-discipline. The principal difference was that the Stoics arrived at their universalism and egalitarianism by assuming a universally operating force of rationality, whereas the Jews drew their conclusions from man's assumed relationship to a universal and omnipotent Creator-God.

It was this central conception of the Hebrew Creator-God that gave to Judaism a strength of conviction that the more intellectual precepts of Stoicism could not match. The Stoics,

too, subscribed to the notion of a universal divinity. But whereas
the existence of the Stoics' God was a matter of inference from
man's rational view of the universe, the God of the Hebrews
was represented as a personalized absolute whose being was to
be accepted by faith in divine revelation. "In the beginning,"
proclaims the Book of Genesis, "God created the heavens and
the earth." Thus in the eyes of the Jews God was self-existent
and transcended all speculative inquiry. Synonymous with belief
in this God, moreover, was an iron commitment to the way of
life with which he was identified. All men were equally subject
to his omnipotence and thereby commanded to observe the code
of ethical rules represented by his will.

In the earliest beginning, it is true, the Hebrew God
had been little more than a tribal deity whose purpose it had
been to fight his people's wars against the rival gods of other
tribes. Gradually, however, from the eighth century B.C. onward,
the great Jewish prophets transformed this primitive conception
into the universal, ethic-conscious God that has been central to
the development of our civilization ever since.

For one thing, the Jewish prophets redefined God's relationship to the Jews from something collective, concerned with them
as a people, to something personal, addressed to them as individuals. Second, they foretold the appearance of a Messiah who
would lead the Jews in the establishment of a great new religious
kingdom. And finally, they extended the possibility of belief in
the Hebrew God to all of mankind. In the words of Isaiah,
predicting what would be God's mission for the Messiah when
he should come: "It is too slight a thing that thou shouldst be
My servant to raise up the tribes of Jacob and to bring back
the dispersed of Israel: I will make thee a light of the nations,
that My deliverance may extend to the ends of the earth." [5]

However, while the tradition of the great Hebrew prophecies
thus sought to liberalize and make universal faith in the Jewish
God, the Jews' political and religious officials were bent upon
identifying their traditional religion with the exclusive cause of
Jewish nationalism. Particularly in the eyes of the powerful
party of the Pharisees, the Jews' first objective was to maintain
their solidarity as a people and to expel the occupying Romans.
To serve this purpose, they insisted that belief in the God of

the Jews was inseparable from submission to a strict program of priestly supervised ritual and required an unwavering identification with the fate of Israel politically.

Had Jesus of Nazareth accommodated his mission to this conservative and nationalistic outlook, he would undoubtedly have been hailed by the Jews as a great politico-religious patriot. But he did not. Instead of a narrow and militant Judaism, he advanced the doctrines of noncoercion and man's universal brotherhood under an omnipotent Father-God. Instead of a utopian Jewish political kingdom of this world, he urged a world-wide fellowship of faith, hope, and charity in contemplation of the happiness that would be achieved by the virtuous in the next. Instead of a religion primarily identified with the socially successful and accepted, he expounded a faith that offered self-respect to all who would embrace it and act according to its precepts. And instead of the customary emphasis on formal religious practices, he assigned greatest priority in the eyes of God to the purity of inner motive and man's responsibility to his fellow man as expressed in loving good works.[6]

Because he thus repudiated national Judaism and insisted upon drawing from Jewish monotheism the most universalistic and liberal inferences he could, Jesus paid with his life. Yet, in so doing, he came to symbolize a religious, ethical, and political inspiration richer than mankind had ever before known. Indeed, as interpreted in the New Testament and developed by the Church, his message became the dominant moral force of our entire civilization. It provided the unifying basis of medieval Christendom. In its postmedieval secular versions it has constituted a determining, if often unconscious, element in modern man's striving for democracy and social welfare. And, perhaps most important of all, it has helped fashion and maintain the unique Western ideal of the sovereign and inviolable individual conscience.

The Church Fathers

The specifically political implications of the Judaic-Christian tradition first began to be worked out in the writings of the so-called Church Fathers. The purpose of these early Christian

leaders and intellectuals was essentially threefold: to absorb
into Christian doctrine whatever elements of Stoicism might be
compatible with it; to develop this intellectually enriched
Christian theology as the basis for a universal Christian community to succeed the rapidly disintegrating Roman Empire;
and to formulate the Church's position on the various social
and political problems with which its growing aspirations and
responsibilities constantly confronted it.

The period between the third and sixth centuries after
Christ in which these Church thinkers wrote was one of extreme
political instability. By the middle of the third century Christianity had been adopted as the Roman Empire's official religion.
Yet the Empire that had taken this step was at the time rapidly
collapsing. And as Rome's military and administrative capabilities deteriorated, the far-flung imperial frontiers began to
yield and crumble. Into the former Roman provinces poured
wave after wave of Germanic barbarians. After Rome itself had
been pillaged by the invaders, the seat of the Empire was moved
eastward to Constantinople. And though the Empire in theory
continued to include Italy and the other Western areas, it
became more and more apparent that the only effective authority
that remained in the West was that of the bishop of Rome—
the pope.

Among the more important problems faced by the Church
Fathers in their application of the Christian religion to secular
affairs was that of determining the Church's stand on law. They
agreed that the Roman conception of three kinds of law—
civil law, *jus gentium,* and natural law—was in principle wholly
acceptable. Their only objection was to the category of natural
law. This, they felt, should in Christian thought be replaced by
the concept of divine law based upon Revelation. According to
Stoicism, man had originally lived in a "state of nature," had lost
this happy condition because of a failure of rationality, but
could regain his lost perfection by rationally contemplating
and following the dictates of natural law. As reinterpreted
by the Church Fathers, in contrast, the Stoic "state of nature"
became the innocent condition of man before his Fall from
the Garden of Eden; the cause of his degradation was translated

into his disobedience to the command of God, that is, Original Sin; and the hope of salvation from earthly sinfulness and suffering was depicted as lying in obedience to the divine law of Christianity.

A second practical problem confronting the Church Fathers was that of reconciling the Christian ideal of human freedom and equality with the actual fact of universal inequality and slavery. Their reasoning was as follows: Because God created man (and because he lived in the Garden of Eden and would have continued to live but for Original Sin) he was completely free. The condition of slavery in the case of any specific individual is thus something wholly accidental and extends only to his body; in his mind and soul every man is free and equal to everyone else. Slavery as an institution, on the other hand, is a this-worldly arrangement resulting from man's evil this-worldly motivations as symbolized by Original Sin. In view of this evil human motivation, slavery may even serve a useful purpose as a corrective to man's sinful propensities. Yet though slavery may have to be accepted as humanly inevitable, it exists only among men. In the eyes of God, the only real slave is the this-worldly sinner. True freedom, regardless of an individual's earthly status or condition, consists of believing in and living according to God's word. This will be recognized and rewarded on the Day of Judgment. Godless men who in this world were free will be condemned to Hell; true Christians, whether on earth they have been free men or slaves, will be rewarded with eternal life.

The Church Fathers resorted to a similar formula in explaining man's seemingly contradictory situation in being free under God yet at the same time finding himself subject to the discipline of the state. They began with the Aristotelian assumption that man is an innately social animal who lived in society even in the state of nature, or, in Christian terms, before his Fall from Eden. Yet in this happy original condition, they maintained, there was neither state nor government. Since man was perfect, neither was necessary. What brought them into being—as with the institution of slavery—was Original Sin, that is, man's beginning to seek after the things of this world rather than devoting himself to God. The state and government must

therefore be viewed as serving the divine purpose of providing
sinful man with the discipline necessary for living as stable and
Christian a life as possible.

A fourth subject upon which the Church Fathers felt
compelled to formulate a Christian position concerned the matter of property. The same reasoning that they had used in
explaining other human institutions brought them an acceptable
solution here. Before the Fall, all property was held in common.
The development of private property was a consequence of
Original Sin and man's turning to this-worldliness and avarice.
And as long as man remained sinful, private property was not
only a necessary institution but one divinely ordained. Like
government, it helped man live an orderly life and devote his
greatest possible attention to the contemplation of God.

Perhaps the most pressing problem confronting the Church
Fathers was that of defining the proper relationship between
the Church and secular authority. At the time, of course, Christianity was the Empire's established religion. The Church highly
valued this relationship because it could thereby count upon the
emperor's support in the suppression of its internal heresies.
Yet at the same time, it was fearful that such support might
easily be extended even to unsolicited and arbitrary governmental interferences in Church affairs. It was therefore to ac-
commodate these two considerations that the Church Fathers
advanced what came to be called the "doctrine of the two
swords."

The essence of this doctrine, as first formulated by the
fifth-century pope Gelasius, was the proposition that there were
two coequal spheres and centers of authority. On the one hand
was the authority of the Church, which was concerned with man's
spiritual condition and extended to the spiritual aspects of even
the emperor's life. And on the other was the secular authority,
which properly encompassed all phases of man's temporal existence. Both of these authorities were said to be divinely ordained
and of equal and interdependent necessity; for, in Pope Gelasius'
words: "Christian Emperors need bishops for the sake of eternal
life, and bishops make use of imperial regulations to order the
course of temporal affairs." [7]

Taken together, these formulations on law, slavery, property, government, and the relationship between spiritual and secular authority became the philosophical basis of Christian politics for nearly a thousand years. The Church's defense of them occasioned the bulk of the political thinking of the Middle Ages in Europe. What in turn marked the breakdown of the European medieval order were social, cultural, and political developments for which these formulations of the Church Fathers had at last become irrelevant.

It will be noted that running through this early Christian political doctrine was a sharp liberal-conservative ambivalence, and that the positions taken were undeniably severely conservative and authoritarian. Human institutions were in effect downgraded to the status of penalties for man's sinful nature. Submission to them was enjoined as a divine command. In the words of St. Paul, upon which this ecclesiastical endorsement of established authority was in the last analysis founded:

> Let every soul be subject unto the higher powers. For there is no power but of God: the powers that be are ordained of God. Whosoever therefore resisteth the power, resisteth the ordinance of God; and they that resist shall receive to themselves damnation. For rulers are not a terror to good works, but to the evil. . . . For this cause pay ye tribute also: for they are God's ministers, attending continually upon this very thing. Render therefore to all their dues: tribute to whom tribute is due; custom to whom custom; fear to whom fear; honor to whom honor.[8]

Yet as significant as this conservative political orientation of the Church was to prove, particularly during the Middle Ages, the Judaic-Christian tradition at the same time also offered several much more liberal doctrinal possibilities. In the first place, its insistence on the necessity of external obedience to authority was matched by a no less firm insistence that the political order and its various institutions must never absorb the individual completely. Unlike the citizen of the Greek city-state, not only was the true Christian to acknowledge his duties to the political community; while doing so, he could and should always think of his highest significance and identity in terms of his individual spiritual relationship with God.

Second, as seriously as the Church Fathers' religious ration-

alizations of the *status quo* might be taken, Christ's original
espousal of the interests of the poor and downtrodden and his
emphasis on good works could never be wholly forgotten. Indeed, they provided a constant undercurrent of standards by
which the performance of human institutions tended in the long
run to be measured. That is, while Christianity commanded
obedience to the rules and rulers of this world, it suggested a
basic morality that human rules and rulers ought to serve and
be judged by.

A final important liberalizing aspect of Christian doctrine
was its recognition of the two separate spheres of secular and
ecclesiastical authority. In all non-Christian societies, authority
has been justified in both human and divine terms. Even in
Christian societies, the constant temptation has been for authority to become absolute: for secular authority to identify
itself with religious sanction, and for religious authority to
secure the unconditional support of secular power. Yet as far as
such concentration of political and religious authority has at
times progressed, it has never reached the point of absolute and
unchallenged identification. Caesar has had to make his concessions to God, but he has never been wholly appropriated
by him. And while God has at times been in danger of
being enslaved by Caesar, he too has managed to retain his
identity. Indeed, as the history of the European Middle Ages
indicates, it was in the unconquerable no man's land between
battling secular and religious authority that our unique Western
ideal of collective secular order with individual spiritual freedom
was first born.

Perhaps the historically most fortunate aspect of the over-
all Christian political orientation has been its very ambiguity.
Had Christianity's political stand been clearly and uncompromisingly conservative, it would very soon have been rejected. If it
had been openly and consistently revolutionary, it would have
enjoyed even less chance of survival. Being *both* conservative
and liberal in its potential appeals, it was, admittedly, vulnerable
to attacks and misuse by reactionaries and radicals alike. Yet in
return for this price, it possessed a flexibility of meaning that
has been one of the most important circumstances in the

development of Western civilization. By the time, in the Reformation, when this flexibility was at last overtaxed, Christianity as a religion had been firmly instilled in all of the peoples of Europe. The foundation had therewith been laid for a common European cultural and political heritage.

St. Augustine

In concluding this consideration of the development of the Christian approach to man's secular life, especial mention must be made of the Church Father who contributed by far the most creatively and comprehensively to the elaboration of Christian doctrine, St. Augustine (354–430). Born in North Africa, where he eventually became a bishop, Augustine is generally acknowledged as one of the most penetrating Christian thinkers of all time. In his greatest work, *The City of God,* he worked out the philosophy of history inherent in Christianity, its implied goal of a world-wide Christian commonwealth, and its theory of human psychology.

In the circumstances, aim, and scope of his work, Augustine can most closely be compared with Plato. Both men wrote in response to their society's cultural and political breakdown; both sought to master the moral confusion of their times by going back to ethical first principles; and both attempted to see and remedy man's problems in the context of a total intellectual and spiritual system.

Substantively, of course, the ideas of the two men were very different. Plato saw man's salvation in the use of his rationality and, hence, constructed his utopia in purely rationalistic terms. Augustine's point of departure was the revealed Christian truth that God had created the world and that all beings, things, and events can therefore be assumed to express God's power and wisdom. The problem for Plato was to show how men would live if the implications of their rationality were fully worked out. Augustine's purpose, in contrast, was to interpret what the omnipresent force of God in the world could and should mean for man. In the words of a recent commentary on Augustine's work,

For Augustine there is no philosophers' city floating like Mahomet's coffin between the actualities of history and the community of the blessed spirits. . . . We are not to embark upon a dialectic which detaches us from the actual, but to discuss the spiritual forces which are and have been actually at work in the history of the human race. . . . Augustine is more concerned to describe this vale of tears, and to fortify us for our life in it, than to excogitate ideal types for an ideal environment. . . . Both are looking for a meaning, but whereas Plato finds it by relating an event to a type, Augustine finds an immanent meaning in events themselves.[9]

The occasion for the composition of *The City of God* was the capture of Rome by the Goths in the year 410. Many prominent non-Christian Romans alleged that the chief reason for this debacle was that Christianity had undermined the old Roman civic and military virtues. It was this accusation which Augustine was determined to refute.

Augustine's central theme in *The City of God* attributed human suffering, including the military defeat of Rome, to man's innate self-centeredness as expressed in his idolization of the things and pursuits of this world. According to Augustine, it was this excessive love of self, with its attendant insecurity, acquisitiveness, and vanity, which had furnished the driving force for all of history's empire building. And as past empires, including Rome, had grown by this-worldly insecurity, acquisitiveness, and vanity, they were doomed sooner or later to fall victim to these same base and short-sighted forces. The only possible escape from such a fate was for men to devote themselves to God and to deal with the things of this world not for their own sake but as mere instruments for creating the peace and stability that would be most conducive to a truly God-oriented Christian life.

Those who glorified the things of this world for their own sake, Augustine called the citizens of the earthly city, the *Civitas Terrena;* those who regarded the pursuits of this life as a necessary evil and consecrated themselves to God, he distinguished as the citizens of the heavenly or divine city, the *Civitas Dei.* And though Augustine did not insist that membership in the Christian Church was synonymous with membership in the heavenly city, he believed that those who belonged to the Church were the most likely to be and remain God-loving people. The Church, Augustine was convinced, was the great new agency that could at last aid man to look to God and overcome his self-centeredness and this-worldliness. That is, if the peoples of the whole world could be brought into the Church and thereby induced to live a true Christian life, the sources of viciousness and suffering among men could at last be permanently eliminated.

The essence of Augustine's message is well summarized in the following sentences on the relationship between the earthly and heavenly cities, taken from Book XIX of *The City of God:*

> The families which do not live by faith seek their peace in the earthly advantages of this life; while the families that live by faith look for those eternal blessings which are promised, and use as pilgrims such advantages of time and of earth as do not fascinate and divert them from God, but rather aid them to endure with greater ease, and to keep down the number of those burdens of the corruptible body which weigh upon the soul. Thus the things necessary for this life are used by both kinds of men and families alike, but each has its own peculiar and widely different aim in using them. The earthly city, which does not live by faith, seeks an earthly peace, and the end it proposes, in the well-ordered concord of civic obedience and rule, is the combination of men's wills to attain the things which are helpful to this life. The heavenly city, or rather the part of it which sojourns on earth and lives by faith, makes use of this peace only because it must, until this mortal condition which necessitates it shall pass away. Consequently, so long as it lives like a captive and a stranger in the earthly city, though it has already received the promise of redemption, and the gift of the spirit as the earnest of it, it makes no scruples to obey the laws of the earthly city, whereby the things necessary for the maintenance of this mortal life are administered; and thus, as this life is common to both cities, so there is a harmony between them in regard to what belongs to it. But, as the earthly city has had some philosophers whose doctrine is condemned by the divine teaching, and who, being deceived either by their own conjectures or by demons, supposed that many gods must be invited to take an interest in human affairs, and assigned to each a separate function and a separate department . . . it has come to pass that the two cities could not have common laws of religion, and

that the heavenly city has been compelled in this matter to dissent, and to become obnoxious to those who think differently, and to stand the brunt of their anger and hatred and persecutions, except in so far as the minds of their enemies have been alarmed by the multitude of the Christians and quelled by the manifest protection of God accorded to them. This heavenly city, then, while it so-journs on earth, calls citizens out of all nations, and gathers together a society of pilgrims of all languages, not scrupling about diversities in the manners, laws, and institutions whereby earthly peace is secured and maintained, but recognizing that, however various these are, they all tend to one and the same end of earthly peace. It therefore is so far from rescinding and abolishing these diversities, that it even preserves and adopts them, so long as no hindrance to the worship of the one supreme and true God is thus introduced.[10]

It was this Augustinian vision of a universal heavenly city on earth that the Church struggled a thousand years to translate into reality. And though Christianity's orthodoxy and leadership in the end became more and more fragmented, the original ideal of a universal community of morality and intellect has remained very much with us, even though in secularized form.

SELECTED BIBLIOGRAPHY

BAILEY, CYRIL. *The Legacy of Rome,* London, Oxford University Press, 1951, Chaps. 1–7, pp. 9–264.

BARROW, R. H. *The Romans,* London, Pelican, 1955.

DE BURGH, W. G. *The Legacy of the Ancient World,* London, Pelican, 1955, Vol. II, Chap. 9, "Christianity," pp. 319–387; and Chap. 10, "The Decline and Fall," pp. 388–436.

EBENSTEIN, WILLIAM. *Political Thought in Perspective,* New York, McGraw-Hill, 1957, Chap. 4, "The Stoics," pp. 93–107; and Chap. 5, "St. Augustine," pp. 108–124.

MULLER, HERBERT J. *The Uses of the Past,* New York, Mentor, 1956, Chap. 6, "The Rise of Christianity," pp. 144–197; and Chap. 7, "The Fall of Rome," pp. 198–230.

SOHM, RUDOLF. *Outlines of Church History,* Translated by May Sinclair, Boston, Beacon Paperback, 1958, Division I, "The Beginning," pp. 1–73.

VERSFELD, MARTINUS. *A Guide to the City of God,* New York, Sheed & Ward, 1958.

« 4 »

Political Thought
of the Middle Ages

THE PERIOD KNOWN as the European Middle Ages is generally considered to have lasted from the sixth to the fifteenth century. The most important accomplishment of this era from the point of view of subsequent Western history was the conversion of the peoples of Europe to Christianity. In the course of this development, a number of new elements were also introduced into the West's orientation to secular affairs. Among the most significant of these were the medieval notion of the organic community; the feudal idea of the reciprocity of obligations between the ruler and the ruled; Thomas Aquinas' philosophical reconciliation of faith and reason; and the principle that the only admissible justification of authority was its utility to those for and over whom it was exercised.

The Course of Medieval History

The first five centuries of the European Middle Ages were characterized by constant barbarian invasions and civil strife. First came the successive incursions and migrations of the Germanic tribes; then the invasions of Vikings, Moslems, and Magyars. Peace and order were achieved for a time under the emperorship of the Frankish king, Charlemagne. Yet soon after his death in the year 814, the barbarian disruptions began anew, to be aggravated, moreover, by the struggles for power among the deceased emperor's successors.

Until the barbarian onslaughts had stopped and more effective relationships had been established for the maintenance of internal order, a stable way of life in Europe proved impossible. Needless to say, there was little occasion for political philosophy. The Church continued to base its policies on the positions set forth earlier by the Church Fathers. And Europe's secular population still lacked the kind of organized political units to which systematic thinking about politics might have been addressed.

The Church during these centuries continued its work of spreading and administering the Christian faith under difficulties that were truly staggering. At times, indeed, the attacks of the barbarians from outside and the loosening of discipline from within threatened to ruin its mission altogether. During the ninth century, for example, the situation on the Continent had become so precarious that a revival of orthodox Christian teaching and uncorrupted Latin was possible only through the work of missionaries who came to Europe from Ireland, where the barbarians had not penetrated.

In fending for itself and its work in these critical early circumstances, the Church was compelled to resort to a good many policies of expedience, some of which contained the seeds of difficulties that were to prove most troublesome in the latter Middle Ages. Most pressing, for example, was the problem of protecting its spiritual and organizational base, the seat of the Papacy in Rome. Here the Church followed a two-pronged strategy. On the one hand, it established its own territorial and political organization in the so-called Papal States of central and southern Italy. On the other, it adopted a permanent policy of playing the European secular powers against one another.

Yet although these strategies served their purpose in aiding the Church in its external defense, they seriously weakened its internal organization, for there soon developed in the Papal States a military barony that came to make and break popes from among its own members with little regard for the Church's universal religious mission. And through the policy of seeking to divide and rule, the Papacy found itself embroiled in almost constant warfare in which military defeat inevitably meant disruptive outside interference in the Church's innermost affairs.

As a result of this weakening of the Church during the early Middle Ages, the Papacy's spiritual and organizational control over its representatives in the field, and particularly its bishops, became more and more tenuous. Still nominally spiritual authorities, the bishops tended increasingly to become appointees of Europe's local secular rulers and to consider the exercise of their secular duties of hardly less importance than their original spiritual ones. According to the Church Fathers' still-current doctrine of the two swords, the Papacy and secular authority remained in theory coequal. Yet in actual practice, the Church's power had been steadily diminished and subordinated.

By the tenth century, European life was at last settling into more or less stable and clearly defined patterns. And with this development began the process that more than any other dominated the political history of the latter Middle Ages: the efforts of the Church to reassert its former power and prestige. Internally, this objective was pursued in several ways: by the elimination of the influence of the Italian barony upon papal elections; by a revitalization of Church doctrine and discipline through the establishment of a number of monastic orders responsible directly to the Papacy in Rome; and by the adaptation of Roman law into a systematic body of Canon or Church law designed to enable the Papacy more effectively to control the Church's organization and personnel. Externally, on the other hand, the Church's strategy took two main forms. First, the Papacy engaged in a succession of determined political offensives against Europe's secular rulers. And second, it sought to justify its claims to equal power with secular authority by resorting to various aggressive theological arguments.

Although the Church's measures for internal reform proved highly successful, its external policies failed badly. Indeed, after each succeeding encounter with secular authority it found its power further reduced. Unfortunate as this long and bitter medieval Church-state struggle proved to be for papal power, it served as an invaluable stimulus to political thought. For, in seeking to advance themselves and discredit one another, both the champions of the Papacy and the advocates of Europe's secular rulers were led to examine the nature and justification of political authority with a thoroughness that had been lacking since the days of the Greeks.

That in the end it was the Papacy that lost out in the medieval Church-state struggle was no proof of the superiority of the arguments of its opponents. The decisive factor, rather, was the growth of a measure of regional differentiation in Europe—as expressed politically by the new emerging nation-state monarchs—that could no longer be contained by one spiritual orthodoxy or directed from one administrative center. Yet the Roman Church's work was by no means lost. Even after the Reformation and the consolidation of the European nation-states, Europe remained Christian and until our own day has maintained its basic Greco-Roman and Judaic-Christian cultural and political orientation. The interpretation and application of our evolving Western heritage simply passed into more numerous and diverse hands.

The Notion of the Organic Community

Most of the ideas introduced into the West's political orientation during the Middle Ages were in essence merely readaptations of positions enunciated earlier by the Church Fathers. At least two medieval lines of political thought, however, were entirely new and were rooted in the native history and way of life of the European peoples themselves, rather than in the cultures of their Mediterranean civilizers. One of these, originating in the traditions of the pagan Germanic tribes, was the notion of the organic community. The other was the principle of the reciprocity of obligations between the ruler and the ruled which derived from the medieval social and economic system of feudalism.

The medieval Germanic notion of the community as something organic meant simply that it was envisaged as an entity consisting of more than merely the sum total of its constituent members. Besides and beyond these, it was envisaged as representing a unique common history, an inviolable body of common custom, and, even, an inherent collective guiding spirit. It was not something that its individual members, including its political authorities, were free to stand above and manipulate. Rather, it was conceived of as an almost sacred collective cultural organism whose ways and interests demanded reverence and obedience.

In the course of subsequent Western political history, this conception of the organic community came to be employed for two quite different purposes, one supporting the development of liberal democracy, the other helping to impede it. By way of contributing to the early growth of responsible government, for example, it served as an excellent argument against royal absolutism: if a community's traditions were truly revered and held to be inviolable, its laws should be framed in strict accordance with them rather than be thought up and imposed upon the people by the whim and will of an arbitrary king. Thus the famous Common Law of England was not legislated law or law derived from systematic legal codes; it was drawn from precedents and from the judges' own understanding of the English people's traditional standards of fairness and equity. And when, in the early 1600's, King James I attempted to reimpose royal absolutism on England by his claim to "the Divine Right of Kings," his most determined opponents were judges who insisted that matters concerning the life and liberty of Englishmen could not be settled by appeal either to divine or natural reason but had to be decided according to the Common Law of the land.

Moreover, it had been this same notion of law as inherent in the traditions of the community that had inspired the English in 1264 to call their first representative assembly the "High *Court* of Parliament." Their reasoning, of course, was that lawmaking was not a matter of telling the community what to do but, rather, of consulting as to what, in regard to any specific question, its customs and traditional ways of doing things seemed to dictate. As one advocate of this point of view put it at the time: "Therefore let the community of the kingdom advise, and let it be known what the generality thinks, to whom their own laws are best known. Nor are all those of the country so ignorant that they do not know better than strangers the customs of their own kingdom which have been handed down to them by their ancestors." [1]

While the notion of the inviolability of the heritage of

the community thus served as a powerful argument against the arbitrary exercise of political authority, it also lent itself to championing the superiority of the collective will of the community over the freedom of the individual. In England, where the achievement of national statehood and individual liberty progressed the most quickly of any country in Europe, this latter dimension of the medieval myth of the community was never seriously invoked. In Germany, in contrast, the situation was very different. Here national statehood was not attained until the latter half of the nineteenth century. And in its absence, the Germans, split up into dozens of small principalities and exposed to the inroads of their politically more advanced neighbors, were constantly preoccupied with the maintenance of at least the cultural solidarity of their people. To achieve this objective, they therefore discouraged the individualism and universalism current in Britain and France and depicted the Germans as members of one unique cultural community to whose destinies every individual German's life should be proudly subordinated. And whereas during the nineteenth century this romanticized collectivism merely begot an excessive German cultural chauvinism, in the twentieth it came to be used as a decisive weapon of political propaganda. For, it was largely in the name of the allegedly organic German ethnic and cultural community, the so-called German *Volksgemeinschaft,* that Hitler won the support of the German people for his Nazi totalitarianism and the fateful policies which he alone had the power to decree that the people should follow.

Political Implications of Feudalism

A second set of concepts that exercised a significant impact upon subsequent Western political thought and action derived from the medieval social and economic system of feudalism. Originating in the ninth century in response to the general anarchy that followed the collapse of Charlemagne's empire, feudalism was essentially a system of landholding conditioned by service and always combining the claims of two persons to each unit of property—the rights and duties of the lord with the rights and duties of the vassal. Highest in feudal society was the

king; lowest was the landed serf. Between them ranged a rigid
hierarchy of superiors and inferiors, each of whom was the lord
of those immediately below him and the vassal of him immediately above. Each lord owed his vassals security, economic
sustenance, and justice. And each vassal was committed to furnish
his lord with whatever military, agricultural, or administrative
service upon which his landholding and other benefits had been
conditioned.

At first these feudal arrangements were largely improvised:
the landless peasant sought the protection of a knight; the
knight offered his fighting services as a vassal to a larger land-
holder; the latter in turn subordinated himself as vassal to a
still more powerful man, such as a count; and so on. Yet with
the passing of time, the feudal system became more and more
regularized. At whatever the level, the landholding, or *feudum*,
became hereditary and the rights and duties attached to it came
to be precisely stipulated by contract. If the terms of the contract
were broken—whether by lord or vassal—the aggrieved party
could seek redress in various types of feudal and royal courts.

Politically speaking, feudalism operated in terms of two
quite contrary principles, the first making for absoluteness of
authority, the other emphasizing its conditional nature. On the
one hand, as a contemporary medieval scholar has put it,
feudalism

> tended to construe all authority as proprietary, and to treat the
> rights of a king as simply a particular agglomeration of property-
> rights, established within the framework of the same legal prin-
> ciples as governed the property-rights of his subjects. Feudal
> thought encouraged the king to regard his power as his private
> affair, to make no distinction between the administration of a
> kingdom and that of any seignory, to merge his public and his
> private treasury, to infeudate governmental functions, to recon-
> stitute the national council as a council of vassals.[2]

At the same time, however, feudalism also tended very
definitely to circumscribe the exercise of authority:

> . . . to the extent that the king was entangled in the contractual
> system, his rights appeared to be limited by law like all proprietary
> rights, and his claim to obedience appeared as legally contingent

on his performance of the stipulated duties which a lord owed his vassals. Feudal law consistently sanctioned the withdrawal of obedience from a king as from any lord who failed to give his vassals justice and protection.[3]

For a time, while the nation-state kingships of Europe were in process of consolidation, the proprietary interpretation of royal power was clearly in the ascendant. Thereafter, however, when the European peoples' chief problem came to be the limitation and democratization of kingly rule, by far the greater influence was exercised by the argument that authority had always to justify itself by its service to its subjects. Indeed, this principle of the conditional nature of authority, along with the other medieval notion of the inviolability of the community's traditions, served as two of the most powerful weapons in the West's early anti-absolutist political armory. No matter how loudly the sixteenth- and seventeenth-century monarchs claimed to be ruling by divine right, the general expectation persisted that authority was legitimate only to the extent that it was conducted within traditional limits and in the interest of those over whom it was exercised.

Thomas Aquinas: Of Faith and Reason

The Church during the feudal period found itself engaged in a constant twofold struggle. The one was its battle for power with Europe's secular rulers. The other concerned its efforts to defend its orthodox religious dogma against the challenge of various heresies. This latter struggle was, if anything, even more crucial than the former. For, if the Church hoped to continue as the sole spiritual agency of a universal Christendom, it could do so only by maintaining a body of common doctrine which it alone retained the right to interpret.

Unlike many of the earlier heresies with which the Church had had to cope, the challenge that Christian doctrine confronted in the thirteenth century concerned no mere theological detail. What was at issue was the compatibility of the two central elements of evolving Western civilization's very essence—the Judaic-Christian as then represented by Catholic dogma, and the Greco-Roman as expressed in the writings of Aristotle.

Could one be a Christian, committed to the revealed truth of the Bible, and at the same time believe in the supremacy of man's rational intellect? Or was it necessary for the true Christian believer to reject the empirical rationality of science?

The dilemma had been inherent in the West's philosophical orientation from the beginning. During the primitive conditions of the early Middle Ages it had simply never been articulated. By the thirteenth century, however, with the achievement of greater stability and the gathering of full-time scholars at Europe's newly founded universities, it was bound to come to the fore. When it did, the immediate issue was the resumption of the study of Aristotle, whose ideas had become available from rediscovered classical manuscripts as well as from commentaries on his works by Arab scholars who had entered Europe through the Moslem occupation of Spain.

The extreme position against the Church's claim to the exclusive validity of revealed Christian truth was taken by a group whose best-known spokesman was a man named Siger of Brabant. According to this scholar there were *two* truths open to man: the truth of the supernatural world as revealed in Christian dogma, and the truth of the natural world as discoverable after the example of Aristotle through philosophy and science. These two truths, he maintained, were contradictory and incompatible. While we are being scientists and philosophers, as he put it, we must regard Christian revelation as nonsense; yet when we speak as Christians, we must affirm that Christian revelation is true even though by scientific and philosophical standards it *is* nonsense. It was his own personal conviction, Siger of Brabant frankly admitted, that "there is no more worth-while occupation in this world than the study of philosophy. The only wise men are philosophers."

Conservative elements in the Church fully agreed that revealed Christian truth and the philosophical truth of Aristotle were contradictory and incompatible. They merely drew the opposite conclusion: that the only wise man was the Christian believer and that in order to protect him from confusion and corruption, all scientifically oriented philosophy should be suppressed. Fortunately for the Church, however, there was one brilliant thinker in its ranks who refused to accept this short-sighted solution. This man was the Italian-born Dominican priest, scholar, and university teacher who was later to be honored as St. Thomas Aquinas (1225–1274).

If Christianity were to survive, Aquinas believed, and if at the same time men were not to be forced to deny their wonderful and unique gift of empirical rationality, it had to be possible for an individual to be both a true Christian believer and an empirically inquiring philosopher. The Christian's revealed truth and the sense-perceived and speculative truth of the philosopher could not be mutually exclusive; they had to be conceived of as merely different expressions of one and the same total truth and, therefore, as compatible and complementary. What Aquinas hoped to demonstrate was that such an all-inclusive and transcending system of truth in fact existed.

The intellectual comprehensiveness of the total conception that Aquinas suggested for this purpose may be seen in his theory of knowledge. The whole of human knowledge, he maintains, forms a single piece. At the least general level are the particular sciences, each with its own subject matter and, taken together, dealing with all phenomena perceivable by the senses. Above these is philosophy, which he defines as a rational discipline whose purpose is logically to formulate the empirically derived insights of the various particular sciences. And above philosophy is revealed Christian truth, which Aquinas sees as the consummation of the whole system.

Though revelation is thus above reason, Aquinas emphasizes, it is in no way contrary to it. It merely discloses insights about man and the universe that are inaccessible to reason. That is, theology merely completes the total system of truth of which the sciences and philosophy form the less comprehensive stages. What this means is that a man can be an empirical scientist and a philosopher and yet at the same time, and without doing violence to his empirical rationality, believe in revealed Christian truth as well. The reason this is possible is that God and revealed truth are not matters in regard to which empirical inquiry and philosophical reasoning are forbidden, but in regard to which they are insufficient.

Aquinas carries this same large thesis into his systematization of law. There are, he maintains, four types of law. The highest of these, eternal law, represents the plan by which the whole universe is ordered. It is, essentially, the reason of God. And though it is in no way contrary to human reason, human reason is not developed enough to understand it. Below eternal law, Aquinas suggests the category of natural law. This he sees as consisting of those principles of the universe which *are* accessible to human reason, that is, insights about man and nature that in our present-day scheme of things are discoverable through the physical and social sciences. Aquinas' third category of law is what he calls human law. This is made by man through the use of his rationality for the purpose of creating and maintaining social and political order. What it aims to do in the more limited realm of human relations is what God's perfect and all-pervasive reason effects in the orderly working of the whole universe. And finally in Aquinas' legal systematization, there is the category of divine law. This consists chiefly of those guides to human conduct—such as the Ten Commandments— that have been made available to man through God's grace. The reasons for this final type of law Aquinas explains as follows:

> Because man is ordained to the end of eternal beatitude, which is beyond the attainment of his natural faculty, . . . it was necessary that he should be directed to his goal by a law divinely given, in addition to natural and human law. Secondly, as a result of the uncertainty of human judgment especially in regard to contingent and particular things, it happens that different judgments about human acts are formed by different men, and from these proceed different and contrary laws. Therefore, that man may know without any doubt what is to be done and what avoided, it was necessary that in regard to particular actions he should be directed by a law divinely given, which assuredly cannot err. Thirdly, man can make law for those things of which he can judge. But man cannot judge of inner happenings, which are hidden, but only of external acts, which are apparent. And yet, for the perfection of virtue, righteousness is required in both kinds of actions. Therefore human law could not sufficiently control and ordain internal acts, but it was necessary that a divine law should supervene for this purpose. Fourthly, . . . human law cannot punish or prohibit all evil deeds, because, while it was seeking to remove all evils, it

would also cause the loss of many good things, and would prevent them from serving the common good as is necessary for human intercourse. Therefore, in order that no evil should remain unforbidden and unpunished, it was necessary that a divine law should supervene, by which all sins are prohibited.[4]

Such, in brief summary, was the metaphysical system in terms of which Aquinas undertook to reconcile Christian revelation and Aristotelian reason. Its great significance has lain in the fact that at a key juncture in our civilization's development it made scientific investigation respectable and gave it an ultimately spiritual meaning. Had it not been for Aquinas' work, the Church might well have altogether rejected the free empirical approach to the physical world. If it had done so, the consequences both for Christianity as well as for philosophy and science would have been most unfortunate. The Church would almost certainly have been forsaken by some of its finest minds. And science and philosophy would have been compelled to work under the heavy stigma of being allegedly un-Christian. Through the spiritual-empirical system suggested by Aquinas, however, it became possible for a man to satisfy his desire for spiritual significance, as a Christian, as well as for scientific knowledge, as a free-thinking intellect.

In Aquinas' system as well as in the essentially similar conception of seventeenth-century Protestants, moreover, man's Christian spirituality and his empirical rationality seemed actually to support each other. That is, it appeared almost to be a good Christian's duty to study the workings of the God-created physical universe. And by the understanding of nature a man would also develop a deeper reverence for God. It was, in fact, these very sentiments that constituted the inspiration and self-justification of our civilization's earliest men of science. Thus, in the words of the great chemist, Robert Boyle, one of the founders of England's Royal Society, ". . . God loving, as He deserves, to be honour'd in all our Faculties, and consequently to be glorified and acknowledg'd by the acts of Reason, as well as by those of Faith, there must be sure a great Disparity betwixt that general, confus'd and lazy Idea we commonly have of His Power and Wisdom, and the Distinct, rational and affecting notions of those Attributes which are form'd by an attentive

Inspection of Those Creatures in which they are most legible,
and which were made chiefly for that end." [5]

In a fundamental way, this notion has remained one of the
directing ideas of our secularized Western civilization. And in
both its Christian-motivated respect for science and its science-
inspired reverence for the workings of the God-created universe,
it amounts to little more than the way of thinking proposed by
Thomas Aquinas in the thirteenth century. The fact that the
original Thomistic system has been subjected to various philosophical refutations is unimportant.[6] What matters is that
through the example of Thomas Aquinas, our Judaic-Christian
tradition (representing man's spirituality) and our Greco-Roman
tradition (representing his speculative rationality) could be kept
from becoming mutually exclusive. It is true, of course, that
there have been constant tensions between these two traditions
and what they represent in the human make-up. And it is also
true that just as during the Middle Ages man's spirituality received the greater attention, so today it is man's empirical
rationality that is most emphasized. Yet because, nevertheless,
these two traditions have always on some terms or other remained complementary and mutually reinforcing, Western civilization has undoubtedly been able to maintain a much greater
cultural dynamism and range of philosophical and political
meaning than it would otherwise have been able to do.

Church versus State

The intellectual defense of Christian universalism, so brilliantly argued by Thomas Aquinas, was only one aspect of the
permanent two-front campaign that the medieval Church was
compelled to wage. The other was its conflict with Europe's
secular rulers, those powerful feudal lords who after the eleventh
century began to establish themselves as nation-state kings. In
the course of this centuries-long struggle between Church and
state, a most important advantage was gained for the West's
political future: that is, all nonrational and nonutilitarian justifications of authority—whether advanced by papalists or secularists—were intellectually severely shaken.

For a time after the conclusion of the late-medieval Church-state struggle, the new monarchs, advancing the argument of the Divine Right of Kings, in fact did enjoy absolute political supremacy. Yet the effectiveness of their argument, and in a number of important cases even their *de facto* supremacy, proved short-lived. For, while the late-medieval secularists had destroyed the Papacy's claims to authority by divine sanction, the spokesmen for the Church—even before it was fully consolidated— had no less devastatingly attacked the Divine Right claims of monarchical absolutism. As a result, there remained only one argument in defense of political authority that seemed truly irrefutable: the utilitarian principle that the only permissible purpose and justification of government was service to the needs of those who were being governed and on whose behalf government existed.

This utilitarian principle of authority has become one of the basic principles in our Western political credo. And though its practical implementation required a number of centuries, its establishment was, in large part, the final and unwitting contribution of the long Church-state controversy with which, politically speaking, the European Middle Ages came to an end.

In the development of the Church's campaign against unlimited secular power the first major blow was struck during the so-called Investiture Controversy, which broke out in 1073. When, in that year, Pope Gregory VII attempted to reassert the Church's authority over the appointment and investiture of bishops, the German emperor, Henry IV, strongly resisted. His reason was that since bishops had over the years acquired such important secular as well as spiritual functions, their control by the Papacy would threaten considerable papal interference in secular affairs. The Pope, however, was adamant. As did every other Christian's, he argued, the moral and spiritual life of a secular ruler fell within the absolute authority of the Papacy. If, therefore, the Pope saw fit, he could go so far as to excommunicate a secular ruler. But such a step would not merely affect the ruler personally. It would, at the same time, mean that he no longer belonged to the body of true Christians and that he could therefore no longer retain the loyalty of his Christian subjects. What the Pope thus claimed was that his right to excommunicate was also a right to depose rulers by absolving their subjects from their oath of allegiance. The Pope, this implied, was the final arbiter not only in religious affairs but in matters of government as well.

The view of secular kingship with which Pope Gregory VII buttressed this claim was not a lofty one. "Who does not know," he wrote, "that kings and rulers took their beginning from those who, being ignorant of God, have assumed because of blind greed and intolerable presumption, to make themselves masters of their equals, namely men, by means of pride, violence, bad faith, murder, and nearly every kind of crime, being incited thereto by the prince of this world, the Devil?" [7] Church authorities, Gregory urged, should always bear this allegedly criminal origin of secular kingship in mind: "So act, I beg you, holy fathers and princes, that all the world may know that, if you have power to bind and loose in Heaven, you have power on earth to take away or grant empires, kingdoms, principalities, dukedoms, marches, counties, and the possessions of all men according to their merits. . . . Let kings and all the princes of the world learn how great you are and what power you have and let these small men fear to disobey the command of your church." [8]

A more analytical assault on growing royal power inspired by the continuing Church-state conflict was contained in John of Salisbury's book, the *Policraticus,* which appeared in 1159. The central thesis of this work was that the all-important test of a true king was whether or not he observed the people's and universal laws. A king who ruled in defiance of these laws was a tyrant and deserved not only to be deposed but, if necessary, killed. Salisbury's reasoning in support of this earliest defense of tyrannicide ran as follows:

> Between a tyrant and a prince there is this single or chief difference, that the latter obeys the law and rules the people by its dictates, accounting himself as but their servant. It is by virtue of the law that he makes good his claim to the foremost and chief place in the management of the affairs of the commonwealth. . . . Let the white-washers of rulers . . . trumpet abroad that the prince is not subject to the law, and that whatsoever is his will

and pleasure, not merely in establishing law according to the model
of equity, but absolutely and free from all restrictions, has the
force of law. . . . Still I will maintain . . . that kings are bound
by this law.[9]

As the churchmen's examination of kingship thus became
progressively more utilitarian in point of view, the popes themselves continued their battling in terms of ever more extravagant
theological claims. The climax in this papal aggressiveness toward secular authority came during the bitter dispute between
Pope Boniface VIII and King Philip the Fair of France. The
latter, in his efforts to consolidate his position as the monarch
of a centralized French nation, in the year 1296 undertook to
levy taxes upon the Church's very extensive properties in France.
The Pope offered all-out resistance. It was in the course of this
resistance that he issued the famous papal bull *Unam Sanctam*.
In this proclamation Boniface enunciated two basic principles
that he held to be essential to the Church's entire position.
The first was that the pope was supreme among Christians and
that subjection to him was necessary to salvation. The second
was that both secular and spiritual spheres of authority fell
ultimately under the supreme authority of the Papacy. It was not
that Boniface wanted the office of secular ruler eliminated altogether; what he asked, however, was that the power of kings
should be exercised "at the command and with the permission
of priests." In the words of one of Boniface's theological supporters, "As in the universe itself corporeal substance is ruled
by spiritual—for the heavens themselves, which are the highest
among corporeal beings and have control over all bodies, are
ruled by spiritual substances as moving intelligences—so among
Christians all temporal lords and all earthly powers ought to be
governed and ruled by spiritual and ecclesiastical authority,
and especially by the pope, who holds the summit and the
highest rank among spiritual powers and in the church." [10]

Ironically, the more sweeping these papal claims became,
the less, in fact, did they bear any realistic relationship to the
Papacy's actual power vis-à-vis secular authority. Indeed, not long
after Boniface's dispute with the French king, the Christian
world was disrupted by the so-called Great Schism. For nearly

forty years, between 1378 and 1417, there simultaneously existed two popes, one at Rome and the other, a protégé of the king of France, at Avignon. For a short period there was even a third claimant to the highest Christian office. Each of these would-be popes was ever ready to defame his competitors as "anti-Christs," and all of them, while seeking to manipulate secular rulers for their own advantage, were, in fact, serving these rulers as instruments in the latters' campaigns for national aggrandizement. The result for Europe as a whole was an unprecedented profaning of Christian spirituality and a disastrous aggravation of political instability.

Not surprisingly, this disruptiveness of the Church's organizational crisis prompted the most serious reflections on the position of priests and religion in general as well as on the urgent problem of European political organization. If, as it appeared, a universal religious and political community under the leadership of the Papacy was no longer possible, what type of relationship and system of authority *could* keep the peoples of Europe at peace?

Thinking on this problem among European scholars, churchmen, and secular rulers culminated between 1414 and 1449 in the so-called Conciliar Movement. The purposes of this movement were twofold. The first was to re-establish a single legitimate pope to serve once again as Christianity's top spiritual executive. And the second was to democratize the Church's decision-making procedure by shifting ultimate authority in Church affairs from the pope to a representative general council of Christianity's most distinguished lay and ecclesiastical subjects. The democratic inspiration that underlay this latter plan was clearly summarized in the following statement of principle by Nicholas of Cusa, the Conciliar Movement's most prominent philosophical spokesman:

> Accordingly, since by nature all men are free, any authority by which subjects are prevented from doing evil and their freedom is restrained to doing good through fear of penalties, comes solely from harmony and from the consent of the subjects, whether the authority resides in written law or in the living law which is the ruler. For if by nature men are equally strong and equally

free, the true and settled power of one over the others, the ruler having equal natural power, could be set up only by the choice and consent of the others, just as law is also set up by consent.[11]

The Conciliar Movement's efforts to save medieval political and religious universalism by democratizing its organizational structure came to naught. Once the Papacy had been re-established in Rome, its opposition to such democratization proved unshakable. Yet in spite of the Conciliar Movement's failure in practice, its significance in the evolution of Western political principle was most substantial. What it once and for all laid to rest was the proposition that authority—whether ecclesiastical or political—could be justified by appeal to Divine Right. What it permanently fixed in the Western political tradition was the conviction that all authority exists for the purpose and by the consent of the governed. How such consent was to be made effective was bound to raise most difficult theoretical and practical problems. That such consent was indispensable could never again in good conscience and with any measure of political realism be denied.

SELECTED BIBLIOGRAPHY

CRUMP, C. G., and E. F. JACOB, *The Legacy of the Middle Ages,* London, Oxford University Press, 1951, Chaps. 6–10, pp. 287–533.

DE BURGH, W. G. *The Legacy of the Ancient World,* London, Pelican, 1955, Vol. II, Chap. 11, "The Legacy of the Middle Ages," pp. 437–497.

EBENSTEIN, WILLIAM. *Political Thought in Perspective,* New York, McGraw-Hill, 1957, Chap. 6, "St. Thomas Aquinas," pp. 125–146; and Chap. 7, "Dante," pp. 147–166.

FREMANTLE, ANNE. *The Age of Belief,* New York, Mentor, 1954.

MULLER, HERBERT J. *The Uses of the Past,* New York, Mentor, 1956, Chap. 8, "The Birth of Western Civilization," pp. 231–279.

PIRENNE, HENRI. *Economic and Social History of Medieval Europe,* New York, Harcourt, Brace, Harvest Book HB-14.

RANDALL, JOHN HERMAN, JR. *The Role of Knowledge in Western Religion,* Boston, Starr King, 1958, Chap. 2, "Religion and Natural Science" pp. 43–75.

« 5 »

The Reformation
and the Nation-State

B Y THE MIDDLE of the fifteenth century, the medieval European
social and religious order was on the verge of final disintegration. The growth of cities, commerce, and money economies had taxed the older feudal arrangements to the breaking
point. And cultural and political differentiation among the
peoples of Europe had reached a stage where it could no longer
be accommodated within one doctrinal orthodoxy or managed by
one common religious institution. The Reformation was a
dramatic expression of this passing into a new era as well as a
decisive event in determining the characteristics that the new
era was to assume. Its two most general effects were, on the one
hand, to give new emphases to the freedom and responsibilities
of the individual and, on the other, to facilitate the consolidation
of the nation-state.

The Impact of Lutheranism

Human action without the guidance of ideas would be
impossible. Yet which of the many ideas available at any given
time will be selected for guidance depends largely upon prevailing circumstances. If, for example, instead of being born in
1483, Martin Luther had been born a century earlier, his ideas
would probably have attracted little attention. At worst, he
might have been burned at the stake for heresy; at best, he

would have been ignored. Appearing at a time of mounting tensions within the traditional Catholic order, his ideas provided the medium through which that order was at last formally disrupted.

Luther himself was little interested in secular affairs. His original and always primary concern was with other-worldly salvation. He objected to the Catholicism of his day because he felt that through its concern with human institutions and its emphasis on various types of ritual it was encouraging this-worldliness, smugness, and an avoidance of true Christian humility. For Luther, in contrast, man was by nature an abject and hopeless sinner; he should always bear this in mind; no priestly effort or formal religious practice could assure his escape from this condition; all he could do was humbly to contemplate his sinfulness and hope that God's love and grace might save him.

In Luther's original view, moreover, the Church was neither an institution nor a hierarchy. It consisted simply of the sum total of all individual Christian believers. And its final authority was not the pope, but the Word of God as written in the Scriptures and understood by each private conscience. Between man and God there was no institutional intermediary. Man was on his own, with nothing but his own understanding of the Bible to guide him and with no hope of salvation except through the promise of God's love and the doing of his inscrutable will. And politics? As far as Luther was concerned, the authority of the state was at best a necessary evil. Rather than resist it, one should, in order not to divert oneself from one's private preoccupation with salvation, merely submit to it and accord it obedience.

Why did these deeply subjective and apolitical ideas of Luther's exercise such a resounding impact? As already suggested, the reason lay less in the ideas themselves than in the discontents of those who were ready to appropriate and apply them. For one thing, there had long been deep resentment throughout northern Europe against the cultural and religious pre-eminence of Rome; here at last, in the ideas of Luther, was a medium in terms of which Europe's other cultural and ethnic groups could reject the age-old Roman tutelage. Second, Luther's ideas proved particularly useful to the various German princes, whose tiny states, under the over-all rule of the so-called Holy Roman Emperor, at the time comprised the German cultural and political area. By endorsing Luther these authorities were able to strengthen their own local prestige and power at the expense of both the pope and the Catholic Holy Roman Emperor. Finally, the implied antitraditionalism of Luther's position strongly appealed to those who for one reason or another felt themselves at a disadvantage in the crumbling feudal order. Among these latter were chiefly two groups. One was the impoverished and exploited peasants. In these, Luther's ideas inspired a number of tragically unsuccessful outbreaks of revolt. The other was the new and growing urban commercial class. The members of this group saw in Luther's religious protest a larger and more meaningful rationale for their own social and economic discontents.

How did these variously motivated appropriations of Luther's ideas affect the West's subsequent historical development? Most immediately, they hastened the consolidation of the European nation-states. In some countries, as to a greater or lesser extent in Germany, the Netherlands, England, and Scotland, Protestantism became the unifying bond of the forces striving for nation-state centralization against internationalist Catholicism. Elsewhere, as in France, where the nation-state monarch had allied himself with Catholicism, Protestantism became the religious cause of those who fought against national centralization. Yet here too the effect was to further nation-state development. For in rallying in the name of Protestantism, the anticentralizers achieved greater solidarity, became more readily identifiable, and, in the final battles, proved the easier for the monarchists to eliminate.

Of even more fundamental importance than its ideological role in the building of European nation-states were the new emphasis and dimensions that Protestantism gave to the freedom and responsibilities of the individual conscience. For, although the Protestant preoccupation with individual freedom and responsibility was in the first instance religious, it soon extended itself into a great many areas of secular life as well. Paradoxically, however, the expression of Protestant individualism in secular affairs took two quite different forms: it operated as a religious inspiration for economically and politically activistic *public* individualism; and it became a religious influence encouraging *private* individualism in the spiritual realm but enjoining external passivity and obedience.

Lutheran Protestantism, particularly in Germany, tended from the very beginning to play this latter type of conservative role. In part, this resulted from the situation in which Luther found himself when he first expounded his message. Being exposed to the wrath of the Catholic Church, it was only natural that he gratefully accepted the protection of the local German princes. Yet once he had entered that alliance and had come to depend upon it, there was little he could do but pay its price. When the peasants, aroused by Luther's own ideas, broke out in revolt against the established secular order, Luther felt obliged not only to refuse them his support but to urge their submission and, in the end, to condone their ruthless suppression. And in doing so, he unwittingly established a pattern of adjustment to life that has been associated with German Lutheran Protestantism ever since: an inclination to intense individualism in private and personal matters, accompanied by an equally pronounced tendency to suspend individual conscience in regard to public affairs.

In a larger sense, however, German Lutheranism's conservative impact is rooted less in historical circumstances than in its founder's theological outlook. Not that Luther himself was a conservative by intention. Indeed, his great stress on the inwardness of religious experience and his doctrine of the equality and personal priesthood of all believers mark him as at heart an almost anarchistic Christian utopian. Lutheran conservatism resulted, rather, by default: first, from the fact that Luther considered secular affairs of subordinate importance as compared with inner spiritual concerns; and second, from his failure to envisage any special religious institution by which his theories could be put into practice. He thereby discouraged his followers from active participation in public affairs and left the administration of religious matters in the hands of the state. Thus, as the German Lutheran theologian and philosopher, Ernst Troeltsch, pointed out almost half a century ago:

The passivity of Lutheranism involved the habit of falling back upon whatever power happened to be dominant at the time. When it was suggested that this attitude left Christians at the mercy of every rogue and brutal tyrant, Luther replied that the Government ought to see that this did not happen, and that if it failed to prevent it, then certainly the Christian must simply suffer for it. Thus everywhere Lutheranism came under the influence of the dominant authority. The yielding spirit of its wholly interior spirituality adapted itself to the dominant authority of the day. This meant, however, that the form Lutheranism took was controlled by the various forms of government with which it was connected.[1]

Calvinist Protestantism

In sharp contrast to the tendency to secular passivity encouraged by Lutheranism in Germany was the economically and politically activistic individualism engendered in countries like Switzerland, Holland, Scotland, and England by the ideas of the great French Protestant Reformer, John Calvin (1509–1564). There have been two main reasons for this difference of political impact between Lutheranism and Calvinism. The one has been a matter of basic theological differences between the two versions of Protestantism. In Luther's view, for one thing, man's sinfulness not only was predetermined by his human nature but was beyond remedying by anything that he himself might undertake. There was little he could do but resign himself to his helplessness and hope for God's grace. In Calvin's interpretation, it is true, man's eternal salvation was also a matter of divinely decided predestination. Yet as Calvin saw it, although man could not know for certain whether he had been elected by God for salvation, there were a number of possible indications and evidences from which he might presume to take hope. Thus, according to Calvin, the elect were always people who had faith, who participated in certain religious sacraments, and who led upright, industrious, and frugal lives.

But if a man accepted these presumptive evidences of salvation suggested by Calvin, what was the rational course for him to follow? Obviously—to do his utmost to make his way of life conform to these standards so that he might presume that he too had been marked by God for salvation. It was, indeed, in its tendency theologically to induce this kind of thinking and behavior that Calvinism distinguished itself decidedly from Lutheranism. For whereas Lutheranism, minimizing the efficacy of individual efforts to achieve salvation, tended to act as a religion of acquiescence, Calvinism was very definitely a spiritual incentive to economic and political action.

A further significant theological difference between Luther and Calvin related to their different conceptions of the nature and role of the Church. Luther had provided for no specifically religious organization whatsoever and had instead left the administration of the faith to secular authority. The more practical-minded lawyer Calvin held a tight religious organization to be a vital necessity for the maintenance of Church discipline as well as for the more advantageous management of the Church's relations with secular authority. For, as he explained in his principal work, the *Institutes of the Christian Religion,*

> if no society, and even no house, though containing only a small family, can be preserved in a proper state without discipline, this is far more necessary in the Church, the state of which ought to be the most orderly of all. As the saving doctrine of Christ is the soul of the Church, so discipline forms the ligaments which connect the members together, and keep each in its proper place. . . . For what will be the consequence, if every man be at liberty to follow his own inclinations? . . . Discipline, therefore, serves as a bridle to curb and restrain the refractory, who resist the doctrine of Christ; or as a spur to stimulate the inactive; and sometimes as a father's rod, with which those who have grievously fallen may be chastised in mercy, and with the gentleness of the spirit of Christ.[2]

This same forcefulness characterized Calvin's stand on the Church's relations with secular authority. As a general proposition, he subscribed to what amounted to the old Catholic doctrine of the two swords: as the Church was responsible for all spiritual matters, so the civil ruler's power extended to all things temporal. Rather than in any way minimizing the importance of secular authority, moreover, Calvin warned that "the first duty of subjects towards their magistrates is to enter-tain the most honorable sentiments of their functions, which they know to be a jurisdiction delegated to them from God. . . . Here let no man deceive himself. For it is impossible to resist the magistrate without, at the same time, resisting God himself." [3]

Yet if allowed to stand alone, this exhortation to submission to established secular authority would be seriously misleading. For, Calvin made it quite clear both in his writings and in his theocratic management of the city of Geneva, where he maintained his headquarters, that though secular government deserved to be respected, it should always remain under the supervision of his ascetic and militant version of Protestant spirituality. As he put it in his *Institutes,*

> Great kings ought not to think it any dishonor to prostrate themselves as suppliants before Christ the King of kings, nor ought they to be displeased at being judged by the Church. As they hear scarcely any thing in their courts but mere flatteries, it is more necessary for them to receive correction from the Lord by the mouth of his *ministers;* they ought even to wish not to be spared by the *pastors,* that they may be spared by the Lord.[4]

What made these theological differences between Calvinism and Lutheranism the more significant was the different nature of the situations in which Calvinism took root. In countries like England and Scotland, for example, a battle for power between the traditionalist and pro-Catholic royalists and the new urban and commercial classes had been shaping up for some time. What these latter groups had lacked had been a justifying, unifying, and directing new world view. It was this that they found in the Calvinist type of Protestantism. In the Calvinistic spiritual militancy they could express their own social restiveness. With Calvin's insistence that the state should be guided by Christian spirituality, they could identify their impatience to see government give greater recognition to their own interests and way of life. And in Calvin's presumptive tests of salvation—piety, hard work, and various kinds of asceticism—they saw a rejection of the luxury, ostentation, and cynicism they associated with the traditional privileged classes and a sanction for their own more austere middle-class virtues.

The resulting interaction between Calvinist religious ideas and the economic and political behavior of the Anglo-Saxon middle classes is generally recognized to have been one of the most important contributing factors in the development of both capitalism and liberal democracy. For, as the English historian R. H. Tawney has pointed out in his classic study, *Religion and the Rise of Capitalism:*

> Such teaching [that is, the various versions of Calvinist Protestantism], whatever its theological merits or defects, was admirably designed to liberate economic energies, and to weld into a disciplined social force the rising bourgeoisie, conscious of the contrast between its own standards and those of a laxer world, proud of its vocation as the standardbearer of the economic virtues, and determined to vindicate an open road for its own way of life by the use of every weapon, including political revolution and war, because the issue which was at stake was not merely convenience or self-interest, but the will of God. Calvinism stood, in short, not only for a new doctrine of theology and ecclesiastical government, but for a new scale of moral values and a new ideal of social conduct.[5]

In concluding this brief consideration of the secular impact of Lutheranism and Calvinism it is necessary to note one further important contribution to the evolution of the West's political orientation for which the Reformation was at least indirectly responsible. That was its long-range effect in destroying the practicability and morality of insistence on any kind of total spiritual or political orthodoxy. It is of course true that in the first stages of the Reformation the enforcement of orthodoxy— among Protestants and Catholics alike—was more uncompromising and brutal than ever. Yet it was in response to that very situation that men were compelled to develop a solution that had never before existed since Christianity's establishment as the West's official religion. That solution was the acknowledgment —as a compromise live-and-let-live denominator among all religions and sects—of the universal right of freedom of conscience.

It was this right of freedom of conscience that became the inspiration of all of the West's subsequent civil liberties. Referring at first primarily to religious matters, it was extended in the course of time to apply to all forms of intellectual as well as political expression. Through the right and responsibility that it has assigned to the individual conscience it has helped to motivate our civilization's finest cultural and political achievements. Without the toleration that it has represented, the bringing to fruition of these achievements—including the entire liberal democratic way of life—would have been impossible.

Machiavelli and Political Power

When traditional political institutions seem to be performing the functions that are expected of them, there is usually little preoccupation with matters of political power. The fact that society is organized in certain patterns and that certain people have authority over others is accepted as entirely proper. When, in contrast, there is large-scale discontent with the working of traditional political institutions, the question of who has authority and of how and for what ends it is being exercised— that is, the question of political power—becomes not only important but paramount.

During the Middle Ages, political power as such was seldom talked about. The feudal system and its traditional relationships of authority were generally held to be adequately serving their purposes and, therefore, occasioned little probing. Once the feudal order began to break down, however, it was necessary not only to devise new units of political organization that would be workable under the changed conditions, but also to decide by what relationships of authority these new political units might best be established and maintained. It was in the process of contemplating and fighting out these decisions that the modern world first became aware of the problem of political power.

The new units of political organization which were fashioned from disintegrating feudalism and Catholic universalism were, of course, the European nation-states; the principle of political authority by which they were established and at first maintained was that of royal absolutism; and wherever this development occurred, as early modern European history dramatically records, it was through a thorough knowledge and ruthless use of political power.

In cases where a particular monarch or succession of mon-

archs proved successful in the consolidation of nation-state
authority (as, for instance, in England), there was little inclination or need to subject the principles and techniques of
power to systematic formulation; it sufficed—and, indeed, was the
better part of wisdom—merely to know the dictates of power
and to act accordingly. Where, in contrast, such royal nation-
building proved unsuccessful and was felt to be creating serious
hardships, the whys, hows, and wherefores of power quite
naturally became the subject of a good deal of theoretical discussion. Thus, not surprisingly, it was the European political
situation which was least successful of all in developing centralized nation-state authority, namely Italy, which inspired modern
Europe's earliest and most impassioned dissertation on the nature
and employment of power, Niccolo Machiavelli's *The Prince*.

At the time of Machiavelli's writing, Italy was politically
organized into five states—the Papal States, the Kingdom of
Naples, the Duchy of Milan, and the Republics of Venice and
Florence. Partly because of the Papacy's efforts to prevent Italian
nation-state consolidation and partly as a consequence of regular
interventions in Italian affairs by the Holy Roman Emperor
and the monarchs of France and Spain, these five Italian states
lived in a condition of constant disorder and war. It was this
chaotic situation that Machiavelli was concerned with remedying.
And the only way he believed this could be done was if the
Italian area itself were welded into a strong and unified nation-
state.

As Machiavelli shows in such other of his writings as *The
Discourses* and *The History of Florence,* the form of constitution he held to be ideal was that of a free, representatively
governed republic. Yet he was convinced that a first stage that
Italy would have to pass through in pursuit of that ideal was a
period of absolute one-man rule. And the dominant feature of
such one-man rule, he believed, would have to be its possession
and morally uninhibited use of centralized political power. It
was as a plan for the development of such leadership, and a
handbook of rules for its most effective possible exercise, that
Machiavelli intended his short book, *The Prince*.

Born in Florence in 1469, Machiavelli not only had personally experienced the pains of Italy's disunited political situ-

ation but had had extensive firsthand contact with the intra-Italian and international political intriguing that was its cause. For fifteen years, as what amounted to Florence's secretary in charge of diplomacy and war, he had conducted his city-state's military and foreign policies, had visited Europe's royal courts, and—beneath the façade of royal splendor—had seen how unscrupulous the kingly conduct of nation-state politics really was. At the age of forty-four, as a result of a *coup d'état* in which he found himself on the losing side, Machiavelli was forced to leave Florence in exile. Never again permitted to return, he took up residence not far away and, for the rest of his life, poured his patriotism, frustrated ambition, and knowledge into his writings.

That he did not believe in absolute power for its own sake but as a means to what he was convinced was the urgent end of achieving an independent Italian nation-state, Machiavelli showed in the fervent exhortation with which he concluded *The Prince*—an exhortation to Duke Lorenzo di Medici, the man to whom he looked to take up the challenge of uniting Italy:

> This opportunity must not, therefore, be allowed to pass, so that Italy may at length find her liberator. I cannot express the love with which he would be received in all those provinces which have suffered under these foreign invasions, with what thirst for vengeance, with what steadfast faith, with what love, with what grateful tears. What doors would be closed against him? What people would refuse him obedience? What envy could oppose him? What Italian would withhold him allegiance? This barbarous domination stinks in the nostrils of everyone. May your illustrious house therefore assume this task with that courage and those hopes which are inspired by a just cause, so that under its banner our fatherland may be raised up . . . .[6]

While Machiavelli's analysis dealt with a great many aspects of power, his prescription of the rules to be followed by Italy's strongman focused above all upon one principle: that the Prince, as Machiavelli calls him, be a realist in his view of human nature as well as in his manipulation of it for his political purposes. He must, in other words, face up to the fact—as Machiavelli sees it—that most men are motivated by desire, fear, and vanity, and that anyone who would do anything with or for them can succeed only by acting accordingly:

There are two methods of fighting, the one by law, the other by force: the first method is that of men, the second of beasts; but as the first method is often insufficient, one must have recourse to the second. It is therefore necessary for a prince to know well how to use both the beast and the man. . . . A prince being thus obliged to know well how to act as a beast must imitate the fox and the lion, for the lion cannot protect himself from traps, and the fox cannot defend himself from wolves. One must therefore be a fox to recognize traps, and a lion to frighten wolves. Those that wish to be only lions do not understand this. Therefore, a prudent ruler ought not to keep faith when by so doing it would be against his interest, and when the reasons which made him bind himself no longer exist. If men were all good, this precept would not be a good one; but as they are bad, and would not observe their faith with you, so you are not bound to keep faith with them. Nor have legitimate grounds ever failed a prince who wished to show colourable excuse for the non-fulfillment of his promise. . . . But it is necessary to be able to disguise this character well, and to be a great feigner and dissembler; and men are so simple and so ready to obey present necessities, that one who deceives will always find those who allow themselves to be deceived. . . . Thus it is well to seem merciful, faithful, humane, sincere, religious, and also to be so; but you must have the mind so disposed that when it is needful to be otherwise you may be able to change to the opposite qualities. . . . Let a prince therefore aim at conquering and main-taining the state, and the means will always be judged honourable and praised by every one, for the vulgar is always taken by ap-pearances and the issue of the event, and the world consists only of the vulgar, and the few who are not vulgar are isolated when the many have a rallying point in the prince. A certain prince of the present time, whom it is well not to name, never does any-thing but preach peace and good faith, but he is really a great enemy to both, and either of them, had he observed them, would have lost him state or reputation on many occasions.[7]

Machiavelli's thesis that the first stage in the development of national political unity must be one of enlightened despotism and amoral power politics has made him the subject of mixed and often heated reactions for five centuries. Actually, of course, he merely described the process by which the Euopean nation-states had everywhere been established. Yet even so, it is not difficult to understand why he should have engendered the strong

feelings that he has. In most Western countries, on the one
hand, the kind of situation with which Machiavelli was concerned has long been transcended. Since power has by now
become regularized and accepted to the extent that its exercise
seems wholly natural and moral, Machiavelli's reminder of its
harsh and amoral essence not surprisingly tends to evoke feelings
of indignation and unbelief. In those countries that have not
yet achieved political unity and a stably functioning system
of authority, on the other hand, Machiavelli's thesis very often
meets with enthusiastic approval. The reason for this, of course,
is that in such countries—for example, many of the under-developed lands of Asia, the Middle East, and Africa—the political situations that prevail are in many ways comparable to that which confronted Machiavelli in early sixteenth-century Italy.

Bodin and the Concept of Sovereignty

The same general problem of nation-state power that concerned Machiavelli was the central subject of another sixteenth-
century student of politics, the Frenchman Jean Bodin (1530–
1596). Whereas, however, Machiavelli had addressed himself to
the challenge of establishing a nation (and had thereby become
involved in the more vulgar aspects of power), Bodin, living in
a nation that already existed, was occupied with the more
refined problem of consolidating and legalizing national power.

The immediate crisis with reference to which Bodin wrote
was the situation he witnessed at the time in his own country.
The chief feature of that situation was the politico-religious
civil war that had raged for decades in France between those who
supported the centralized nation-state power of the Catholic
French monarchy and the various groups who opposed it. What
Bodin hoped to do in his analysis, as set forth in his *Six Books
of the Republic,* was to show what the functional and legal
essence of the state was, so that it might be better understood
and abided by by all those who wanted it to survive.

According to Bodin, what distinguished the state from all
other associations and institutions was its possession of what he
called *puissance suprême,* or sovereignty. What this basically
consisted of was an unconditional commitment on the part of

all of the state's citizens to accept the state's authority to legislate for them as ultimate, irrevocable, and not subject to the approval of any other. As Bodin analyzed it, such sovereign power has four chief characteristics: it is inherent in the state by definition and is therefore undelegated; it is perpetual, lasting as long as the state itself exists; it is inalienable, because it is the state's very essence and could not be taken away without bringing the state's existence to an end; and it is unrestricted by law, because the state's sovereign power is itself the source of law. Its justification, moreover, is not a matter of either religious or metaphysical sanction. It flows, rather, from the utilitarian necessity of maintaining political order, which can be met only if those who are subjects of the state unreservedly acknowledge their inescapable obligation to accept the state's laws and commands as final and binding. Though Bodin at times creates the impression that sovereignty is synonymous with royal power, his more considered position is that it is in reality the essential attribute of the state itself. Whether, in other words, sovereignty is considered for practical governmental purposes to reside in a king, an aristocracy, or the people, Bodin believed to be an entirely incidental question that did not affect the basic fact of the state's sovereignty as such.

This function and quality of sovereignty, as first described by Bodin, has remained the accepted definition of the legal essence of the state. Yet while the concept of sovereignty has thus been with us for the past four centuries, so has the moral dilemma to which it unavoidably gives rise. On the one hand, Bodin was obviously quite correct about the necessity of the attribute of sovereignty. If in being a citizen of a state one were not committed to acknowledge the state's authority as supreme and ultimate, the state's existence would be highly precarious. Since everyone would be free to obey or not obey whatever laws he pleased, the state would be in constant danger of falling into anarchy or of being conquered from the outside. On the other hand, if in being a citizen of a state one must accept its sovereign will as final, is one not thereby committed, if called upon, to abdicate one's own individual moral standards as a human being in favor of whatever commands the state may decide to impose upon one as a citizen?

This conflict between one's duty to his sovereign country and his commitment to more universal values has been experienced by modern men everywhere. Attempts to resolve it have taken two chief forms. The first has been to see one's own country's policies as representing whatever universal morality he may believe in. If a person can thus convince himself that his own country represents the good (while other countries represent evil), he need feel little compunction about obeying whatever his country may command. Unfortunately, however, since the citizens of other lands may be assumed to be believing the same thing about their country's policies, what results is likely to be merely a self-deceptive abdication of individually held moral standards. Moreover, whatever international clashes may occur will probably be waged more uncompromisingly and brutally than ever. Since obedience to the nation is in each case glorified as the championing of a universal good, individual moral responsibility tends on all sides to give way to unquestioning nationalistic self-righteousness.

The other attempt to resolve the dilemma of conflicting national and universal loyalties has been based upon a much sounder, if more difficult, strategy. That has been the effort to persuade sovereign states so to conduct their affairs that they need not call upon their citizens to engage in actions occasioning conflicts of national and universal loyalties. It is with the development of this latter type of attempt to mitigate the politics and moral dilemma of nation-state sovereignty that the modern Western world's international lawyers have concerned themselves.

Grotius and International Law

One of the earliest and most famous of the lawyer-philosophers to occupy himself with the political and moral implications of nation-state sovereignty was the Dutchman Hugo Grotius (1583–1645). Grotius deeply regretted the breakup of medieval European universalism, but was convinced that whether one approved of it or not, the phenomenon of the nation-state had to be faced. His purpose, therefore, was to develop a method whereby at least the most destructive effects of the anarchical

competition among Europe's new sovereign powers might be
checked and eliminated. Not only was early modern Europe the
scene of almost permanent interstate conflict; the manner of
waging war had acquired a new and unprecedented ferocity. As
Grotius himself described the situation: "I saw prevailing
throughout the Christian world a license in making war of which
even barbarous nations should be ashamed; men resorting to
arms for trivial or for no reasons at all, and when arms were
once taken up no reverence left for divine or human law,
exactly as if a single edict had released a madness driving men
to all kinds of crime." [8]

In his greatest and best-known work, *On the Law of War
and Peace,* Grotius approached the task of remedying this
situation by making two basic initial assumptions about nation-
states, assumptions which we still accept as valid today. The
first was that the political and legal reality of the sovereign
state, as formulated by Bodin, had to be accepted as a permanent
fact. All states had to be considered as completely independent,
not only of one another but also of any supranational authority
such as the Holy Roman Empire or the Roman Papacy. Within
the territory under his control, therefore, each sovereign must
be acknowledged as supreme in all matters. And Grotius' second
and related initial assumption was that all sovereign states, by
the fact of their being such, must be considered as legally and
diplomatically equal. In terms of rights and prerogatives, that
is, there can be no distinction between them. They are all on
a par, whether large or small, old or new, militarily powerful
or weak, and regardless of their type of government.

And how did any particular sovereign actor on the new
stage of freely competitive world politics qualify for recognition
as a full-fledged member in this Family of Nations, as Grotius
called it? His answer, which we still adhere to today, was that
to gain international acceptance as a fully sovereign and equal
nation a state had to show convincing evidence of possessing
four basic attributes: a civilization of the type of the already
established Christian states of the West; an organized government capable of entering into and observing treaties and conventions; a fixed territory within which its sovereignty is complete; and a condition of internal stability which appears likely
to offer to its sovereignty a guarantee of permanence.

Among the sovereign equals of the Family of Nations so defined, Grotius pointed out, there were three possible types of relationships: peace, war, and neutrality. It was to the precise definition of these three types of relationships and to the formulation of rules of international behavior (that is, international law) by which states should conduct them, that Grotius devoted the bulk of his treatise. And since it was the relationship of war which in his day was the most frequent, it was to this that he gave his fullest attention.

As well-intended and impressive as Grotius' and all subsequent formulations of international rules of conduct have been, their effectiveness has from the very beginning hinged on the solution of a most difficult problem. How, if states are defined as sovereign, can they be persuaded or compelled to accept and abide by the rules of international conduct suggested to them as international law?

Grotius himself was only too clearly aware of this question. And the answer he gave has, once again, been essentially the one which international lawyers have had to be satisfied with until the present day: that even though there was no way to *enforce* conformity to international law, it would nevertheless be abided by because it was the expression of the universally self-evident rationality, morality, and common sense of Natural Law. As Grotius defined this originally Stoic and Ciceronian sanction of Natural Law, it was "the dictate of right reason, indicating that an act, from its agreement or disagreement with the rational and social nature of man, has in it moral turpitude or moral necessity, and consequently that such an act is either forbidden or commanded by God the author of nature."

Yet the question remained: how were the dictates of this Natural Law to be known and recognized with any degree of specificity as far as the rules of international conduct were concerned? According to Grotius, there were three reliable guides for the recognition of a given rule of conduct as a dictate of Natural Law: first, if its value and necessity were instinctively perceived by the conscience of the normal individual; second, if it was proclaimed by general agreement among the civilized world's best minds; and, finally, if it was confirmed by the practice of all the most civilized peoples.

Unfortunately once again, whereas these criteria for establishing an international law seem reasonable enough in theory, their effectiveness in practice has remained severely limited. In any major international controversy, particularly if it proceeds to outright war, what appear to be the dictates of right reason tend on each side to be much too strongly biased by local cultural and political conditioning. And even where there is agreement on the course of conduct that would be required by international law, nations all too often simply refuse to comply. Either they excuse their own violations by alleging prior violations on the part of their opponents; or, when they feel that there are very critical military situations, they plead the precedence over the dictates of international law of what they call their own paramount national interest.

Yet in spite of the failure of international law to eliminate the consequences of national sovereignty, it has done much to curb them. It has achieved its successes, however, less through moral exhortation than through appeal to the common *interests* of the various nations. With increasing international trade and communication, the range of such common interests—including such matters as the regulation of postal traffic, sea and air navigation, and patent arrangements—has become ever wider. As global interdependence continues to grow, the significance of such practical-minded international co-operation is certain steadily to increase.

SELECTED BIBLIOGRAPHY

BAINTON, ROLAND H. *The Age of the Reformation*, Princeton, N.J., Van Nostrand, Anvil, 1956.

CORBETT, P. E. *Law and Society in the Relations of States*, New York, Harcourt, Brace, 1951, Pt. I, pp. 3–89.

EBENSTEIN, WILLIAM. *Political Thought in Perspective*, New York, McGraw-Hill, 1957, Chap. 8, "Machiavelli," pp. 167–198; Chap. 9, "Luther," pp. 199–219; Chap. 10, "Calvin," pp. 220–243; and Chap. 11, "Bodin," pp. 244–255.

FROMM, ERICH. *Escape from Freedom*, New York, Rinehart, 1941, pp. 3–135.

MOSSE, GEORGE L. *Calvinism: Authoritarian or Democratic?* (Source Problems in World Civilization), New York, Rinehart, 1957.

TROELTSCH, ERNST. *Protestantism and Progress*, Boston, Beacon, Beacon Paperback, 1958.

« 6 »

The Philosophy
of Liberal Democracy

MODERN WESTERN CIVILIZATION has confronted two fundamental political challenges. The one, in the nature of
things the historically prior, has been the challenge that first
engaged men like Machiavelli, Bodin, and Grotius: the problem
of establishing and regulating the sovereign power of the nation-
state. The other, which has everywhere emerged as central once
the former has seemed on the way to being solved, has been the
problem of deciding how, by whom, and for what purposes the
sovereign power of the nation-state should be maintained and
operated.

The dominant modern Western ideal for governing the
nation-state has been that of some form of liberal democracy.
And everywhere where this ideal has been implemented or
striven for, it has been philosophically argued on the basis of
three major assumptions: first, the utilitarian assumption that
government exists entirely for the benefit of the governed;
second, the liberal assumption that all men are equal and that
all, therefore, enjoy equal and inalienable natural rights, including the right to decide what is in their own best interest;
and third, the democratic assumption that since all men are the
proper and best judges of their own individual interest, the most
equitable and effective way of interpreting and realizing the
collective best interest is by majority decision of those concerned.

The elaboration of these assumptions and their constant

99

reinterpretation in the light of changing circumstances occupied the West's greatest political philosophers from the beginning of the seventeenth to the end of the nineteenth century. Among the most decisive milestones in this development of liberal democratic political philosophy were the arguments for and against political equality occasioned by the so-called Putney Debates at the conclusion of the English Puritan Revolution; the controversy about human nature and its implications for government between Thomas Hobbes and John Locke; Jean Jacques Rousseau's plea for the sovereignty of what he called the general will; Montesquieu's thesis that political liberty depended upon the institutional separation of legislative, executive, and judicial powers; Jeremy Bentham's enunciation of the utilitarian principle of the greatest good of the greatest number; and Adam Smith's liberal economic theory that the greatest collective prosperity inevitably results from the greatest possible reliance on the unfettered self-interest of the individual.

For and against Political Equality

The first people to solve the problem of consolidating the sovereign power of their nation-state were the English. Not surprisingly, therefore, it was in England that the first major actual and theoretical battles came to be fought over the subsequent control of the state's governing authority.

The earliest stages in the consolidation of England as a nation had, as elsewhere, occurred through the instrumentality of an absolute monarchy. Gradually, however, the English gentry and wealthier commercial groups, acting through Parliament, had secured substantial political concessions from the monarchy. So steadily had this trend progressed that by the end of Elizabeth I's reign, in 1603, Parliament had in a number of important respects come to be an almost equal partner in England's government.

Yet this peaceful diffusion of authority was suddenly halted by the efforts of Elizabeth's successors, the Stuart kings James I and his son Charles I, to reverse the trend by reinstituting absolute monarchy in the name of the so-called Divine Right of Kings. Having come from Scotland, and not recognizing the fact that in England this nonutilitarian argument had long ago been rejected, James I no sooner assumed the throne than he embarked on a determined campaign to reduce Parliament to a strictly subordinate and advisory role. Alleging that a king was responsible only to God, James explained and defended his antiparliamentary policies in terms of propositions such as this:

> The state of monarchy is the supremest thing upon earth: for kings are not only God's lieutenants upon earth, and sit upon God's throne, but even by God himself they are called Gods. . . . And so it follows of necessity, that kings were the authors and makers of the laws, and not the laws of kings. . . . That which concerns the mystery of the king's power is not lawful to be disputed; for that is to wade into the weakness of princes, and to take away the mystical reverence that belongs unto them that sit in the throne of God.[1]

Acting under the inspiration of this theory of royal power, James I and subsequently Charles I were guilty of infringement after infringement of rights and privileges that Parliament had long come to believe belonged to it by established English usage. For years Parliament was ignored and subjected to the most arbitrary indignities. Finally, after a long series of increasingly bitter crises, Parliament's resistance to nonresponsible and personalist royal rule broke out into open revolt. The civil war that followed, with the country's Protestant nonconformist sects and antimonarchists on the one side, and Charles I and his royalist and Anglican supporters on the other, amounted to the first of the modern world's great revolutionary fights for the idea and practice of government of, by, and for the governed. Before it was over, in 1649, Charles I had been defeated and publicly executed; England had temporarily been proclaimed a commonwealth; and Europe had for the first time heard a discussion of the pros and cons of liberal democracy whose various arguments were to echo throughout the Western world for at least three centuries to follow.

What makes these earliest discussions of the desirability and implications of liberal democracy the more impressive is that they were not contributed by people who regarded themselves as political philosophers. They resulted, rather, from the impromptu disputations of ordinary Englishmen, officers and men of the revolutionary army who, during the famous Putney Debates of 1647, were resisting disbandment until the lines of the country's political future should be more clearly and definitely settled.

Of the many brilliant interchanges that marked these debates, none is more penetrating than the one in which a Colonel Rainboro pleaded for government by consent and universal suffrage, and in which a Commissary-General Ireton answered that if political equality were claimed on the basis of inherent individual natural right, it would be only a question of time until the same justification would be advanced for all other kinds of equality, including the economic equality of common ownership of property.

Colonel Rainboro's argument in defense of political equality ran as follows:

> Really I think that the poorest he that is in England has a life to live as the richest he; and therefore truly, Sir, I think it's clear, that every man that is to live under a Government ought first by his own consent to put himself under that Government; and I do think that the poorest man in England is not at all bound in a strict sense to that Government that he has not had a voice to put himself under; and I am confident that when I have heard the reasons against it, something will be said to answer those reasons, insomuch that I should doubt whether he was an Englishman or no that should doubt of these things.[2]

The more conservative Commissary-General Ireton's reply to this plea for a vote for every Englishman was that

> If you make this the rule I think you must fly for refuge to an absolute Natural Right, and you must deny all Civil Right; and I am sure it will come to that in the consequence. . . . For my part I think it is no right at all. I think that no person has a right to an interest in the disposing or determining of the affairs of the Kingdom, and in choosing those that shall determine what laws we shall be ruled by here, no person has a right to this, that has not a permanent fixed interest in this Kingdom; and those persons together are properly the Represented of this Kingdom, and con-

sequently are to make up the Representors of this Kingdom, who taken together do comprehend whatsoever is of real or permanent interest in the Kingdom. . . . This is the most fundamental Constitution of the Kingdom, which if you do not allow you allow none at all. . . . If we shall go to take away this fundamental part of the civil constitution we shall plainly go to take away all property and interest that any man has, either in land by inheritance, or in estates by possession, or anything else.[3]

Political developments since the Putney Debates have, of course, borne out the insights of both these seventeenth-century Englishmen. The assumption of inherent natural rights has turned out to be the philosophical rock upon which liberal democracy has been built. And the establishment of full political equality has led to the extension of equality to many other areas of social life as well, including, to a greater or lesser extent, the economic.

Yet these practical implementations of liberal democracy's philosophical assumptions were still to require several centuries. In the short run, argumentations such as Rainboro's proved largely academic. The execution of Charles I was followed by an interim period of dictatorship under Oliver Cromwell, and then by the restoration of a monarchy that appeared for decades to have learned very little from the great events of the past. It was not until the later so-called Glorious Revolution of 1688 that the English Crown came in both law and fact to be a truly constitutional monarchy. And it was only with the first of the long series of electoral Reform Acts, in 1832, that the English Parliament began definitely to travel the road to universal suffrage and actual popular sovereignty.

Hobbes versus Locke

Among the greatest of seventeenth-century political philosophers were Thomas Hobbes (1588–1679) and John Locke (1632–1704). Both of these Englishmen took for granted that government was wholly utilitarian. And both subscribed to the liberal assumption of inherent individual human rights. They gave proof of this common point of departure by setting forth their respective ideas in terms of the famous hypothesis of the social contract.

The main purpose of the social contract hypothesis, which had first been suggested by the ancient Stoics, was to make it clear that man should always be considered to have moral precedence over social and political institutions. To support this view, the social contract hypothesis postulated the existence of an original state of nature in which there had been no social and political institutions and in which man had enjoyed unlimited natural rights, which he had pursued wholly on his own. Eventually, to improve upon his condition in the state of nature, he had subordinated himself to various types of institutions. But he had not done so blindly or as a victim of circumstances. He had taken the step in full consciousness as part of a self-interest–motivated contract with his fellows. And because of this, the institutions in question had always to be viewed as nothing more mysterious or glorious than rational instruments that man has set up and consented to abide by in the interest of achieving his own greatest possible individual happiness.

On the basis of this common utilitarian and liberal beginning, however, Hobbes and Locke built very different analyses and arrived at almost totally different conclusions. Whereas Locke believed that responsible representative government by majority rule was possible, Hobbes insisted that man's nature was such that his welfare required the discipline of a system of iron absolutism. As they expressed this basic difference of conclusion in the more specific terms of their writings, the two men differed in three chief respects: first, in their view of the postulated state of nature in which man lived before civil society was instituted; second, in their conception of the type of contract by which the establishment of society and government was agreed to; and, finally, in their depiction of the relationship that obtained between the individual and government once it had been instituted.

According to Hobbes, in his book *Leviathan,* there is no possible halfway point for man between unlimited natural freedom and complete submission to civil authority. Once man decides to leave the state of nature, he must be prepared to be ruled by a government whose power is completely absolute and whose right to exercise that power is ended only when it is no longer *able* to exercise it. The reason for this is that the act whereby men enter into contract with their fellows to set up the state is more a matter of an irrevocable commitment than of mere consent:

> It is a real unity of them all, in one and the same person, made by covenant of every man with every man, in such a manner as if every man should say to every man, *I authorize and give up my right of governing myself, to this man, or to this assembly of men, on this condition, that thou give up thy right to him, and authorize all his actions in like manner.* This done, the multitude so united in one person is called a Commonwealth, in Latin, *civitas.* This is the generation of that great *Leviathan,* or rather, to speak more reverently, of that *mortal god* to which we owe, under the *immortal God,* our peace and defence. For by this authority, given him by every particular man in the commonwealth, he has the use of so much power and strength conferred on him that by terror thereof he is enabled to form the wills of them all, to peace at home, and mutual aid against their enemies abroad. And in him consists the essence of the commonwealth. . . . And he that carries this person is called Sovereign, and said to have sovereign power; and every one besides, his subject.[4]

Why did Hobbes place such strong emphasis on the absolute and irrevocable nature of civil authority? The reason lay in his highly pessimistic view of human nature or, as he put it, of man's condition in the state of nature. According to Hobbes, man is a creature of appetites and passions which he is constantly driven by nature to satisfy. In this drive for gratification he is guided by a second factor in his natural functioning: his ability to be rational (understood by Hobbes to mean purposeful). The net result of this human makeup is that each man, using his rationality in the service of his passions, is in a constant natural state of war with every other man. And in this condition, Hobbes points out, "there is no place for industry, because the fruit thereof is uncertain; and consequently no culture ●f the earth; no navigation . . . ; no account of time; no arts; no letters; no society and, which is the worst of all, continual fear, and danger of violent death; and the life of man, solitary, poor, nasty, brutish, and short." [5]

But man's basic natural passion is his desire to survive. Because of this fact, and because every man knows that he is neither strong enough nor cunning enough to escape the natural war of all against all, his reason tells him that there is one compromise solution by which he and all other men can minimize life's hazards and maximize its chances for gratification. That solution is to contract with one another to assign to the state all responsibility for maintaining collective order. And since Hobbes viewed human nature as pessimistically as he did, he quite consistently concluded that the authority required to maintain collective order and to save men from the amorality and fear of their natural selves would have to be absolute, total, and unchallengeable.

According to Hobbes, therefore, liberal democratic government is not possible. Man has his inherent natural rights, that is true. And these include the right to be subjected to a government that he has agreed to institute and that exists for his welfare. Yet to protect his basic right and desire—his will to survive in peace and order—he can afford to exercise his natural freedom only once: in his decision to set up and submit to an unlimitedly powerful sovereign. Thereafter, in the practical interest of maximizing his welfare, his only rational course is to resign himself to whatever measure of domination the sovereign state may feel it necessary to impose.

In sharp contrast to this Hobbesian theory was Locke's conclusion that government was nothing but a trust that man had the moral self-sufficiency constantly to watch over and, if necessary, to rebel against. An undoubtedly important reason for this basic difference of conclusion was the different political circumstances in which the two men developed their theories. For Hobbes, whose *Leviathan* appeared in 1651, these circumstances were the violent years of the Puritan Revolution. Locke, in contrast, was inspired by the later and bloodless Glorious Revolution of 1688–1689. It was in that year that the English Parliament and people finally expelled the last of the arbitrary Stuart kings, James II, and invited William of Orange and his English wife, Mary, to assume the throne as truly constitutional monarchs. And though Locke's famous *Two Treatises of Government* (1690) is much more than a mere tract for the times, he admitted in his Preface that its immediate purpose was "to estab-

lish the throne of our great restorer, our present King William,"
and "to justify to the world the people of England whose love
of their just and natural rights, with their resolution to preserve
them, saved the nation when it was on the very brink of slavery
and ruin."

Important as these differences in Hobbes' and Locke's immediate political environments were, however, the really decisive factor making for their contrary conclusions about the
workability of liberal democratic government was the difference
in their views of human nature. For Locke as for Hobbes, man
is a creature of appetites who employs his rationality to achieve
his greatest possible individual satisfaction. But whereas Hobbes
defines rationality as meaning nothing more than the ability
and inclination to act purposefully, Locke understands it as a
capacity including not only purposefulness but also an innate
moral knowledge of good and evil as well as a natural predis-
position actually to *do* good. Thus whereas Hobbes' man in the
state of nature is simply an amoral egotist, Locke's natural man
is an egotist who at the same time, by virtue of his rationality,
tends to do unto others as he would have them do unto him.

Because Locke thus included a moral as well as a purposive
content in the rationality that he ascribed to human beings, he
was able to conceive of the state of nature as much less desperately in need of governmental correction than was the case in
Hobbes' analysis:

> The state of nature has a law of nature to govern it, which
> obliges every one, and reason, which is that law, teaches all man-
> kind, who will but consult it, that being all equal and independent,
> no one ought to harm another in his life, health, liberty or posses-
> sions. . . . Every one, as he is bound to preserve himself, and not
> to quit his station wilfully, so by the like reason, when his own
> preservation comes not in competition, ought he as much as he can
> to preserve the rest of mankind, and not unless it be to do justice
> on an offender, take away, or impair the life, or what tends to the
> preservation of the life, the liberty, health, limb or goods of an-
> other.[6]

Yet in spite of this innate human moral knowledge, Locke
maintained, the state of nature required remedying in three

basic respects. The rationally perceived law of the state of nature had to be clarified; there was need for a third-party judge who had no stake in the disputes that unavoidably arise among men; and it was necessary to have common provision for the enforcement of laws and judgments. To gain these advantages, according to Locke, "Mankind, notwithstanding all the privileges of the state of nature, but being in an ill condition while they remain in it, are quickly driven into society." [7]

Locke's conception of the social contract, however, is a very different one from that of Hobbes. What is transacted by Locke's contract is not an abdication of all rights and powers to an omnipotent and unchallengeable state. It is, rather, the establishment of a sovereign society which is intended, once in existence, to entrust the desired common public functions to a responsible government. The society is not the slave of the state; the state, rather, is the instrument of society. And the creation of this state, understood by Locke as simply the power to legislate on behalf of the members of the society for their own good as they see it, is not a matter of contract at all. Instead, in Locke's terms, it is a trust, set up by society for the performance of specified tasks and responsible to the society as the moral and political force which both set it up and intends to be its beneficiary.

From this difference of view between Hobbes and Locke on the establishment of society and government, resulting from their differing conceptions of human nature, follows, in turn, their completely different understanding of the relationship between government and the citizen. For Hobbes, the relationship was one of complete power in the hands of the state and complete submission on the part of its subjects. For Locke, in contrast, the acting sovereign, the elected legislature, is always responsible to the actual and final sovereign, the community of citizens with their own individual inherent and inalienable rights.

Even in its day-to-day exercise, governmental power is understood by Locke to be strictly limited. What these limitations upon legislation are, he summarizes as follows: The legislators, firstly, are to govern by promulgated established laws, not to be varied in particular cases, but to have one rule for rich and poor, for the favourite at Court, and the countryman at plough. Secondly, these laws also ought to be designed for no other end ultimately but the good of the people. Thirdly, they must not raise taxes on the property of the people without the consent of the people given by themselves or their deputies. . . . Fourthly, the legislative neither must nor can transfer the power of making laws to anybody else, or place it anywhere but where the people have.[8]

If, Locke continues, government abuses its trust and transgresses these limits, the people have the right to overthrow the legislative power and replace it with another that will conform to the purpose and rules of its mandate:

Since it can never be supposed to be the will of the society that the legislative should have a power to destroy that which everyone designs to secure by entering into society and for which the people submitted themselves to legislators of their own making: whenever the legislators endeavour to take away and destroy the property of the people, or to reduce them to slavery under arbitrary power, they put themselves into a state of war with the people, who are thereupon absolved from any farther obedience, and are left to the common refuge which God hath provided for all men against force and violence. Whensoever therefore the legislative shall transgress this fundamental rule of society, and either by ambition, fear, folly, or corruption, endeavour to grasp themselves, or put into the hands of any other, an absolute power over the lives, liberties, and estates of the people, by this breach of trust they forfeit the power the people had put into their hands for quite contrary ends, and it devolves to the people, who have a right to resume their original liberty, and by the establishment of a new legislative (such as they shall think fit), provide for their own safety and security, which is the end for which they are in society.[9]

What Locke's political philosophy thus added up to was the first exposition of the modern theory that government not only for and of the people, but also by the people, is possible. In expounding this theory Locke was also the first to make explicit the liberal democratic assumption as to why government by

popular sovereignty has been held to be workable. That assumption has been that men by nature (that is, by their rational
recognition of the dictates of natural law) behave so as not to
need governmental direction to induce them to co-operate for the
common good.

It has been on the validity of this assumption about human
behavior that the liberal democratic theory of government has,
in the last analysis, had to stand or fall.[10] That is, to the extent
that men are rational in the Lockean sense and do by nature act
not only purposefully but also morally, to that extent their insistence on their natural rights and their resulting limitation of
governmental power will be compatible with collective order and
welfare. To the extent, however, that men do not naturally
and voluntarily act with consideration for one another and the
public interest, to that extent they will either suffer from various
collective disharmonies or, in order to prevent them, will be
compelled to resort to the governmental supervision and limitation of their assertion of their natural rights. Some of the ways
in which this theoretical debate as to the workability of liberal
democracy has beset modern governmental practice are considered in Part II below.

Montesquieu and the Separation of Powers

In full agreement with the position of Locke was the thinking of the Frenchman, Baron de Montesquieu (1689–1775).
Montesquieu, however, was less inclined to political philoso-
phizing than to the empirical study of precisely how free
representative government could be made to work in actual
practice. In the pursuit of this interest he traveled extensively
throughout Europe and spent two years observing the governmental system of England. He eventually incorporated the results
of his studies and reflections in his famous treatise, *The Spirit
of the Laws.*

Montesquieu's purpose in *The Spirit of the Laws* was to
analyze the interdependence of all the elements of which a
society's life is composed, and to demonstrate how these affected
the problem of achieving political liberty. What came to be the
most influential part of this analysis was the section he devoted

The Philosophy of Liberal Democracy

The Philosophy of Liberal Democracy   *111*

to a consideration of the dynamics of English government. In this Montesquieu hit upon one of the most germinal of all modern Western political insights: that an indispensable precondition for preventing the abuse of governmental authority and for maintaining political liberty was the institutional separation of legislative, executive, and judicial powers. The logic of this insight, which was later to become one of the fundamental principles of the Constitution of the United States, Montesquieu explained as follows:

> The political liberty of the subject is a tranquillity of mind arising from the opinion each person has of his safety. In order to have this liberty, it is requisite the government be so constituted as one man need not be afraid of another.
>
> When the legislative and executive powers are united in the same person, or in the same body of magistrates, there can be no liberty; because apprehensions may arise, lest the same monarch or senate should enact tyrannical laws, to execute them in a tyrannical manner.
>
> Again, there is no liberty if the judicial power be not separated from the legislative and executive. Were it joined with the legislative, the life and liberty of the subject would be exposed to arbitrary control; for the judge would be then the legislator. Were it joined to the executive power, the judge might behave with violence and oppression.
>
> There would be an end of everything, were the same man or the same body, whether of the nobles or of the people, to exercise those three powers, that of enacting laws, that of executing the public resolutions, and of trying the cause of individuals.[11]

Rousseau and the General Will

Though Montesquieu's analysis accurately described the institutional dynamics of political liberty in England and the future United States, it had little relationship to the political situation prevailing at the time in his own France. The eighteenth-century thinker who did concern himself with that situation was Jean Jacques Rousseau (1712–1778). His greatest work in political philosophy, the *Social Contract,* was in effect a brilliant attack against the continuing absolutism and exploitation on the part of the French monarchy. Postulating the

premise that "man is born free, and everywhere he is in chains,"
it sought to show how this situation had come about, why it was
unjust, and how it could and should be corrected.

As the title of his work indicates, Rousseau utilized the
hypothesis of the social contract. Like Hobbes and Locke, he
portrayed the state as having originated in a voluntary agreement among individuals who in the state of nature were wholly
free and equal. The essence of that agreement Rousseau described as reducible to the following terms: "Each of us puts in
common his person and his whole power under the supreme
direction of the general will; and in return we receive every
member as an indivisible part of the whole." And once this
agreement is entered, he added, "Instead of all the contracting
parties, this act of the association produces a moral and collective body, which . . . receives from this same act its unity,
its common self, its life, and its will." [12]

Up to this point in his theorizing Rousseau is fully in
accord with Locke: government is something entirely utilitarian;
it rests upon the inalienable natural rights of the governed;
and it should express the sovereignty of the people. After having
taken this initial liberal democratic position, however, Rousseau
adopts a much sterner, Hobbesian view. He insists, for example,
that "there should be no partial associations in the state, and
that every citizen should express only his own opinion." The
reason for the necessity of this injunction, he explains, is that
"when factions, partial associations, are formed to the detriment
of the whole society, the will of each of these associations becomes
general with reference to its members, and particular with reference to the state; it may then be said that there are no longer
as many voters as there are men, but only as many voters as
there are associations." [13]

Rousseau is even more firmly insistent upon the unchallengeable supremacy of the sovereign general will in its relations
with the individual citizen:

> That the social pact may not be a vain formulary it tacitly
> includes this engagement, which can alone give force to the others,
> —that whoever refuses to obey the general will shall be constrained
> to do so by the whole body; which means nothing else than that
> he shall be forced to be free; for such is the condition which,

uniting every citizen to his native land, guarantees him from all personal dependence; a condition that insures the control and working of the political machine, and alone renders legitimate civil engagements, which, without it, would be absurd and tyrannical, and subject to the most enormous abuses.[14]

What these provisions of Rousseau's political philosophy indicate is that once he had established the cause of popular sovereignty, he envisaged it as no less of an absolute power over the citizenry than was Hobbes' Leviathan. It has been because of this seeming two-sidedness of Rousseau's thinking that his ideas have been appropriated no less frequently by totalitarians seeking to justify the stifling of political liberty than by liberal democrats engaged in extending and defending it. In the long run, moreover, the more Hobbesian aspects of Rousseau's theory of democracy have proved all too prophetic. On the one hand, the effectiveness of government by popular sovereignty has often tended to be undermined by various partisan and group interests. And on the other, popular government—as Rousseau went so far as to recommend—has upon occasion shown itself capable of intolerances hardly less severe than those practiced in avowedly authoritarian systems. Both circumstances were eventually to occasion very serious liberal democratic rethinking. Yet the need for such rethinking was not to become pressing until the end of the nineteenth century. In the meantime, particularly in the Anglo-Saxon countries, the original optimistic Lockean view of liberal democracy reigned more or less supreme.

Jeremy Bentham's Utilitarianism

As the political individualism initiated during the Puritan Revolution was reinforced by the economic individualism unleashed in the course of the Industrial Revolution, the unfettered rational freedom of the individual became enthroned not only as an end in itself, but as the very key to society's achievement of peace, welfare, and progress. It came to be assumed, that is, that the surest way to attain the greatest individual and collective good was to keep the role of government to a minimum and to rely instead upon every individual to pursue his own self-interest as he himself saw it. What this in effect amounted to was the adoption of what economists were to call *laissez faire* as the central principle of social organization.

One of the most characteristic expressions of this optimistically liberal philosophy as applied to political behavior was the so-called Utilitarianism of the English social thinker, Jeremy Bentham (1748–1832). It was Bentham's conviction that there was one principle at work in man that if allowed freely to operate would assure the highest possible human fulfillment:

> Nature has placed mankind under the governance of two sovereign masters, *pain* and *pleasure*. It is for them alone to point out what we ought to do, as well as to determine what we shall do. On the one hand the standard of right and wrong, on the other the chain of causes and effects, are fastened to their throne. They govern us in all we do, in all we say, in all we think: every effort we can make to throw off our subjection, will serve but to demonstrate and confirm it. In words a man may pretend to abjure their empire; but in reality he will remain subject to it all the while. The *principle of utility* recognizes this subjection, and assumes it for the foundation of that system, the object of which is to rear the fabric of felicity by the hands of reason and of law.[15]

The result of the operation of this principle in all individuals, Bentham concluded, would add up to the minimization of pain and the maximization of pleasure by society as a whole, that is, in its attainment of the greatest good of the greatest number. This would be so in all aspects of society's life, including its politics: Bentham did not exempt even the matter of political obligation from the operation of his principle of utility. He maintained, rather, that subjects should obey the commands of the sovereign state "just so long as it is in their interest, and no longer."

Bentham himself, who all his life urged and practiced the ideal of pleasure derived from altruism and public-spiritedness, was certainly not an amoral hedonist. Yet in its general formulation, his principle of maximized pleasure and minimized pain could be given any kind of content—moral or amoral—that the free individual might choose. As in the case of Locke's reliance on the moral-directedness of human rationality, the decisive question on which the workability of Bentham's formula depended was therefore this: *would* the individuals concerned freely choose to find pleasure in acting with consideration for one another and the larger public interest? If they would, the discipline required for a sound and stable collective life would be assured and the role of government *could* be kept to a minimum. If, however, such a natural preference for socially constructive behavior was lacking, the consequence would be either social conflict or, in the Hobbesian sense, the necessity of resorting to the corrective planning and coercion of the state.

Adam Smith and Economic Liberalism

This same crucial question underlay the outstanding statement of the Lockean type of liberal democratic theory as applied to the realm of economics. The author of that statement was the Scottish moral philosopher, Adam Smith (1723–1790), who in 1776 published his epoch-making *The Wealth of Nations*. Smith's point of departure in this work was that of a true utilitarian and liberal. On the one hand, he believed that "consumption is the sole end of all production." On the other, he was convinced that unhindered human freedom was not only an end in itself but man's best assurance of maximized individual as well as collective well-being.

How, according to Smith, does the coincidence of unrestrained individual self-interest and the interest of the society as a whole come about? It comes about, first, because self-interest acts as the best possible incentive to men to turn to whatever kind of work that society (that is, the collectivity of men freely deciding what they need and want) is willing to pay for. Thus, says Smith, "it is not from the benevolence of the butcher, the brewer, or the baker that we expect our dinner, but from their regard to their self-interest. We address ourselves, not to their humanity, but to their self-love, and never talk to them of our necessities, but of their advantages." Second, in thus pursuing their self-interest, men are restrained from exploiting one another, in Smith's analysis, by the fact that if any individual charges too much for his goods and services, it will become profitable for someone else to offer them more reasonably; and if someone is not prepared to pay enough for the goods and services he wishes, sellers will refuse him these goods and services because they can obtain more from other would-be buyers. In the same manner, Smith maintained, the operation of individual self-interest assures that desired goods and services will be produced, that they will be produced in the right quantities, and that they will be allocated in ways which assure a maximum of individual and social satisfaction. In each case, Smith sought to demonstrate, the market is in effect self-regulated by the mechanism of free competition operating through the laws of supply and demand. In order to give these laws free reign and to maximize economic wealth and progress, Smith therefore concluded, the role of governmental planning and regulation should, except as a passive umpire of the process, be kept to a minimum.[16, *]

As was the case with Bentham's principle of utility, Smith's liberal economic theory thus rested upon the same crucial assumption: that rational man *would* make the decisions that were most in his own interest as well as best for society. Yet though this assumption came to be progressively qualified, it was never rejected outright for almost a century. The reason for this was simply that it seemed at the time to accord so fully with the plainly visible facts of actual political and economic developments and, hence, to offer the most reliable possible guidance in making sure that these developments would continue.

The facts of these eighteenth- and nineteenth-century developments that classical liberal democratic theory was intended to describe are well known. They pertain to that vast economic and political transformation that almost overnight came to distinguish the Western world from all the civilizations that had preceded it. In but a few decades, through the secular application of the forces of political and economic individualism, first England and then major areas of continental Europe were turned from traditionalist agricultural societies into economies based upon mechanical power, credit, manufacturing, and free monetary exchange. Great new cities and immense industrial plants had mushroomed. To keep themselves supplied with raw ma-

---

* Smith further qualified the purity of his model free-market system by asserting the duty of the sovereign to provide public works and public institutions "which it can never be for the interest of any individual, or small number of individuals, to erect and maintain."

terials and to market their unending flow of manufactures, the European nations had quickly set about to involve in their orbits every part of the world that was willing to deal with them or too weak to offer effective resistance. And what had been the net result of it all? The most rapid rises in gross national products, the most intensive development of trade and commerce, the most astronomical accumulations of capital, and the most encouraging hope for universal plenty that mankind had ever known.

And what appeared to be at the root of the entire unprecedented development? It was the very force that the classical liberal democratic philosophers were celebrating and seeking to free from various outdated economic and political restrictions. That force was the incentive, resourcefulness, and freedom of choice of the new urban middle classes who had shown themselves to be the liberal-industrial revolution's chief driving agents.

The earliest and most penetrating tribute ever to be paid to the accomplishments of these new middle classes—and, indirectly, to the liberal democratic philosophers who argued the logic of their economic and political role—was penned by none other than Karl Marx, the early liberal democratic period's severest critic. "The bourgeoisie has played a most revolutionary role in history," Marx wrote in his *Communist Manifesto* in 1848.

> The bourgeoisie, wherever it has got the upper hand, has put an end to all feudal, patriarchal, idyllic relations. It has pitilessly torn asunder the motley feudal ties that bound man to his "natural superiors," and has left no other bond between man and man than naked self-interest, than callous "cash payment." It has drowned the most heavenly ecstasies of religious fervor, of chivalrous enthusiasm, of philistine sentimentalism, in the icy water of egotistical calculation. It has resolved personal worth into exchange value, and in place of the numberless indefeasible chartered freedoms, has set up that single, unconscionable freedom—Free Trade. . . .
>
> The bourgeoisie has disclosed how it came to pass that the brutal display of vigor in the Middle Ages, which reactionaries so much admire, found its fitting complement in the most slothful indolence. It has been the first to show what man's activity can bring about. It has accomplished wonders far surpassing Egyptian

pyramids, Roman aqueducts, and Gothic cathedrals: it has conducted expeditions that put in the shadow all former migrations of nations and crusades. . . .

The bourgeoisie, by the rapid improvement of all instruments of production, by the immensely facilitated means of communication, draws all nations, even the most barbarian, into civilization. The cheap prices of its commodities are the heavy artillery with which it batters down all Chinese walls, with which it forces the barbarians' intensely obstinate hatred of foreigners to capitulate. It compels all nations, on pain of extinction, to adopt the bourgeois mode of production; it compels them to introduce what it calls civilization into their midst, *i.e.,* to become bourgeois themselves. In a word, it creates a world after its own image. . . .

The bourgeoisie keeps more and more doing away with the scattered state of the population, of the means of production, and of property. It has agglomerated population, centralized means of production, and has concentrated property in a few hands. The necessary consequence of this was political centralization. Independent, or but loosely connected provinces, with separate interests, laws, governments and systems of taxation, became lumped together into one nation, with one government, one code of laws, one national class interest, one frontier and one customs tariff. . . .

The bourgeoisie, during its rule of scarce one hundred years, has created more massive and more colossal productive forces than have all preceding generations together. Subjection of nature's forces to man, machinery, application of chemistry to industry and agriculture, steam navigation, railways, electric telegraphs, clearing of whole continents for cultivation, canalisation of rivers, whole populations conjured out of the ground—what earlier century had even a presentment that such productive forces slumbered in the lap of social labor? [17]

If even its fiercest opponent felt compelled thus to extol its accomplishments, it was little wonder that in at least the earlier stages of this momentous transformation the validity of the liberal democratic assumption about human behavior upon which it was believed to rest should remain largely unquestioned. For the time being at least, nothing seemed clearer than that— as Bentham and Adam Smith had maintained—the individual's free and rational pursuit of his own self-interest actually *did* result in both his own and society's greatest possible prosperity and progress. It was therefore only as the process of industrialization and democratization began to create problems that original liberal democratic theory had not foreseen, and could not suggest solutions for, that this optimistic assumption began seriously to be challenged. What the problems were that occasioned these challenges and with what new philosophical and practical schemes men attempted to come to grips with them is examined in the next chapter.

SELECTED BIBLIOGRAPHY

BURY, J. B. *The Idea of Progress,* New York, Dover, Dover Paperback, 1955.

EBENSTEIN, WILLIAM. *Political Thought in Perspective,* New York, McGraw-Hill, 1957, Chap. 12, "Hobbes," pp. 256–268; Chap. 14, "Locke," pp. 284–323; Chap. 15, "Montesquieu," pp. 324–333; Chap. 16 "Rousseau," pp. 334–347; and Chap. 19, "Bentham," pp. 402–431.

GREENE, THEODORE MEYER. *Liberalism: Its Theory and Practice,* Austin, University of Texas Press, 1957.

HEILBRONER, ROBERT. *The Worldly Philosophers,* New York, Simon & Schuster, 1953, pp. 3–95.

Political Consequences
of Industrialization
and Democratization

THE PROCESS OF REPLACING the disrupted Catholic and feudal
order of the Middle Ages had taken several hundred years.
By the middle of the nineteenth century it appeared well on
the way to being completed. The entire Western world seemed
destined to be politically organized in terms of nation-states and
governed through some form of liberal democracy. Within the
new Western political order, however, two developments were
occurring that rapidly created problems with which the nation-
state and its evolving liberal democratic institutions found it
more and more difficult to cope. The one development was the
transformation of Western economic and social life by the spread
of industrialization. The other was the progressive democratization of human relationships through the extension and intensification of popular sovereignty.

The problems raised by industrialization and democratization presented themselves differently in every country. Yet everywhere, in one form or another, they involved the following six
principal issues: first, the demand of the newly urbanized industrial workers for the right to vote (that is, for the implementation of the political equality that had so long been claimed for
them); second, the widespread insistence on a more equitable

120

distribution of the benefits of industrial production than that provided by the economics and politics of laissez faire; third, the correction of the tendency of the laissez-faire economic system to suffer from costly slumps and depressions; fourth, the task of educating the newly sovereign democratic majorities in the complexities and responsibilities of popular government; fifth, the continuing problem of ordering the relations among nations, aggravated after industrialization and democratization by their immensely increased warmaking potential and their constantly growing economic interdependence; and, finally, the necessity of preventing democratic-industrial society's new organizational pressures and material expectations from stifling in the individual his own independence of moral conscience.

The emergence of these problems indicated that the optimistic assumptions about liberal democratic politics and laissez-faire economics held by thinkers like Locke, Bentham, and Smith were in need of serious re-examination. Clearly, the fundamental questions of politics—by whom, how, and for what purposes humanity's inherent freedom should be managed—could not be left to the completely chance verdict of the economic and political market place. The individual's innate rationality and morality could not automatically be counted upon to enable him to make the most of his own and his society's potentialities. What appeared to have become necessary, therefore, were efforts of a more planned and collectivistic kind that might increase the individual's and society's opportunities for fulfillment by frankly recognizing and compensating for this fact. It is, at any rate, as attempts to provide such planned and collectivistic efforts that one can best understand the three chief political solutions that have been proposed for dealing with the problems resulting from industrialization and democratization. These have been Marxism, fascism, and the democratic welfare state.

Liberalism versus Democracy: Burke, De Tocqueville, and J. S. Mill

Even before these major programmatic reactions to the working out of liberal democracy, there had long been developing a strong undercurrent of doubt about the possible political

and cultural implications of popular sovereignty. These doubts
focused chiefly on the question whether the majority, once
enthroned in power, would not prove an even more irresistible
tyrant than had been the earlier monarchical despots. Put differently, the question was raised whether the ideals of democracy,
concerned with the freedom and power of the *majority,* would
in the long run be compatible with the ideals of liberalism which
were a matter of the freedom and power of the *individual.*

One of the earliest warnings in this connection was that of
the English politician and man of letters, Edmund Burke
(1729–1797). Writing in 1790 in his book, *Reflections on the
Revolution in France,* Burke stated it as his firm conviction

> that in a democracy, the majority of the citizens is capable of exer-
> cising the most cruel oppressions upon the minority, whenever
> strong divisions prevail in that kind of polity, as they often must;
> and that oppression of the minority will extend to far greater num-
> bers, and will be carried on with much greater fury, than can
> almost ever be apprehended from the dominion of a single sceptre.
> In such a popular persecution, individual sufferers are in a much
> more deplorable condition than in any other. Under a cruel prince
> they have the balmy compassion of mankind to assuage the smart
> of their wounds; they have the plaudits of the people to animate
> their generous constancy under their sufferings; but those who are
> subjected to wrong under multitudes, are deprived of all external
> consolation. They seem deserted by mankind, overpowered by a
> conspiracy of their whole species.[1]

The same point was elaborated a half century later by the
French aristocrat and political observer, Alexis de Tocqueville
(1805–1859). After an extensive visit to the United States, De
Tocqueville penned what is generally agreed to be the most
penetrating work on America ever written by a foreigner, his
Democracy in America. De Tocqueville's purpose in this book
was to study democracy where he believed it to be most advanced
and firmly established. "I confess," he wrote, "that in America
I saw more than America. I sought the image of democracy itself,
with its inclinations, its prejudices, and its passions, in order to
learn what we have to fear or to hope from its progress."

What struck De Tocqueville most sharply about democracy

as he saw it developed in America was the seemingly total power of public opinion:

> It is in the examination of the display of public opinion in the United States, that we clearly perceive how far the power of the majority surpasses all the powers with which we are acquainted in Europe. . . . At the present time the most absolute monarchs in Europe are unable to prevent certain notions, which are opposed to their authority, from circulating in secret throughout their dominions, and even in their courts. Such is not the case in America; as long as the majority is still undecided, discussion is carried on; but as soon as its decision is irrevocably pronounced, a submissive silence is observed; and the friends, as well as the opponents of the measure, unite in assenting to its propriety. The reason of this is perfectly clear: no monarch is so absolute as to combine all the powers of society in his own hands, and to conquer all opposition, with the energy of a majority, which is invested with the right of making and of executing the laws.
>
> The authority of a king is purely physical, and it controls the actions of the subject without subduing his private will; but the majority possesses a power which is physical and moral at the same time; it acts upon the will as well as upon the actions of men, and it represses not only all contest, but all controversy.
>
> I know of no country in which there is so little true independence of mind and freedom of discussion as in America. In any constitutional state in Europe every sort of religious and political theory may be advocated and propagated . . . ; for there is no country in Europe so subdued by any single authority, as not to contain citizens who are ready to protect the man who raises his voice in the cause of truth, from the consequences of his hardihood. If he is unfortunate enough to live under an absolute government, the people is upon his side; if he inhabits a free country, he may find a shelter behind the authority of the throne, if he require one. The aristocratic part of society supports him in some countries, and the democracy in others. But in a nation where democratic institutions exist, organized like those of the United States, there is but one sole authority, one single element of strength and success, with nothing beyond it. . . .
>
> Absolute monarchies have thrown an odium upon despotism; let us beware lest democratic republics should restore oppression, and should render it less odious and degrading in the eyes of the many, by making it still more onerous to the few.[2]

A third major political thinker concerned with the implications of majority rule for the freedom of the individual was John Stuart Mill (1806–1873). Deeply impressed by De Tocqueville's analysis of democracy in the United States, Mill saw the danger of majority tyranny as inherent in every evolving democracy, including his own native England. The only defense against such a development, he was convinced, was to raise the individual's freedom of opinion and sentiment to the status of an *absolute*. Not only was this necessary to protect the individual's freedom; it was no less essential to assure the continued pursuit of truth for truth's sake. Mill thus expressed this moral as well as intellectual defense of individual freedom of opinion in his famous treatise, *On Liberty:*

> If all mankind minus one, were of one opinion, and only one person were of contrary opinion, mankind would be no more justified in silencing that one person, than he, if he had the power, would be justified in silencing mankind. . . .
>
> First, if any opinion is compelled to silence, that opinion may, for aught we can certainly know, be true. To deny this is to assume our own infallibility.
>
> Second, though the silenced opinion be an error, it may, and very commonly does, contain a portion of truth; and since the general or prevailing opinion on any subject is rarely or never the whole truth, it is only by the collision of adverse opinions that the remainder of the truth has any chance of being supplied.
>
> Third, even if the received opinion be not only true, but the whole truth; unless it is suffered to be, and actually is, vigorously and earnestly contested, it will, by most of those who receive it, be held in the manner of a prejudice, with little comprehension or feeling of its rational grounds. And not only this, but, fourthly, the meaning of the doctrine itself will be in danger of being lost, or enfeebled, and deprived of its vital effect on the character and conduct: the dogma becomes a mere formal profession, inefficacious for good, but cumbering the ground, and preventing the growth of any real and heartfelt conviction, from reason or personal experience.[3],*

* Mill's conception of civil liberty is the culmination of a line of thought that is reflected in a series of British constitutional documents. Magna Carta, extracted from King John by his barons in 1215, established the beginnings of due process of law. The Petition of Right (1628) and the Bill of Rights

Read today, at least in the contemporary Western democracies, views such as these seem most relevant and timely.
For the task of protecting the freedom of the individual against
the pressures of the majority has increasingly shown itself to
require the most vigorous alertness and courage. Until very
recently, however, the much more immediate and urgent problem of the day has seemed, rather, to be the task of first fully
establishing the economic and social equality about whose consequences men like Burke, De Tocqueville, and Mill were concerned. And it was to this latter more popularly pressing challenge that Marxism, fascism, and the theory and practice of the
democratic welfare state addressed themselves.

Marxism

Karl Marx (1818–1883) was a German, of Jewish background, who spent the greater part of his adult life as a
refugee in England. In spite of the uses to which his ideas have
been put, their intended import was wholly in the evolving
Western utilitarian, liberal, and democratic tradition. Indeed,
notwithstanding his uncompromising rejection of the then prevailing economic and political order, Marx subscribed to an
even more optimistic faith in man's innate rationality and good-
ness than did most of the liberal thinkers whom he spent
his life refuting.

As was pointed out in the last chapter, Marx was by no
means unaware of the liberal age's accomplishments. What he
chiefly objected to was that the system which had initiated and
was controlling industrialization was not extending its benefits
equitably enough to the mass of the people who were doing the
actual work (the proletariat) and without whose contribution
the whole process would be impossible. According to Marx, the
wherewithal was in man's hands for at last creating a free and

---

(1689) not only increased the power of Parliament but also reaffirmed the
right of habeas corpus, forbade martial law in peacetime, and protected a
subject's right to petition the government without fear of punishment. By
Mill's time thoughtful men on both sides of the Atlantic had become convinced that individual liberty must be protected as vigilantly against the acts
of elected legislatures as against those of absolute monarchs.

world-encompassing society based upon the social ideal of "to
each according to his needs, from each according to his ability."
Yet in actual fact, he maintained, the proletariat was constantly
growing poorer and more numerous, while the capitalists were
becoming richer and fewer. Marx's intellectual purpose was to
explain how this had come about and how in his view it should
and could be remedied.

In accounting for the successes and failures of liberal capitalism Marx devised his theory of dialectical materialism. One of
the central propositions of this theory was that ideas and institutions are not the key variables in human behavior. The determining factors, rather, are held to be the tools with which man
makes his livelihood, which Marx calls the *means of production;*
and the arrangements by which these tools and the distribution
of their produce are operated and controlled, which he refers
to as the *relationships of production.*

As Marx saw it, there was an inevitable tendency for whoever controlled the means of production—in his own time, the
bourgeoisie—to develop a special class interest, to become more
and more conservative and exploitive, and in the end to make
much less of the available technology than its inherent potentialities would warrant. The reason for this, Marx maintained, was
that the economically dominant class always succeeded in getting
control of the political instruments of the state and in justifying
itself in terms of an entire world view, which Marx referred to
as a cultural and political superstructure. Those who were once
raised in such a cultural and political system quite sincerely
believed that the ideas which it advanced and the institutions
through which it operated represented universal absolutes that
could be talked about completely apart from the prevailing
means and relationships of production. Yet this was an illusion,
Marx insisted. For, first, and as the foundation of everything,
had come the particular means and relations of production.
Only later, around them and in various ways consciously and
unconsciously determined by them, had developed the corresponding ideas and institutions.

In assigning this importance to the economic circumstances
of man's life, Marx clearly took his stand as a proponent of what
he himself described as the materialistic, as contrasted with the

idealistic, approach to human behavior. Yet this did not mean that he was a materialist in the vulgar sense of attaching sole or ultimate value to material welfare. On the contrary, the justification he advanced for his preoccupation with material wants was that their adequate satisfaction was the most important step in freeing men from economic insecurity and enabling them to devote themselves to more dignified and creative pursuits. As he wrote in his principal work, *Capital:*

> The realm of freedom does not commence until the point is passed where labor under the compulsion of necessity and of external use is required. In the very nature of things it lies beyond the sphere of material production in the strict meaning of the term. . . . Freedom in this field cannot consist of anything else but of the fact that socialized man, the associated producers, regulate their interchange with nature rationally, bring it under their common control, instead of being ruled by it as some blind power; that they accomplish their task with the least expenditure of energy and under conditions most adequate to their human nature and most worthy of it.[4]

To achieve this ideal condition, Marx urged, it was necessary to put an end to what he alleged was the exploitation of the industrial masses who operated the means of production by the capitalist minority that merely owned them. It was perfectly true, Marx admitted, that the capitalists had initiated industrialization. But the operation of an industrial economy, once initiated, was no longer a minority matter. Either as an industrial producer, or as a consumer of the goods industry produced and had to market, everyone in society was in one way or another involved. In view of this fact, Marx reasoned, everyone should democratically share in the enjoyment of the economy's benefits. In other words, in order socially to utilize the industrial economy's potentialities to the full, the capitalists' economic control through the system of *private* ownership of the means of production should be replaced by a system of *collective* ownership, that is, by a communistic economic order.

Marx predicted that because of the capitalists' culturally and politically entrenched position, one could not expect them to surrender their monopoly of power voluntarily. Fortunately, however, he asserted, capitalist ownership and power were becoming concentrated in fewer and fewer hands. Aside from stripping the capitalists of their moral justification—which he himself hoped to do in his writings—all that was therefore required was to dislodge the power position of a relatively small minority. This, Marx maintained, would necessitate a revolution, followed by a transitional stage of "dictatorship of the proletariat." Thereafter, however, true communism would be established; the state as an exploitive instrument of a particular class would "wither away" (inasmuch as there would *be* only one class—the workers); and through the operation of the .principle of "to each according to his needs, from each according to his ability," everyone would finally be released from all economic insecurities and would be free to develop himself as a full human being.

As we today know, Marx erred in his prediction as to how his utopia would have to come about (that is, by revolution), as well as in his faith in its practicability. The chief reason for his errors was that he generalized too broadly from the particular circumstances that prevailed in his own day. It was indeed true that the working masses in mid-nineteenth-century Europe were exploited and impoverished in the extreme. Crowded into the new industrial centers, without the protection of a patriarchal state, the leverage of political representation, or any effective form of labor organization, millions of men, women, and children worked from twelve to sixteen hours a day under the harshest conditions and for subsistence pay. Contemplating their lot, Marx quite understandably concluded that the revolutionary exploitation of their capitalist employers was the only hope of remedy.

Yet while this condition everywhere continued more or less unmitigated during Marx's lifetime, his mistake was to conclude that it could be improved only by revolution. Even before Marx's death, developments had begun to occur that were to make possible at least an approximation of Marx's welfare state without the necessity of recourse to revolution. Partly because of feelings of social responsibility among capitalists themselves, and partly in response to growing working-class economic and political pressures, the sovereignty of the state eventually *did* in many countries come to be democratically shared and employed for the general welfare.

Contemporary Americans, for example, live in a society that in the terms of Marx's original concepts could be said to approximate the realization of his utopia more closely than does any other. More and more the ownership of the means of production in the United States is becoming so diffused and so extensively regulated by governmental agencies that for all practical purposes its use is being increasingly governed by the dictates of the general welfare. More and more, too, equal economic and social opportunity and minimum standards of living are being assured to the entire citizenry. And though it has not been the proletariat, but the American version of the middle class that has risen to dominance, the net result is the same: an essentially one-class society in which the state, very much in Marx's ideal sense, is no longer an exploitive instrument of any particular group but the administrative agency for serving the interests of the entire collectivity.

The greatest deviations from Marx's original intentions have, in contrast, occurred in those countries that in the name of the ideology of communism have officially claimed to be fulfilling the Marxian program. To date at least, none of these countries has progressed past the Marxian transitional stage of "the dictatorship of the proletariat." There have been two principal reasons for this. One of these has had nothing to do with Marxism itself. It has resulted, rather, from the fact that in most of the communist nations the chief preoccupation of the minority enjoying dictatorial power has been economic rather than political. That is, as it was a politically dominant capitalist minority that led in the industrialization of the West, so it is the politically dominant communist elite that is initiating and controlling the industrialization of countries that by Western standards have until recently been underdeveloped.

The second principal reason why the communist nations have to date failed to achieve any substantial progress toward political democracy goes to the heart of Marxist theory itself. As the industrial masses became urbanized and educated in the West, the originally dominant capitalist industrializers were forced to yield to them more and more political as well as economic concessions. Similar popular pressures are known to be building up in the countries where industrialization is being brought about under communist leadership. Yet there the struggle for political liberty is encountering an obstacle never present in the West. That obstacle, ironically, is Marx's theoretical justification of the allegedly necessary stage of "the dictatorship of the proletariat."

In the West, the dominant political philosophy during the period of industrialization was that of liberal democracy. It was this philosophy in terms of which the capitalists had themselves fought their battles against royalist absolutism and feudal aristocracy. For some decades after they had won these battles, it is true, the capitalists were able to maintain their privileged positions in spite of their adherence to this philosophy of equality and freedom. What was significant, however, was that the dominance of this ruling group was never sanctioned by any generally accepted justification and was therefore from the very beginning philosophically and politically on the defensive.

In the communist countries, officially claiming to be operating in terms of Marxist theory, this deterrent to the permanent monopoly position of a politically entrenched elite is completely absent. On the one hand, the citizenry does not enjoy the political and moral leverage of an accepted philosophy of political freedom. On the other, the communist elite possesses the ready-made Marxian rationale for a period of dictatorship which, in the name of its right to interpret the alleged dictates of Marxism, it is in effect free to prolong indefinitely.[5] That this fact simultaneously hinders those who would challenge the monopoly power of the dictatorial communist group and strengthens the ability of this group to resist the extension of political democracy goes without saying.

The most that can in summary be said of Marxism is that it has proven of immense suggestive value intellectually. As a guide to actual political developments, in contrast, it has shown itself of little intrinsic use, at least in the sense in which Marx himself would have intended. In the West, its objectives are in process of achievement without revolution. In economically less developed countries, it is helping to delay political democratization by seeming to justify the dictatorship of an elite less interested in the establishment of democracy than in rapid industrialization and the maintenance of its own monopoly of power. And internationally, rather than being the inspiration for a supranational global workers' state as Marx envisaged, it has merely served as a propaganda appeal with which nationalistically minded communist powers have sought to subvert the national loyalties of the citizens of their rivals.

Nor does Marxism offer any guidance whatever for societies that are approaching the realization of Marx's utopia of a democratic welfare state. The reason it does not lies in Marx's uncritical faith that once political freedom was established and economic wants were satisfied all of mankind's problems would be permanently solved. To the extent that this is not proving to be so, Marxism must be looked back upon as no more relevant to the problems of the present than are the classical liberal political and economic theories which Marx so vehemently rejected.

Fascism

The key historical instrument in Marxism was the anticapitalist workers' revolution. Fascism, on the other hand, hoped to solve the problems resulting from industrialization and democratization through the use of a restored and intensified nation-state authoritarianism. Where Marxism has served as the official guide to policy, the consensus necessary to implement the desired collective programs has been created by physically eliminating the groups that seemed to stand in the way. This was the fate that was meted out to the aristocracy and middle classes of czarist Russia as well as to the postrevolutionary Kulak peasantry. In industrially and politically somewhat more advanced countries, where such a radical revolutionary solution was for one reason or another not possible, the course taken, under the name of fascism or national socialism, was to attempt to impose a political consensus on conflicting social groups through an all-encompassing system of state coercion.

Whereas Marxism, at least in its vision of the final communist utopia, placed the greatest faith in the inherent rationality of the free individual, fascism represented a deep reaction against the assumption that individuals can be relied upon to make the proper decisions for themselves and their society. Developing after World War I in Italy, Japan, and Germany, countries where feelings of international insecurity coincided with grave internal economic and political difficulties, fascism was in effect the way of last resort where liberal democracy no longer seemed workable and Marxism could not sufficiently appeal because of its uncompromising one-class program and its international tie to the Soviet Union.

Being thus a response to a coincidence of international as well as domestic crises, fascism everywhere stood for a dual program. On the one hand, in order to re-create internal political consensus and stability, it precipitated foreign military adventures with a view both to generating greater national solidarity and to helping justify whatever restrictions of freedom its leadership desired to impose. On the other, in order to mobilize the support required to make its military undertakings successful, it used every means at its command to excite nationalistic fervor and stopped at nothing in its total regimentation of its own citizens and of the foreign peoples that fell under its control.

As it operated in its most ruthless and aggressive form in Hitler's Germany, under the name of National Socialism, fascism involved five basic tenets.[6] The most fundamental of these was the primacy of what Nazi leaders called *Staatsräson*, or national interest. By the doctrine of national sovereignty the ultimate claim of national interest is, of course, acknowledged everywhere. Yet in the case of fascism there was no attempt whatsoever to conceive of sovereign national power as being employable for the implementation of any other more human and universal goals. Nor was there the slightest regret when such other goals had to be sacrificed for what were felt to be the dictates of national interest. As did Machiavelli, therefore, and in part for the same desired objective of strengthening national political unity, fascism subscribed to the doctrine that the end justifies the means. Yet unlike Machiavelli's system, fascism had no end. Being fundamentally a phenomenon of crisis, it did not look beyond its means; its means, indeed, *were* its end—maximized national power for its own sake.

A second tenet of German fascism, designed to strengthen

national solidarity psychologically rather than by the externally imposed claim of national interest, was the myth of an allegedly organic German racial-cultural community, a German *Volksgemeinschaft*.[7] Defined as an almost tribal collectivity of unquestioningly obedient, nationalistically dedicated, and racially superior Teutons, the purpose of this myth was to discredit all expressions of rationalistic individualism of the Western type and to exhort the Germans to accept whatever sacrifices the Nazi leadership might see fit to demand of them.

Rationalistic individualism in economics, fascism denounced as leading to unrest between capital and labor, depressions, and eventually communism. Rationalistic individualism in cultural matters, it condemned as bringing about the relativization of values, skepticism, and ultimately total moral confusion. And individualism and rationalism in politics, it charged, resulted in the fragmentation of society into hostile political groups and, in the end, political stalemate and civil strife. It was because of the effects of such Western doctrines of the importance of the individual, Hitler claimed, that Germany had by 1933 fallen into internal disorder and suffered its grave losses internationally. In order to halt this process of political disintegration and decline, the Germans were to accept the allegedly sounder and more satisfying way of life of the German *Volksgemeinschaft* and permit themselves to be governed by Hitler's one-party Nazi totalitarianism.

A third major tenet of German fascism was anti-Semitism and the doctrine of the alleged superiority of the so-called Aryan race. The purpose of this plank in the Nazi position was a twofold one. On the one hand, it was intended as a scapegoat. That is, it was used to evade the true complexities of the society's crises by attributing responsibility for them to what the Nazis alleged were the lack of public-spiritedness and the subversive internationalism of the group they defined as Jews. And second, the Nazi racial doctrines were designed to build up the Germans' national ego, to help overcome their lack of confidence in their prowess as a world power, and to offer them an alleged justification for following Hitler in whatever foreign conquests he might decide to undertake. In this latter sense, the Nazi tenet of racism was nothing more than a substitute for the long-range utopia that fascism did not possess. Since there was nothing to be for, there was at least something to be against.

A fourth central tenet of National Socialism was the doctrine of the corporate state. This was intended to eliminate individualism and rationalism from German economic life. Its basic feature was a program of centralized state economic management administered through a network of state-dominated industrial syndicates representing both capital and labor. As the Nazis saw it, such an economic system combined the advantages of both capitalism and socialism. On the one hand, it maintained the invaluable incentive of free enterprise. On the other, it placed final control over all economic decisions, including the terms of both capital and labor, in the unchallengeable hands of the one-party Nazi state.

A fifth basic fascist tenet was the so-called leadership principle. This expressed fascism's antiliberalism as applied to the realm of politics. Its premise was that the only sure way to interpret and carry out the collective interest was to reject democratic procedures in favor of the decision-making power and discipline of an authoritarian leader. Hitler phrased this fascist imperative in regard to Germany thus:

> There shall be no decision by majority, only by responsible individual persons; the word "council" must be restored to its original meaning [advice]. Every man shall have his advisers, *but the decision shall be made by one man*. The principle which in days past made of the Prussian army the German people's most wonderful instrument must, in its traditional sense, one day become the basis of our entire national constitution; authority of the *Führers* [leaders] downward and responsibility upward.[8]

Based upon these or essentially similar planks, fascism everywhere rapidly mobilized its subjects, made its all-out imperialistic bid, and disastrously failed. The fundamental reason for its failure was that its program as well as its strategy were much too directly an expression of the crises—national and international—that it hoped to solve. As fascism's opponents warned time and time again, it was no longer possible for a nation to remedy its international insecurities by conquering, annexing, or destroying its neighbors. Nor was it any longer possible to root out the universal ideals of human equality, dignity, and liberty. In seeking to defy this logic of modern Western civilization, fascism was doomed from its very beginnings. It merely struck out with a desperate short-term program and, in thereby making its failure a certainty, accomplished nothing save to aggravate the crises from which it itself had first sprung.

The Democratic Welfare State

Unlike the other principal programs designed to cope with the problems of industrialization and democratization, the ends and means of the democratic welfare state are neither utopian nor cynical. They are, indeed, nothing more nor less than a constantly evolving re-expression of the traditional ideals of liberal democracy as applied to the ever-changing circumstances of the present. By whatever name they may be described, whether *democratic socialism, Christian socialism,* or *welfare capitalism,* they are, in effect, the ends and means that have progressively, if undramatically, been incorporated in economic and social legislation throughout the Western world during the past half century.

Like the liberals of the nineteenth century, contemporary liberals (that is, exponents of the democratic welfare state) are unreservedly committed to the ideals of individual fulfillment and political liberty and their political expression through representative governmental institutions. The exponents of the democratic welfare state differ from the liberals of a century ago chiefly in their thinking on the matter of economic and social organization.

Nineteenth-century liberals advocated a system of unrestricted free enterprise. They did so not for the sake of free enterprise itself, but because they were convinced that, compared with the mixture of royalist regulations and feudal privileges that had prevailed up to that time, the free operation of the laws of supply and demand would assure a much greater means of economic prosperity and social satisfaction. Their ultimate ideal was the achievement of the greatest possible human welfare; and they believed that the most effective possible economic means for achieving that ideal was the system of laissez faire.

It is this same end of the greatest possible human this-worldly fulfillment that is the inspiration of the present-day proponents of the democratic welfare state. The reason these twentieth-century liberals reject pure laissez faire in favor of a greater or lesser measure of supplementary state regulation of economic production and distribution is no less practical than was that for which pure free enterprise was advocated earlier. It is, simply, that after the experiences of the past century, it has become evident that pure laissez faire does not, as once expected, assure the greatest possible productivity and equitableness of distribution. Until the institution of such measures as graduated income taxes, the legalization of trade unions, minimum-wage rates, maximum working hours, and compulsory safety provisions, for example, the much stronger bargaining position of employers exposed the large mass of workingmen to truly damaging economic and social privations. And until the employment of such levers as governmental regulation of interest rates and public spending, the depressions that so frequently beset the free operations of the laissez-faire economy wrought the severest economic and psychological hardships. It has been in order to implement the ideal of maximized social welfare in the light of new and inescapable realities such as these that the twentieth-century liberal has forsaken the letter of earlier liberalism in order the more effectively to realize its spirit.

The extent to which the advocates of the democratic welfare state have rejected the free market economy has largely depended upon the laissez-faire system's performance in fulfilling the purposes for which it was originally permitted to develop. To the extent that the laws of supply and demand have seemed to be operating satisfactorily, the free enterprise system has continued to be valued and has been governmentally supplemented only in the respects in which it has appeared to fall short. Where, in contrast, the free market system of production and distribution has seemed over long periods to be seriously failing, it has been rejected in favor of more or less radical schemes of public ownership and management by the state. In the former type of situation, as in the United States, the economy has remained almost completely private, with the role of government confined to over-all supervision, taxation, the provision of minimum social services, and emergency spending. In the latter, as in Great Britain, the role of the state has been enlarged to include the ownership and management of certain basic industries and the public provision of extensive medical services.

More and more, significantly, discussion of the subject of the democratic welfare state has everywhere tended toward a broadening consensus. The champions of the welfare ideal have by no means lost their zeal, but have become progressively more open-minded in their attitudes and more pragmatic in their tactics. The reason for this is not far to seek: many of the gravest economic injustices of the 1920's and 1930's are now remedied; in contrast to the inefficiencies that have been discovered to characterize total state regimentation, the economic value of the dynamic of free enterprise has won renewed recognition and appreciation; and after the examples of fascism and communism, the power of the state has become suspect regardless of the purposes for which it may be employed. In the words of Norman Thomas, long the leading figure among proponents of the welfare state in America:

> At the same time that we have been learning to guard against statism as an expression of socialism, we have learned that it has been possible, to a degree not anticipated by most earlier socialists, to impose desirable social controls on privately owned enterprises by the development of social planning, by proper taxation and labor legislation, and by the growth of powerful labor organizations.[9]

A similar tempering of earlier militancy on the subject of the democratic welfare state has occurred among the defenders of the laissez-faire position, the members of the business community. Such objectives of the democratic welfare state as full employment, minimum-wage guarantees, equal educational opportunities, and old-age pensions are no longer publicly denounced by even the most conservative private entrepreneurs. This does not necessarily mean, of course, that all concerned are actually convinced of the desirability of such measures. It does, however, represent a very significant realization: that the sovereign democratic majority can and will insist upon the objectives of the democratic welfare state and that the only questions still realistically open to debate are *how* and *at what tempo* these objectives are to be implemented. Can the job be done through the voluntary efforts of business, labor, and other private initiative? Or will it require an extension and intensification of central planning and management by the state?

Indeed, in the light of our whole modern Western historical development, the further evolution of the democratic welfare state—whether one considers it a good thing or bad—would seem to be both culturally logical and politically unavoidable. If, as has occurred throughout the Western and Westernized world, the this-worldly fulfillment of the individual be accepted as the highest good, then it is only natural that this fulfillment should include the individual's political right to share in his community's government. And once men have gained this right, it is no less natural that they should employ it to gain for themselves the highest standard of welfare possible. What this means, was bound to mean, and will doubtless continue to mean, is that the modern world is destined to experience whatever measure of welfare-statism that its sovereign democratic majorities may insist upon, implemented by whatever combinations of techniques— public and private—that they are convinced will prove most effective.

The Future of Liberal Democracy

The normal condition of the vast majority of human beings throughout the ages has been one of want and oppression. Quite understandably, therefore, the utopias to which they have looked have, above all, envisaged a condition in which these scourges would forever be banished.

Thanks to industrialization and democratization, we in the contemporary West, and particularly in the United States, are for the first time in the process of actually attaining this long-yearned-for utopia. And in doing so, we have come to confront a philosophical and political challenge with which no previous age has had the need—and opportunity—to cope: How can we sustain and utilize both our material plenty and our political mastery over ourselves?

From the point of view of politics, the challenge we face may be phrased in terms of one fundamental question. Can the democratic majority remain in effective political direction of the operations of our vast, complex, and dynamic industrial society? Or will the formally sovereign majority find its way of life and political fate increasingly dictated by the motivations, processes, and potentialities of industrialism? This question can be put in terms that go to the very heart of liberal democratic theory. Can the people be entrusted to determine and implement their own and society's best interests? Or are there circumstances in which this assumption is no longer realistic and must give way to some elitist political theory and practice? Current American thinking on this vital question remains hopeful; yet it uniformly warns that the situation is becoming constantly more perilous.

One cause of grave concern, for example, is the matter of the nation's allocation of its resources. Since economic decisions in a free society are made by the majority—either as voters or as consumers—the inevitable tendency is to concentrate overwhelmingly on the production of consumer goods, to aim for the largest Gross National Product possible, and to conceive of rivalry with other nations as chiefly a matter of competing standards of living. But can such economic decision making be counted upon to assure the society's most creative possible fulfillment and, above all, its ability to survive internationally? It was generally assumed that it could—until the Soviet Union's spectacular firing of its first Sputnik.

Reflecting upon why the United States fell behind in the crucial field of guided missile development, the eminent economist, Professor Kenneth Galbraith, has written as follows:

> It has become evident that our failure to match this achievement was the result of the failure to concentrate the requisite resources on the desired ends. Some have even pointed out that in the same week the Russians launched the first earth satellite we launched a magnificent selection of automobile models including the uniquely elegant new Edsel. The lesson was not completely learned. Too much was attributed to fortuitous factors—unwise budget cuts, the perverse personality of the Secretary of Defense,

interservice conflict, and generally poor administration. We have not yet seen that the causes were far deeper—that our economy, and the economic theory that explains and rationalizes its behavior, immobilizes all but a minor fraction of the product in private and, from the standpoint of national security, irrelevant production. We have not seen that the problem is far more than one of a bigger budget—that it is one of our attitude toward the goals of the society itself. A society which sets as its highest goal the production of private consumer goods will continue to reflect such attitudes in all its public decisions. It will entrust public decisions to men who regard any other goal as incredible—or radical. We have yet to see that not the total of resources but their studied and rational use is the key to achievement. . . .

To furnish a barren room is one thing. To continue to crowd in furniture until the foundation buckles is quite another. To have failed to solve the problem of producing goods would have been to continue man in his oldest and most grievous misfortune. But to fail to see that we have solved it and to fail to proceed thence to the next task, would be fully as tragic.[10]

The same anxious note is being sounded with ever greater frequency in regard to the sovereign majority's apparent lack of sufficient knowledge, sense of larger priorities, and institutional competence in the direction of our industrially and democratically advanced society's general cultural life. As a *Time Magazine* editor, Thomas Griffith, has warned in his recent book, *The Waist-High Culture:*

We tolerate what contents us, placidly accept what might require too much exertion to correct, and allow a free play to ambition. The result is a society tightly organized for specific purposes but loosely controlled in general, a society which has surrendered paramount influence over itself to those in no position to encourage or require the best of it. Not profit, which admirably organizes our production and consumption, but rather the leaving to profit of duties it is not best fitted to carry out, is our difficulty. To commit to corporations or to voluntary organizations the determining of our national aims is to leave them in the end to no one responsibly. Our society must find a way first to conceive the common good, and then to honor and reward in proper proportions those activities which best serve, not individual employers, but the community's aims. It is not enough to say of a society that though it feels itself a little frustrated it is generally content, for it may be satisfied with its circumstances while unaware of its true situation.

True, a certain kind of present danger is everywhere acknowledged: our press and our politicians talk of little else but the threat of Communism. Its menace is usefully exploited to persuade us to do things that need doing, though it is also invoked in dubious causes as well. We are urged to hate Communism but to adopt its scientific and military emphasis; and we are encouraged to congratulate ourselves on how superior our own morality is. But though Communism's challenge cannot be minimized, it is not the real root of our difficulties: these would exist if there were no Russian threat. These difficulties arise from the increased tempo of our lives, from the headlong and compulsive strides of our sciences . . . and from the increasing capacity of our distractions to numb our energies. Our difficulties are aggravated by the fact that events everywhere are out of kilter. If a great effort must continually be made against Russian assault, our real expenditure of imagination must be in lighting the chaos inside us, and recovering a clarity of purpose. Only in this way will we regain health as a nation, or hope to inspire others to admire us. The only competition that should matter to us as a nation is not with Communism but with that best we ourselves might be.

All societies create daily equilibriums, and achieve a balance amid conflicting drives. We too make a patchwork equilibrium and enjoy a fortunate civic tranquility, but I believe it to be an equilibrium out of gear with our increasing necessities. It reckons too little on the dynamic propulsion of technological changes within it, and is out of rhythm with the disturbances in the rest of the world.[11]

The Foundations of Individuality

If, as is thus widely maintained, it is true that our democratic-industrial society is suffering from a progressive weakening of its control over itself, how is this danger to our future to be overcome? The problem is generally agreed to involve two principal aspects. Most obviously, it is seen as a question of political *means*. That is, the vaster and more complex the operation of our democratic and industrial way of life becomes, the more effective must be our institutional and administrative techniques for keeping it under responsible over-all direction. The development of such techniques and their adaptation to constantly changing circumstances is considered to be the most urgent task of present-day politics.[12]

In a more fundamental sense, however, the problem we face is increasingly being diagnosed as a matter of modern man's *ends*. For, it is reasoned, while the satisfactions and demands of involvement in an industrial and democratic society are undoubtedly very great, how an individual reacts to them depends always upon his purposes in life. The man whose highest conscious aims are for material well-being and social approval is likely to be easily satisfied by material and social rewards. He is constrained by the nature of his aims and by their satisfaction to accept the society that thus allows him to fulfill himself. He is little prone to inquire beyond it—even to its foundations and implications. And, even if he should feel any lingering discontents, he is unlikely to dwell upon or express them for fear of jeopardizing the material and social rewards upon which he so exclusively depends.

The only man who is able to escape this iron logic of acceptance and reward is he whose ends go beyond mere material satisfactions and social approval. For, valuing other things besides the rewards that democratic-industrial society can give him, he is both motivated to look beyond it and free to judge it even though in doing so he does run risks of jeopardizing its rewards.

What is thus felt to be ultimately at issue is the question of the foundations of individuality. At the beginning of our modern era these foundations were conceived of in largely Christian terms. The satisfaction of material and social wants was not despised, but always held the status of a means to an end. Man's highest significance, in contrast, consisted in the relationship of his own soul and conscience with his Creator and Father God.[13] In the centuries-long postmedieval struggle against want and oppression, this religious foundation of individuality acquired first political, then economic, and finally more and more social dimensions. As this occurred, the originally predominant religious ingredient in individuality became progressively displaced. Utopia came to be something achievable here and now. And while the individual's this-worldly happiness was enthroned as the highest good, his significance came more and more to depend upon the extent to which he participated in the organized pursuit of that good. It was thus that, as the individual increasingly became the master of society, he simultaneously came to be more and more completely engulfed by it: the receipt of its rewards became his highest fulfillment, and obedience to its demands his highest morality.

If this diagnosis of the crisis of modern individuality is correct—and it is subscribed to in one version or another by almost every one of our prominent contemporary social thinkers [14]—upon what does the strengthening of the political direction of our democratic and industrial society appear to depend? It would seem to depend, above all, upon the addition to the ends with which the individual is identified of values other than those of mere material and social satisfaction. For, it is only through the possession of such additional metasocial values that the individual is equipped to see his society in larger perspectives and to contribute creatively and courageously to the direction of its over-all unfolding. Paradoxically, that is, the extent to which our modern type of society remains successful industrially and democratically may depend most crucially of all upon how *un*-successful it proves in absorbing its individual members morally and psychologically.

The strengthening and reintroduction of the needed larger values—whether they be religious or philosophical—is seen by no one as an easy matter. Indeed, in a free society, where changes must in the last analysis be willed by each individual citizen, it is recognized as a task of unprecedented magnitude. Yet as our industrial and democratic social order *gives* more to the individual than any other, it also inevitably *demands* more of him. Whether or not he can face up to this challenge may be the ultimate open question upon which the future of our civilization hinges.

SELECTED BIBLIOGRAPHY

BUTZ, OTTO. *Modern German Political Theory*, New York, Doubleday, Doubleday Short Studies in Political Science, 1955.
EBENSTEIN, WILLIAM. *Political Thought in Perspective*, New York, McGraw-

Hill, 1957, Chap. 22, "Tocqueville," pp. 464–500; Chap. 23, "Mill," pp. 501–526; Chap. 24, "Marx," pp. 527–560.

GRIFFITH, THOMAS. *The Waist-High Culture,* New York, Harper, 1959.

HOOK, SIDNEY. *Marx and the Marxists,* Princeton, N.J., Van Nostrand, Anvil, 1955.

MEYER, ALFRED G. *Marxism: The Unity of Theory and Practice,* Cambridge, Mass., Harvard University Press, 1954.

SCHUMPETER, JOSEPH A. *Capitalism, Socialism, and Democracy,* 3d ed., New York, Harper, 1950.

TONSOR, STEPHEN J. *National Socialism: Conservative Reaction or Nihilist Revolt?* (Source Problems in World Civilization), New York, Rinehart, 1959.

PART TWO

Contemporary Politics and Government

« 8 »

Liberal Democracy
in the United States

IN THE CARRYING OUT of Western political ideas, ideals, and
objectives no nation has pioneered as extensively as has the
United States. Nowhere were governmental institutions as consciously designed to embody the philosophy of liberal democracy.
Nowhere has government been as responsive to the will of the
majority, while maintaining the liberties of its subjects as individuals. And, finally, nowhere has a system of representative
government survived as long while suffering from such persistent
difficulties in generating a sustained flow of political power.

Constitutional Ideas

The structure of American government rests upon two
eighteenth-century philosophical ideas and the recognition of
one universal political necessity. The two philosophical ideas
are, first, the notion that all government must derive its authority from the consent of the governed; and second, the precept
that the exercise of governmental authority is always subject to
prescribed limits. The political necessity recognized in the American system is the imperative that governmental powers, though
limited, must be adequate for the purposes which government
must serve.

The reasons why the American Constitution was so consciously designed to rest upon liberal democratic philosophical

foundations were both historical and political. For one thing, as educated Englishmen, the American Founding Fathers inevitably conceived of politics in terms of the ideas current in the Anglo-Saxon world of their time; and most typical and prominent among these were the Lockean notions of the social contract, of inalienable natural rights, and of government by the consent of the governed. Nowhere, moreover, did the hypothesis of the social contract and its conception of free and self-sufficient individuals living in a state of nature seem to describe more plausibly the actual facts of life than in the largely frontier society of the American colonies.

More important, the claim that government should be by popular consent, as well as the insistence that it be limited to protect man's inherent individual rights, precisely expressed the colonists' grievances against the mother country. The colonists demanded an end to arbitrary interferences with their lives and property. And they asked that *any* kind of governmental regulation be made conditional upon their freely given consent as expressed through their own elected representatives. Whereas liberal democratic political principles had been argued in England by the rising middle classes in their struggles against royal absolutism, in the United States these principles were advanced against the nonresponsible rule of the English Parliament and on behalf of what was to become a whole nation.

The original implementation of liberal democratic governmental ideals in the United States occurred in two stages. The earlier stage, which lasted as long as Americans had a common cause in rejecting the bonds of colonialism, was expressed in the Articles of Confederation of 1781, whereby the colonies first banded together. Denying the central government even such basic powers as the regulation of interstate commerce and the authorization of taxes, the Articles constituted one of the purest national political embodiments of the ideals of popular and limited government ever attempted.

However, as the colonists' united anti-British orientation gave way to more long-range thinking about the ideals and requirements of government, the Articles of Confederation were seen to be inadequate in two chief respects. First, they failed to give the central government sufficient powers to maintain the

new nation's internal unity and to conduct its affairs internationally. And second, in having left such extensive powers to
the governments of the individual colonies, the Articles seemed
not to assure reliable enough protection to individual rights,
particularly private property rights.

This latter view, at least, was held by the politically dominant, propertied group among the colonists. This group desired
a stronger central government to check the more radical type of
democracy that they feared was developing in the politics of the
individual colonies. As James Madison, one of this conservative
group's most prominent members, wrote in *The Federalist*
papers: "To secure the public good and private rights, and at
the same time to preserve the spirit and form of popular government, is the great object to which our inquiries are directed."
It is noteworthy that the papers advocating a new Constitution
were a collaboration between Madison, with his countryman's
concern for personal liberties, and Alexander Hamilton and John
Jay, with their big-city awareness of the needs of business. The
Constitution that was thus framed in 1787 and became the law
of the land in June of the following year was intended permanently to achieve a triple objective for the new American nation:
popular, yet limited, yet effective national government.

Governmental Structure

The system of government adopted in 1788 has served the
United States for some one hundred and seventy-five years.
Organized in terms of its chief operating principles—separation
of powers, checks and balances, and federalism—it has provided
the political framework for some of the most far-reaching changes
ever experienced by a people. Originally conceived for the needs
of a sparsely settled land of farmers and merchants along the
Atlantic seaboard, it has survived as the machinery of government for what has become one of the most dynamic and populous
continental powers in history.

It is tempting to give principal credit for the achievement
of the American system of government to the foresight of the
Founding Fathers. Yet that would be misleading. For as in-
sightful as were the authors of the American Constitution,

the fact is that the system of government they devised came to operate in a very different manner, and survived for very different reasons, from what any of them anticipated. Indeed, as Professor Robert Dahl has pointed out, the most remarkable thing about the deliberations of the Constitutional Convention when considered in retrospect is

> the extent to which the members of this historic assemblage did not know what they were doing. They thought the popular House would be dynamic, populist, egalitarian, levelling and therefore a dangerous center of power that needed restraining; they thought the President would represent the wellborn and the few and that he would use his veto against popular majorities lodged in the House. They were wrong; for the dynamic center of power has proved to be the presidency, and after Jackson the President could claim, and frequently did claim, to be the only representative of a national majority in the whole constitutional system. Meanwhile, the House has scarcely revealed itself as the instrument of those impassioned minorities that the men at the Convention so desperately feared. Today the relationship they envisaged is, by and large, reversed. It is the President who is the policy-maker, the creator of legislation, the self-appointed spokesman for the national majority, whereas the power of Congress is more and more that of veto—a veto exercised, as often as not, on behalf of groups whose privileges are threatened by presidential policy.[1]

The chief reason for the Founding Fathers' erroneous predictions lay in their misunderstanding of the dynamics of American society. They failed to see correctly the social balance of power and political outlook that was to prevail even in their own lifetime. They were quite right in assuming that without feudal traditions and with its open frontier American society would be dominated by a spirit of social egalitarianism. Yet where they were wrong was in concluding that this social egalitarianism would express itself in political hostility toward the institution of private property.

It is true that almost everywhere else social egalitarianism *has* proven politically inimical to private property rights. Yet in the United States this conflict failed to materialize. The chief reason why it did not was that free access to the new lands on the frontier made social egalitarianism and respect for private property not only compatible but even mutually sustaining. Elsewhere in the world access to property could be achieved only by using politics as an instrument to gain greater equality of economic opportunity. In the agrarian and frontier society of the United States, this battle did not have to be fought with anything like the same urgency. As a result, social radicalism and economic conservatism were able to exist side by side, for the best assurance of fulfilling the ideal of free individualism that underlay both seemed to be the individual's acquisition and ownership of private property.

During the Depression of the 1930's this unique American idiom came very close to breaking down. Yet, in spite of the disastrous dimensions of this collapse of the industrialized American free enterprise economy, a major adjustment, rather than a rejection of the original formula, proved enough. After 1937, with the Supreme Court's confirmation of the social and economic legislation of the New Deal, social egalitarianism and respect for private property could again peaceably coexist. The price, admittedly, was acceptance of the principle that private property rights are not absolute but, rather, are subject to whatever limitation and regulation the politically effective majority may demand. Once American propertied interests had resigned themselves to this price, however, the path was cleared for the traditional American formula of social egalitarianism combined with what the rest of the world might consider economic conservatism. Once again, therefore, even in the changed conditions of the twentieth century, the political fears of the Founding Fathers failed to be justified.

Because of the unique American combination of popular democracy and respect for private property rights, the primary task confronting the American governmental system has not been that of restraining all-out conflicts of economic class or political principle. The continuing challenge, rather, has been to provide the country's politically significant interest groups with enough access to the decision-making process to assure them what they consider a fair hearing and an equitable share in the society's over-all benefits.

It has been in response to this challenge that the institutions devised at Philadelphia have acquired the altered functions that they have come to serve. And it was in the course of making this response that the American political system developed its most characteristic feature. That feature, to quote Professor Dahl once more, has been "the high probability that any active and legitimate group in the population can make itself heard effectively at some crucial stage in the process of decision . . . that one or more officials are not only ready to listen . . . but expect to suffer in some significant way if they do not placate the group, its leaders, or its most vociferous members." [2]

Governmental Trends

In adapting its democratic responsiveness to changing conditions and popular needs, American government has been undergoing two major long-term changes. One has been a continuing expansion of the powers of the federal government. The other has been a steady growth in the political importance of the presidency.

Like all changes in American domestic politics, the expansion of the powers of the federal government has been wholly nonideological. In the course of the country's commercial and industrial development, its various financial, business, and labor organizations became simply too large-scale and far-reaching in their importance to the nation's life as a whole to be regulated by the individual states. In other words, bigger and more complex economic operations, together with continually rising popular expectations as to personal welfare, created the practical necessity of concentrating ever greater responsibilities for economic and social administration in the hands of the central government.

The means of adapting the originally enumerated federal powers were at hand in the instrument of judicial review. Save for the Sixteenth Amendment (1913), giving Congress the power to tax incomes without apportioning the burden proportionately to the population of each state, the changes effected required little formal constitutional alteration. Instead, they were interpreted by the Supreme Court as already *implied* in certain of the existing constitutional provisions. The precedent for the Supreme Court's assumption of the role of final arbiter as to the constitutionality of an implied power was Chief Justice John Marshall's ruling in the case of *McCulloch versus Maryland* (1819): ". . . Let the end be legitimate, let it be within the scope of the constitution, and all means which are appropriate, which are plainly adapted toward that end, which are not prohibited but consist with the letter and spirit of the constitution, are constitutional."

The three most important of the enumerated federal powers to be so enlarged have been those of the so-called commerce, elastic, and supremacy clauses. According to the commerce clause (Article I, Section 8), "The Congress shall have the power to regulate commerce with foreign nations, and among the several States. . . ." According to the elastic clause of the same section, "The Congress shall have the power to make all laws which shall be necessary and proper for carrying into execution the foregoing powers, and all other powers vested . . . in the government of the United States, or in any department, or officer thereof." And according to the supremacy clause (Article VI, Section 2), "This Constitution, and the laws of the United States which shall be made in pursuance thereof . . . shall be the supreme law of the land; and the Judges in every State shall be bound thereby, anything in the Constitution or laws of any State to the contrary notwithstanding."

After Chief Justice Marshall's death, and particularly from about 1895 onward, the Supreme Court showed a tendency to reverse the direction of expanded federal powers. With the year 1937, however, and the Supreme Court's upholding of the sweeping New Deal legislation, the former trend was resumed and accelerated. Most significantly, perhaps, the commerce clause was reinterpreted to grant Congress the right to regulate interstate commerce on virtually any terms it might choose. This, combined with the further rule adopted in 1937 that Congress could use its tax power for regulatory purposes "to provide for the general welfare," placed at the disposal of the federal government full legal authority to frame whatever national economic and social policies the exigencies of the twentieth century and the needs of the American electorate might demand.

Hand in hand with this expansion of the powers of the federal government, and lending it all the greater significance, has been the rapid growth during the past quarter century in the governmental initiative and responsibilities of the Presidency. Also an entirely nonideological matter, this development has been a response to the nation's new internal circumstances as well as to its changed role in world affairs.

Typical of the new presidential responsibilities resulting from the American people's changing internal circumstances and needs are the tasks assigned to the Chief Executive under the Employment Act of 1945. Affirming the dedication of American society to the values of the free enterprise system, this act envisaged the government as the ultimate compensatory agent responsible for the nation's over-all economic health. By its fiscal, monetary, and credit policies, and by its public works programs, the government was to keep the economy in full production at all times. With the help of a Council of Economic Advisers, housed in the Office of the President, the President was to maintain a continuous surveillance of the economy as a whole and to report to Congress whatever policies he might deem necessary. In effect, as Professor Sidney Hyman has put it, the President "is expected to turn the spotlight on economic injustices; fortify the strength of the individual Americans; encourage the expansion of commerce, industry and agriculture; control bigness; guarantee a steady flow of low-cost goods; ensure the existence of mass purchasing power; guarantee access to raw materials—but to respect the structural lines of a constitutional instrument built in a different economic climate." [3]

A similarly far-reaching planning and administrative function has fallen to the Presidency as a result of the role of the United States in the changed circumstances of present-day world politics. The most striking expression of this development lies in the comprehensive responsibilities assigned to the President under the National Security Act of 1947. Formerly limited to the supreme command of military and naval forces engaged against an enemy, the President must today direct a program of military preparedness that reaches deeply into every phase of the nation's economic life and consumes upward of one half of its annual governmental budget. He is responsible for huge standing armies. He is dependent upon the professional advice of whole phalanxes of experts. And as a result of the development of nuclear weapons, he in effect possesses the power of life and death not only over Americans but over the entire world.

Perhaps the most obvious illustration of these enlargements of presidential functions is the vast size and complexity of today's executive branch in pure organizational terms. For currently aiding the President in his various domestic and foreign responsibilities are 10 departments headed by "secretaries" of cabinet rank; 40 agencies and commissions; some 30 special advisory commissions; and about 200 interdepartmental committees. More than 2,500 people work in the Executive Office of the President, including 50 senior assistants and 350 clerical employees in the White House Office alone. All in all, the executive branch today comprises some 2.3 million civilian workers and 2.6 million members of the armed forces—involving an annual payroll of approximately $21 billion.

Although these new concentrations and dimensions of American government are often looked upon with regret and uneasiness, they are generally recognized as in the last analysis unavoidable. For they have been in no wise the result either of constitutional usurpation or of doctrinaire planning. "The legitimate object of government," Lincoln once wrote, "is to do for a community of people whatever they need to have done but cannot do at all or cannot do so well for themselves in their separate or individual capacities." The growing responsibilities and size of the federal government, and of the executive branch in particular, have been the organizational price that has had to be paid for the carrying out of the ideal of democratic responsiveness in the conditions of our here and now.

Civil Liberties

The United States was "conceived in liberty, and dedicated to the proposition that all men are created equal," as Lincoln said in 1863 in the Gettysburg Address. His phrase about the equality of all men is borrowed from Jefferson's ringing words in the Declaration of Independence, which are followed by the assertion that men "are endowed by their Creator with certain unalienable Rights, that among these are Life, Liberty, and the pursuit of Happiness." The antecedents of these ideals in the Western political tradition have been discussed in Part I of this volume.

Chapter 7 has shown how Englishmen began by demanding individual rights from their king and ended by insisting that these liberties be guaranteed by Parliament as well. In like manner, the American colonists started with grievances against George III and later insisted that civil liberties be protected against possible curtailment by a government of the revolutionists' own creation. Between 1776 and the drafting of the federal Constitution in 1787, the thirteen new states emulated the mother country by adopting constitutions with explicit bills of rights. The federal Constitution itself has several aspects of a bill of rights, both expressed and implied. Article I enumerates specific limitations upon the powers of Congress and of the states, including prohibitions against suspending the writ of habeas corpus in peacetime or passing bills of attainder, and Article III defines treason narrowly for the citizen's protection. Moreover, the careful enumeration of the government's powers implies that they are limited to those listed. These provisions, however, did not satisfy either the libertarian conservatives attending the Constitutional Convention, notably James Madison and George Mason, or the radical democrats who were absent. Ratification of the Constitution, indeed, was not sure until a bill of rights in the form of the first ten amendments was promised.

The Bill of Rights, adopted in 1791, begins with the celebrated First Amendment guarantees against abridgment of religious freedom and of freedom of speech, press, or assembly; continues with specific guarantees against arbitrary governmental acts, particularly in respect to due process of law; and concludes by "reserving" to the states or the people all powers not constitutionally granted to the federal government. Jefferson hailed the Bill of Rights as a safeguard "the people are entitled to against every government on earth."

The first major test of civil liberties in the United States came in 1798, when a conservative Congress passed a Sediton Act in a display of panic at the radicalism of the French Revolution. This law, which made a mockery of the First Amendment, was overturned at the polls by the election to the Presidency of

Thomas Jefferson. The second major test came in the Civil War. The war itself established the principle that states' rights do not include the right of secession. The war also led to the Thirteenth, Fourteenth, and Fifteenth Amendments, which abolished slavery, defined citizenship ("All persons born or naturalized in the United States, and subject to the jurisdiction thereof . . ."), and guaranteed the political and civil rights of all citizens regardless of "race, color, or previous condition of servitude." The third major test of civil liberties in the United States is still current and involves the question of whether a citizen can be treated as "second class" either because of his racial ancestry or because of his exercise of First Amendment freedoms. For the most part the question is being answered in terms of the assertion of human equality in the Declaration of Independence.

While American government has continued effectively to realize its *democratic* ideal of responding to the wishes of the majority, it has done hardly less creditably—at least over the long run—in executing its *liberal* ideal of protecting the civil liberties of its citizens as individuals. Whereas the former success largely has been the achievement of the Congress and of the executive branch, the latter—in recent years—has been the work of the United States Supreme Court, exercising its power of judicial review.

Save for a few espionage and sedition cases arising in the course of World War I, however, the Supreme Court's preoccupation with the issue of civil liberties is a relatively recent development. An important exception was a post–Civil War decision that found a Missouri loyalty oath, aimed at Confederate sympathizers, unconstitutional as a bill of attainder. There are two chief reasons for the recency of the Supreme Court's concern with civil liberties. One is that until 1937 the principal concern of the Court was with the property rights of American citizens. Before 1937 the Supreme Court's chief role was, in effect, that of a judicial censor of Congress and the state legislatures in the regulation of the economy. After the Court's acceptance of basic New Deal legislation in 1937, on the other hand, it completely abandoned its defense of the principle of unrestricted free enterprise and has not declared a major regulatory act of Congress unconstitutional since that date. Instead, it has turned its attention to the redefinition and enlargement of the rights of individuals, including new protections against the actions of expanding and proliferating big government.

Most significant of the Supreme Court's civil liberties decisions have been those upholding the rights of labor unions and those invalidating state segregation laws. Beginning about 1890 some twenty states had enacted laws requiring the segregation of non-Caucasian persons in various public and private facilities, including schools and common carriers. Such laws were upheld by a divided Supreme Court in 1896 on the basis of a "separate but equal" doctrine. Reversing this doctrine in 1954, the Court began a series of decisions calling for desegregation "with all deliberate speed" on the ground that the "Constitution is color-blind."

The other principal reason for the recency of the Supreme Court's concern with civil liberties is that it was not until the past decade that such cases became at all frequent. Their greater incidence during this period has, of course, resulted from the number of critics of American Cold War policies who were affected by new legislation enacted to control subversives or by Congressional investigations exploring the need for such anti-subversive legislation. In the course of the administration of these Cold War measures many new cases presented themselves to the Supreme Court. These involved chiefly such issues as the discharge of employees of the federal government on loyalty grounds, the rights of witnesses before Congressional committees, the rights of organizations to refuse to register with the Attorney General, the rights of states to enact and enforce antisubversion laws, the legality of the Communist party, and the indictability of defendants for advocating and teaching the overthrow of government by force and violence. To some degree the debate over these issues is bound to continue as long as there are international tensions, for the debate rests on a highly subjective value judgment as to the relative importance of national security and individual liberty—or, in another form, as to whether there is any necessary conflict between the two.

Until 1954 and the easing of Cold War tensions, the Supreme Court consistently supported the authority of the President,

Congress, and the states to undertake whatever antisubversive measures they deemed necessary. Its findings thus tended to be almost uniformly against defendants. After 1954, however, the Court's position rapidly changed. Previous decisions in favor of the federal government were modified and clarified, new rules were developed in favor of the rights of defendants, and defendants began regularly to win their appeals. The movement in this direction reached its climax in the Supreme Court term of 1956–1957. And taken as a whole, as one observer has put it, it marked a new and unprecedented

> surge of zeal for the protection of individuals and their civil liberties. . . . The Court, obviously, deliberately, and consciously, seeks to keep . . . the "great system of balances upon which our free government is based," and one of these lines of balance is the relation of the Government and the individual, between the claims of the majority and the rights of the minority. The policy of the Warren Court in recent terms has been to weigh this balance towards the rights of individuals and minorities.[4]

Political Parties

Although it is generally agreed that the American system of government has performed well in its democratic responsiveness and its protection of the liberties of the individual, there is somewhat less satisfaction among experts in regard to its achievement of an adequate flow of sustained political power. Weakness and confusion in American leadership are found to be particularly glaring and damaging to the national interest in the area of foreign policy. It is not denied that in periods of crisis and emergency the United States has never yet failed to come up with the political decisiveness that the particular occasion has demanded. The question that is asked, however, is whether such an *ad hoc* pattern of political response remains adequate for the present. Will it do for a world of continuous cold wars, big bureaucracies, and chronic national and international crises in which there are no more periods of what once was called normalcy? Thomas Finletter has written in his *Can Representative Government Do the Job?*

The question thus is whether the *means,* that is the procedure of our government, are adequate in relation to its objectives, or its *ends.* The usual pattern has been long periods of negative government interlarded with short periods of strong action. . . . The irregular flow of power endangers representative government in the United States. . . . A government of fits and starts is no longer good enough for our purposes.[5]

A large measure of responsibility for this alleged absence of sustained political leadership is ascribed to Congress. The legislative branch, in this view, fails to enunciate and support statesmanlike and clear policies upon the major national issues. For one thing, it is charged, this failure of Congress discourages coherent political thinking among the people as a whole. And, no less important, it results in the abdication of more and more over-all governmental responsibilities—with less and less effective political accountability—to the executive branch. According to Sidney Hyman,

Our constitutional rules and our pressing physical needs are still in a state of conflict. What we expect the President to do under the law continues to encounter the opposite pull of what we expect of the presidential institution. How can the tension be reduced? It can be reduced if Congress does its *legislative* part in meeting national and international expectations. If it fails to do what it is competent to do, then the people, in their search for pragmatic solutions, will enlarge the Presidency to a dangerous point where it might become an autonomous source of action, indiscriminate in its objects, and beyond the immediate effective reach of the other organs of government.[6]

Indeed, there appears to be considerable doubt whether Congress can any longer even be expected to make the required contribution to national leadership and the tightening up of presidential responsibility. In the opinion of Professor V. O. Key, for example,

Representative bodies, the institutional embodiment of democratic ideology, have by the compelling force of events lost both power and prestige. Their role in the initiation of public policy has been diminished by losses to pressure groups and administrative agencies; their authority to decide many issues has, of necessity, been delegated to the administrative services. They have been driven towards a role of futile and uninformed criticism, at its worst motivated either by partisan or picayune considerations.[7]

To the extent that the complexities of modern government and the separation of powers would permit Congress to contribute more forcefully to national leadership than it does, what can be done to enable it better to realize its potentialities? With the posing of this question the key problem of present-day American government is shifted to the condition of the country's political parties. For it is generally agreed that, barring formal constitutional changes, the most obvious and valuable way to stabilize national power and keep it responsible would be through a long-overdue organizational realignment of the American party system.

Professor Stephen K. Bailey has observed in a recent essay on *The Condition of Our Political Parties:*

> The root of the weakness is that while the two national parties for years have genuinely competed for the Presidency they have not made a similar effort in the election of United States Senators and Members of the House of Representatives. Nor have they been of sufficient help to the President and the Congress in providing candidates of high quality for the grand patronage of departmental and agency direction. So long as we lack strong national parties operating as catalysts in the Congress, the executive branch, and the national government as a whole, and between the national government and state and local governments, power will continue to be dangerously diffused or, perhaps what is worse, will whip-saw between diffusion and presidential dictatorship.[8]

Professor Bailey cites five major consequences of the present amorphous and decentralized condition of the two major parties in the United States. First, he points out, it virtually ensures a government by fits and starts:

> Presidential requests for an adequate United States Information Agency budget have been listened to one year and ignored the next by the House Appropriations Committee. As a result, cultural officers abroad have had to spend much of their time hiring and firing—inflating and deflating programs like an accordion. This has made us look ridiculous as a nation, and has made it extremely difficult for a coherent information program to develop

as a vital element in our foreign policy. The same has been true
of foreign economic aid.

No less damaging, moreover, have been the discontinuities of
policy resulting from the inability of the executive department
and Congress to agree on any co-ordinate methods of applying
the kind of devices needed in economic stabilization, defense
policy, atomic energy policy, welfare policy, and conservation
policy. And these discontinuities "have been quite as apparent
when the Presidency and both Houses of Congress have been
in one party as when the control of the government has been
divided." [9]

A second consequence of the present structural limitations of
the American parties is what Professor Bailey describes as

> the lack of rationality and consistency in the substance of much
> public policy. . . . In a world in which, for example, the indis-
> criminate dumping of rice on the world market in order to ease
> a temporary glut in Louisiana could cost us the friendship of
> Burma, there are huge dangers in having unlinked centers of power
> making their own policy for the nation. And yet, parochial groups
> in Congress (often in league with sections of the executive branch
> and with outside pressure groups) still carry an inordinate amount
> of power.[10]

A third consequence of the absence of coherent party
machinery is that the government cannot be truly responsive to
popular majorities. Professor Bailey sees a tendency for Congressional compromise

> to fall with considerable regularity on the side of minority rather
> than majority interests. Committee chairmen from "safe," and often
> sparsely populated, one-party states and districts; the minority-
> weighted bipartisan rules committee; and the myths, rules, and
> influence structure which enable Congressional leaders to ignore
> demands for greater majority representation in policy decisions—
> all these combine to inflate the power of minority interests at the
> expense of the national popular majority.[11]

This leads directly to what Professor Bailey cites as a fourth
consequence:

> The increasing danger of public cynicism and apathy toward the
> Congress, partly because its power is too diffuse or too subtle to

comprehend; partly because when power *is* clearly identifiable it seems to work more consistently for minorities than for the majority.

Finally, Professor Bailey asserts, the absence of a unified party structure results in the dissipation and discouragement of badly needed criticism of both domestic and foreign policy:

> There is no effective vehicle for responsible opposition criticism of programs; there is no machinery for anticipating the implications of social changes and their effects on policy. With the help of a huge and in part brilliant staff, Members of Congress may fill the air and the *Congressional Record* with daring solutions to our dilemmas. But without some sort of party sanction, these ideas are worth little more than an inch or two in the *New York Times*.[12]

All of these results, in Professor Bailey's analysis, follow from the fact that neither the Republican nor the Democratic party is truly competitive across the entire nation; that neither has a sufficiently unified structure to enable it to dramatize its program around its basic ideology; that neither has the power, even if it had the right structure, to carry out its program; and that neither has sufficiently clear and unambiguous lines of political accountability running to the voters. Until these defects in the American party system are corrected, this expert therefore concludes, the ineffectiveness of Congress's contribution to sustained national political leadership is bound to continue.

Political Attitudes and Circumstances

There is little doubt that the political needs to which Professor Bailey's and similar analyses are addressed are well founded. The further question, however, is whether the majority of the American people and their elected representatives *perceive* these needs and *feel* them sufficiently strongly to be moved to undertake the indicated measures.

To date, at least, save among a handful of American statesmen and the country's political scientists, there is little visible general concern about the long-range trends, dangers, and requirements of the American political process. There would seem to be four major reasons for this. One is the deeply ingrained laissez-faire assumption that if every private interest takes care of itself, the best interests of the society as a whole will automatically be served as well. A second is the related notion that the sole concern of a free society is the limitation of governmental authority and that that government is best which governs least. A third is the fact that what political concerns we *do* feel are largely directed toward our relationship with the Soviet Union. And the fourth, and undoubtedly most important, is our absorption in our ever-rising and seemingly secure material prosperity which, as one observer has recently alleged, "results in part from our new way of getting rich, which is to buy things from one another that we do not want, at prices we cannot pay, on terms we cannot meet, because of advertising we do not believe." [13]

Can these attitudes and circumstances be overcome and the necessary political adjustments effected? Or will pursuit of the ideal of maximized democratic responsiveness have to be sacrificed—either because of internal developments or because it is incompatible with the exigencies of the country's international situation? Is a successful industrial and democratic society in the long run politically possible? Or is it doomed politically to fall victim to its very industrial and democratic success? In confronting questions such as these at the height of its fulfillment, the United States is once again—as it was at its inception—the modern Western world's great political pioneer.

SELECTED BIBLIOGRAPHY

DAHL, ROBERT A. *A Preface to Democratic Theory*, Chicago, The University of Chicago Press, 1956.

HINDERAKER, IVAN, ed. *American Government Annual, 1958–1959*, New York, Holt, 1958.

HUTCHINS, ROBERT M. *Is Democracy Possible?* The Fund for the Republic, Bulletin, February, 1959.

KEY, V. O. *Politics, Parties, and Pressure Groups*, 4th ed., New York, Crowell, 1958.

LUBELL, SAMUEL. *The Future of American Politics*, New York, Harper, 1952.

« 9 »

Great Britain:
Parliamentary Democracy

No people has been as fully and consistently successful in the implementation of Western political values as the British. The only nation in which liberal democracy developed without interruptions from wholly native roots, Great Britain has also been the only country in which that type of government is universally agreed to have been an unqualified blessing. It has contributed most creatively to Britain's fulfillment as a nation and has in no significant way detracted from the ability of the British to maintain internal political stability and to adjust rationally to the changing realities of international politics. Throughout the world, for these reasons, the British political system is considered the great classic of liberal democratic government.

The British Consensus

The most important circumstance underlying the evolution of the British system of government was Britain's early and full development of a national political consensus. The British were the first and most successful among the Western peoples in achieving the agreement on collective ends and means that makes it possible for a society to function freely and effectively as a nation.

The development of the British political consensus has, in

165

turn, been the outcome of a great many factors. Undoubtedly the most important has been the fact that the British have enjoyed the inestimable advantage of being able to fashion their history as the inhabitants of an island. Although the English Channel is at its narrowest point hardly more than twenty miles wide, its presence—"which serves . . . as a moat . . . against the envy of less happier lands," as Shakespeare put it—has been the joy of Englishmen and the regret of continental Europeans for more than five centuries.

The most obvious advantage of British geographical insularity has been in the realm of defense. Since the Norman William the Conqueror invaded the country in 1066, Englishmen have had the opportunity of developing their destinies free from all foreign intervention. The evolution of their national solidarity and political institutions has never since been interrupted by foreign invasion or occupation. Unlike the land powers of Europe, they did not experience the manpower and financial drain of centuries of war in the establishment and defense of strategic or ethnic boundaries. The Royal Navy was the only major defense arm that Britain required during its crucial formative centuries. And although the maintenance of this sea power was not financially inexpensive, it demanded neither large masses of men nor the development of the entrenched military machines that have dogged civilian supremacy elsewhere.

In addition to facilitating national defense, Britain's insularity has also been a factor of key importance in the country's internal evolution. Because of the nation's inaccessibility from abroad, the modus vivendi that came to exist among the classes and groups that at any given time comprised English society had always to be fought out on the basis of their own domestic strength and without possible recourse to aid from abroad. When, for example, Henry VIII began his suppression of the English Catholics' tie with the pope, it was impossible for his victims to summon assistance from the Roman Catholic kings and peoples of the Continent. It was similarly impossible for Charles I to call in foreign forces to support him in suppressing the resistance of Parliament to his royal absolutism. At these and other decisive junctures of British history, that side carried the day which *within* the country could muster the greatest strength and support. And as unfortunate as this was for those who had no alternative but to yield, for the stable evolution of the nation as a whole it was a rare blessing: it meant that prolonged resistance to the dominant direction of developments was hopeless. Unlike the situation on the Continent, where it was always possible to look to the intervention of like-minded groups from across the border, the only rational course in Britain was to accept the new relationships on the best terms one could get, that is, to compromise. And with each compromise, of course, the political consensus was broadened and the advisability of future compromises made more compelling.

The early development of this spirit of compromise was facilitated by the absence among the English of irreconcilable economic and cultural differences. In part this was a matter of the country's size. Less than one thirtieth the area of the United States, Britain has had the great advantage of being able to operate as a unitary state, without the divisive and politically limiting effects that have had to be reckoned with in nations where vast size or deep-rooted regionalism has made necessary a federal structure of government. Even in British economic life, such differences as have existed have tended to be complementary rather than mutually exclusive; the last major showdown came in the 1840's, when British agriculture was deprived of its tariff protection and forced to compete freely on world markets. Thereafter, Britain was firmly committed to its role as a manufacturing nation, with each sector of the British economy prepared—on the best terms it could get—to play its part accordingly.

The steadily growing political consensus expressed in these developments had all along benefited from still another fortunate circumstance: the early emergence of a distinctly British world view. On the Continent, where forces of change and reaction remained deadlocked for centuries, political discussion often hardened into the assertion of impassioned dogmas which impeded stable political evolution even further. In Britain, in contrast, where such sterile impasses were avoided, there developed a much more pragmatic attitude to the problems of the collective life.[1]

The British people's practical view of politics was strengthened by the country's commercialization and its consequent world-wide contacts with foreign peoples. Astride the trade routes between the Old World and the New, the British for hundreds of years served as the Western world's most active explorers, missionaries, merchants, businessmen, and bankers. In the process, their successive ruling groups—first the aristocracy, then the middle classes, and, finally, the general electorate —became the most realistic and statesmenlike sovereigns that the modern world has known. The result was the development of a national sense of confident matter-of-factness that has enabled the British to adjust to change—if not always to master it—with a measure of success that has been the envy of all Western peoples.

The Sovereign Parliament

The most significant of all the expressions of Britain's evolving political consensus was the development of the sovereignty of Parliament. For, to the extent that the political consensus grew, it was governmentally registered in the increasingly sovereign power of Parliament; and to the extent that the sovereign power of Parliament broadened, it came to be in and through Parliament that Englishmen compromised with one another in solving their collective problems and thereby contributed to the further strengthening of their political consensus.

Perhaps the most striking expression of the agreement upon political fundamentals that developed among the British is the fact that the constitution by which Parliament became sovereign has always been an unwritten one. The code by which the British have come to govern themselves consists of an unsystematized historical accumulation of documents, statutes, conventions, and precedents, each marking some stage in the evolution of Parliamentary sovereignty. There is in this tradition of British Parliamentary sovereignty no provision for the American type of separation of powers, no explicit cataloguing of human rights, and no judicial review. Since no special amending process is provided for, and no authority above Parliament can declare an act of government unconstitutional, the country is, in law and fact, left to the unrestrained rule of the sovereign Parliament.

The reason the British have been willing to leave their collective decision making so freely in Parliament's hands has, of course, been their faith that it would not transgress the limits of the underlying political consensus of which it was nothing more nor less than the electorally responsible government expression. In countries like the United States, France, and the Soviet Union, written constitutions became necessary because entirely new political systems were being created. The ends and means of these new systems had to be articulated as fighting statements against the past, as inspirations for the future, and as specifications of the relationships that were to prevail among the participants in the new regimes. In Britain, in contrast, political ends and means were historically inherent and merely evolved in gradual adjustment to changing circumstances. What earlier rejections of the past there were—directed always against royal absolutism—were only partial and could therefore be stipulated in documents much less all-prescribing than formal constitutions. For the rest, adjustment and adaptation through acts of Parliament proved sufficient.

The organizational media through which the British consensus is made politically operative are the country's two dominant political parties. After the middle of the nineteenth century these two parties came to be the Conservatives and the Liberals. The former was the traditionalist party of those who inclined toward the pre-industrial ideal of the paternalistic state; the latter was the free enterprise party supported by the business community. The crucial test of this traditional two-party system, as of the larger political consensus that underlay it, came with the development of a growing and increasingly assertive urbanized working class that followed upon large-scale industrialization. On what terms could this new group, fast becoming the most numerous in the society, be absorbed into the traditional political consensus? How could it be permitted to participate in the Parliamentary expression of that consensus?

In spite of grave misgivings on the part of the traditional ruling groups, none of the successive extensions of the franchise

to the lower-middle and finally the working-class citizens of
Britain led to any radical change in the political consensus
or to any disruptions of continued gradual Parliamentary evolution. There were two chief reasons for this. One was the
highly esteemed position of Parliament itself. As the middle class
had done earlier, even Britain's working class proved willing to
exercise restraint and moderation as it waited for greater access
to Parliament and the opportunity to employ Parliamentary
powers in its own economic and social interest.

An even more important circumstance that facilitated the
gradual and peaceful absorption of the British working class
into the nation's political consensus and governmental process
was the "lower-class" Englishman's social submissiveness and
readiness to accept the leadership of his "betters." Unlike the
members of militant democratic movements today, the mass of
nineteenth-century Englishmen were not driven by the notion
that they were as fully capable of governing as anyone else in
their society. For nearly half a century, indeed, the laboring
citizens of Britain submitted to their lot with nothing to look
to for improvement save a badly restricted incipient union
movement and Parliamentary representation through the Liberal
party—the party of the very interests with which labor stood in
economic conflict. As late as 1891, for example, George Bernard
Shaw, in an address to a meeting of British workingmen, thought
it necessary to remind his audience that "until the workers learn
to trust one another and choose one another as representatives,
instead of running after the tall hats and frock coats, they will
never have a genuine Labour Party in Parliament." [2] And
in the same year, another middle-class champion of working-
class representation, Robert Blatchford, warned a similar gathering that "what they needed was to get a few energetic men who
were not too respectable. A Labour candidate who went to
Parliament with a stand-up collar, a tall hat and a very nice
black coat and waistcoat, and was always afraid that he was
going to say something that the educated gentlemen there would
not approve, was not much use to a Labour Party." [3]

Finally set up in 1906, the present British Labour party
was the offspring of a Labour Representation Committee which,
in turn was the result of the convergence of three forces: the

so-called Independent Labour Party, founded in Scotland in
1893; British trade-union groups; and the famous Fabian
Society. The latter, set up in 1893, was a society of middle- and
upper-middle-class intellectuals whose purpose was to help the
Labour party map out its program and explain its position to
the public at large. Its membership included such prominent
people as Beatrice and Sidney Webb, George Bernard Shaw,
and, for a time, H. G. Wells.

The tradition of gradualist reform that came to be associated
with the Fabian Society continued to dominate the direction of
the Labour party from its first gain of twenty-nine Parliamentary
seats in 1906 to its sweeping electoral triumph under Clement
Attlee in 1945. Providing the British with a bridge of social
consciousness between classes, and supplying the Labour party
with the respectability and learning of some of the country's
finest minds, the Fabian Society played a most important part
in guarding the British political consensus from major defections
to either communism or fascism.[4,*] It accomplished this, in the
words of one of its early members, by presenting "the case for
Socialism in plain language which everybody could understand.
It based Socialism, not on the speculations of a German philosopher [Marx] but on the obvious evolution of Society as we see
it around us. It accepted economic science as taught by the
accredited British professors; it built up the edifice of Socialism
on the firm foundations of our existing political and social
institutions: it proved that Socialism was but the next step in
the development of Society, rendered inevitable by the changes
which followed from the industrial revolution of the 18th
century."[5]

As Labour's power in Parliament gradually grew, the traditional British party alignment underwent a major change.
That was the progressive demise of the old Liberal party. In
1922, for example, the Liberals were still able to capture 29.1
per cent of the votes cast, against Labour's 29.5 per cent, and
the victorious Conservatives' 38.2 per cent. In the 1945 general

* Only in the 1930's was there some serious doubt as to the ability of the
British consensus to survive the transition to a welfare state. The question
was whether the British propertied classes would peacefully yield to a Labour
party electoral victory—and to the anticipated social and economic changes
that would follow.

election that swept Labour into power with 39.8 per cent of the vote, the best the Liberals could do was 9.0 per cent. And on the occasion of the Conservative victory in 1955, the Liberals' electoral support had dropped to a negligible 2.7 per cent.* What had happened was that the Liberals had been attracted away in the direction of both Right and Left. Its supporters who were attached to nineteenth-century free enterprise had shifted to the Conservatives, and those with a welfare-state conception of liberalism had joined the ranks of Labour.

To keep their respective sectors of the national consensus mobilized for political action, both Labour and Conservatives maintain permanent national organizations. In the Conservative party the purpose of the national organization's work, including its annual conference, is primarily to advise and support rather than to originate policy. The dominant figure, selected by his predecessor in informal consultation with other party promi-nents, is the party leader, the man who is either head of Her Majesty's Government or leader of Her Majesty's Loyal Op-position.

The national organization of the Labour party accords a somewhat higher measure of responsibility to the party member-ship. In composition the Labour membership is of two kinds: individual members and "affiliated" members. The latter are various types of organizations—trade unions, co-operative socie-ties, socialist societies, professional organizations, and constitu-ency Labour parties. Though it is its Parliamentary leadership that actually determines Labour's policies and tactics, whatever decisions are arrived at must be formally discussed at the party's important annual conference.

In spite of their very different origins and traditions, the policies offered to the voters by these two dominant British parties have become more and more similar. By choice as well as circumstance, Labour has become more conservative, and the

* In the election of October 8, 1959, the Liberals more than doubled their share of the popular vote by tallying 5.8 per cent. Since the Conservatives retained just under half of the total, whereas Labour's percentage dropped from 46.4 to 43.9, Liberal leaders predicted a return to their old place as the second major party. Most neutral observers considered such predictions premature.

Conservatives have become more progressive. Labour, for its part, has lost most of its original militant leadership. Its directors today are mainly middle-class intellectuals and representatives of the managerial echelon of the labor unions. Now that such major industries as coal and transport have been nationalized, Labour's remaining objectives are simply those of the democratic welfare state: full employment and government-assured standards of wages, working hours, and health. Since these, according to all indications, are the objectives of the majority of the British electorate, the Conservatives have had little choice but to follow Labour's lead. And this they have in fact done. What practical differences therefore remain between the two parties are differences largely of tempo and technique.

As in other advanced liberal democracies, questions of basic political purpose and structure have for the most part been settled. Even in foreign affairs, the requirements of Britain's economic situation, its relative loss of world power, and the dimensions of present-day weapons leave open fewer and fewer real alternatives. The political parties inevitably reflect this fact. And to the extent they do, their rivalry is no longer one of differences in world view or fundamental method. They compete, rather, in terms of personalities and the details of political administration. Yet even in this less basic appeal to the voter, their function is nonetheless vital. For it is the fact that there *are* alternative personnels vying for power and scrutinizing each other's performances which assures that the democratic consensus will be honestly represented and its problems responsibly formulated and attended to.

Governmental Institutions and Processes

The system through which the British Government politically operates is dominated by the House of Commons, the lower house of the legislature. It is this which makes Britain's governmental arrangements, in contrast to the American, a *parliamentary* system. In the United States, executive and legislative powers are separated and must be exercised within the mandate of the Constitution as interpreted by the courts. In Britain, executive and legislative powers are concentrated in one locus, the House of Commons, and are not subject to measurement against a written constitution through judicial review.

The most significant feature of the House of Commons is that it simultaneously controls, and is controlled by, the Cabinet. Composed of members of the House of Commons who must constantly work through and with the House, the Cabinet is, in effect, the executive committee of the House of Commons. And since it is the majority party from which the Cabinet's membership is drawn, it is the prominent men in the majority party who occupy the Cabinet offices and whose leader is the head of the Cabinet, the Prime Minister.

It is the Prime Minister and his majority-party associates in the Cabinet who make up the Government. In the carrying out of its legislative and executive mandate the Government must constantly reckon with the members of the minority party, the Loyal Opposition. It is the latter's function to scrutinize all Government action and to be prepared at any time to assume Government power and responsibility with an alternative program and personnel of its own. For this reason even the party in opposition has its leaders, ever ready to assume the House's executive functions. When the Conservatives are in opposition, their leadership is called the "Shadow" Cabinet; when it is Labour which is in the minority, its direction is in the hands of its Parliamentary Committee.

The genius of this British system is its ability to avoid stalemates between the executive and the legislative. Its executive, the Cabinet, stands and falls with its legislative, the membership of the House of Commons. The principal reason for this is the Prime Minister's right of dissolution. For if the Prime Minister fails to secure majority support for any major policy, he is empowered to dissolve the House and call for new elections. The legislative, for its part, is able at any time to withdraw its majority support of the Government and thereby to force it to resign.

Though this arrangement suggests an equal interdependence of powers between the House and the Cabinet, in actual practice the superior initiative rests overwhelmingly with the latter. For in view of the highly disciplined British party system and the domination of the Cabinet by the party leadership, the rank and file of the Members of Parliament—called "back benchers" —enjoys little practical choice but to support Cabinet policies. It has been because of this circumstance, aggravated in recent years by the growing volume and complexity of legislation, that British "parliamentary" government has in actual fact become more and more a matter of "cabinet" government.

The members of the British Cabinet are selected by the Prime Minister from among the membership of his party's majority in the House of Commons. In sharp contrast to the American arrangement, each minister is expected to occupy a seat in the legislature. He must be ready at any time to support legislation involving his own department and to participate in Question Time to answer queries regarding his department's administration. In his relations with the Prime Minister and the other members of the Cabinet, each minister is committed to the principle of collective responsibility. Once Government policy is decided upon, it is each minister's duty to support this policy in full and, if called upon, to defend it during Question Time before the House.

The powers of the elective House of Commons are shared with an upper chamber, the hereditary House of Lords. Comprised today of some 865 peers, the House of Lords in times past exercised legislative powers even greater than those of the Commons. Indeed, as late as 1911 its legislative opposition to the Cabinet and lower house on a budget bill threatened to bring the process of government to a complete stalemate. Not surprisingly, this bold action of the Lords was followed by a series of measures by which the legislative power of the upper house was progressively qualified and limited.

At the present time, the functions of the House of Lords remains essentially threefold. The first, which is the same as it has always been, is its role as the highest appeal court of the land. In the exercise of this function it is not the entire chamber which is involved but a select group of legal experts who are either already members of the Lords or who have been raised to the peerage specifically for its judicial purposes. The second function is the general one of exploring complex areas that may become subjects of future legislation and of discussing the implications of legislation already proposed. Finally, the chamber has the power to review legislation voted in the Commons and either to approve it or send it back for revision. Compared with earlier times, however, this power is today carefully circumscribed. Since the Parliament Act of 1911, the House of Lords cannot reject any money bills. And since the Parliament Act of 1949, a bill may become law despite the opposition of the Lords if it has been passed by the Commons in two successive sessions and if one year has elapsed since the time of its second reading. How long even this one-year suspensive veto power will last will probably depend upon whether and how it is used. If employed to obstruct strongly supported social and economic legislation, the result—as some Labour spokesmen have long recommended—may well be the abolition of the legislative functions of the House of Lords altogether.

A second seemingly anachronistic institution in the British governmental system is, of course, the monarchy. Unlike the House of Lords, however, the monarchy is neither redundant nor in danger of being abolished. Even though only formally, it is involved in every phase of the governmental process. Beyond that, its influence pervades the nation's entire political life. In lending to British democracy the aura and color of traditional royalty, it enables the state to function at once more freely and with greater discipline than is possible in pure republics.

The function of the monarchy in the process of government is essentially that of a symbolic sanction. Legislation, in order to become law, must be signed by the monarch (even though the occupant of that office has no alternative but to sign and has not refused since the eighteenth century). The program of government submitted by the Cabinet at the beginning of each legislative session is read by the monarch and is called the Speech from the Throne. Major appointments are made by the monarch (after being decided by the Cabinet); the formal naming of Governments and the acceptance of their resignation is handled by the monarch; and the operation of the whole system is not merely in the hands of a small group of party politicians called the Cabinet but of an august body of royal servants with the status of Her Majesty's Government. Since the monarchy has been the central feature of the British state for more than seven centuries, it is not difficult to understand the result: a most effective inducement to the citizenry to look upon government with seriousness and esteem, and a valuable inspiration to politicians to see and exercise their functions with the greatest possible responsibility and dignity.

The monarchy serves a further important function: it attracts to itself all the reverence which inevitably attaches to the head of a state. The Prime Minister, the actual and practicing leader of the government, can be viewed and judged respectfully but unemotionally in terms of himself as a person and of the job he is doing on the public's behalf. On the monarch, who has no independently exercisable powers, can safely be heaped whatever adulation toward the nation the people may be moved to feel and express.

The advantage of this British arrangement is apparent when one compares it with the situation prevailing in systems where the head of state is also the operating executive head of government. In the United States, for example, the evaluation of the President is rendered much more difficult by the fact that it is often impossible to separate the man as the symbol of America from his role as a politician. As a result, it is difficult to criticize the President as a politician without seeming to be guilty of lack of reverence for the nation as represented by him in his simultaneous function as head and symbol of state.

The Uniqueness of British Democracy

The monarchy is only one of the factors which create in British political life that combination of freedom and self-discipline that is so vital to liberal democracy's successful functioning. Another, already alluded to above, is the exceptionally high degree of social and economic homogeneity of the British population. There is no doubt that when measured by absolute standards, the American system of government is much more cumbersome than that of the British. Such arrangements as federalism, the separation of powers, and the sharing of legislative functions between the two houses of Congress impede policy making and often narrow the limits within which policy is possible. Yet in large part at least, the price in inefficiencies that is paid by Americans in these and other respects is the inescapable price of a diverse and populous continental society. Although one may admire and envy the British system and its advantages, he must admit that little short of a regime of one-party totalitarianism (that would impose through coercion the consensus and discipline that do not exist spontaneously) could force the unruly American political process into the type of cabinet-led parliamentary pattern that works so admirably among the British.

An additional important factor that makes possible the unusual performance of the British system of executive-parliamentary leadership is the British people's willingness to be politically represented by men who in their background, education, and public dedication are frankly recognized as above average. For centuries, British politics was in the hands of a relatively small aristocracy—men who had attended one of the country's top preparatory schools (public schools), who had put in their years at Oxford or Cambridge, and who looked for their highest fulfillment and recognition in national service, either in Parliament or in some nonpolitical branch of government. The motivation and training of this aristocracy of birth was transmitted during the nineteenth century to the sons of the new aristocracy of business and industry, and has been passed on in the present century to the aristocracy of ability of all classes. And throughout the entire period, the British voter has continued not only to accept the leadership of people so motivated and trained but actually to prefer it.

The situation in the United States in these respects is, of course, quite different. American society's egalitarianism, its revolution-born hostility to executive authority, and its long historical experience of the open frontier and international isolation have resulted in a persistent tendency to undervalue and reject the role of government. And the ideal of the political leader has not been the man of superior intellect and culture but a somewhat romanticized image of the self-made man. In Britain, an Oxford accent and a cultivated bearing are almost certain to inspire the workingman's respect and confidence; in the United States, traces of an Ivy League education tend, if anything, to put an individual culturally on the defensive and to arouse in the electorate feelings ranging from uncertainty to animosity.

These and other differences between British and American democracy clearly converge in the prevailing conceptions of the ideal role of the legislative representative. In the United States, the role of the member of Congress—in both expectation and fact—tends more often to be that of a delegate of his constituents' interests and views than that of a representative exercising his independent judgment of the requirements of the country's situation as a whole. In Britain, even though constituency pressures upon Members of Parliament are not lacking, both ideal and practice are decidedly the other way. In part, again, this is a question of the traditionally more urgent sense of the over-all national interest among British electors and of fewer diversities in need of being asserted in the formulation of national policy. In part, however, it is also a matter of the historically more earnest and aristocratic spirit of British politics already discussed above. The implications of this more aristocratic British political idiom for the role of the legislative representative have nowhere been interpreted more clearly and movingly than in the formulation of Edmund Burke, made nearly two centuries ago in a speech to his constituents in the city of Bristol. Burke's thesis, which continues to be accepted as the ideal relationship between the elected politician and his constituents even today, ran as follows:

> Their [the voters'] wishes ought to have great weight with him; their opinion high respect; their business unremitted attention. It is his duty to sacrifice his repose, his pleasures, his satisfactions, to theirs; and above all, ever, and in all cases, to prefer their interest to his own. But, his unbiased opinion, his mature judgment, his enlightened conscience, he ought not to sacrifice to you, to any man, or to any set of living men. These he does not derive from your pleasures; no, nor from the law and the Constitution. They are a trust from Providence, for the abuse of which he is deeply answerable. Your representative owes you, not his industry only, but his judgment; and he betrays, instead of serving you, if he sacrifices it to your opinion . . . if government were a matter of will upon my side, yours, without question, ought to be superior. But government and legislation are matters of reason and judgment, and not

of inclination; and what sort of reason is that, in which the determination precedes the discussion; in which one set of men deliberate, and another decide; and where those who form the conclusion
are perhaps three hundred miles distant from those who hear the
arguments? . . .

Parliament is not a congress of ambassadors from different and
hostile interests; which interests each must maintain, as an agent,
and advocate, against other agents and advocates; but Parliament is
a deliberative assembly of one nation, with an interest, that of the
whole; where, not local purposes, not local prejudices, ought to
guide, but the general good, resulting from the general reason of the
whole. You choose a member indeed; but when you have chosen
him, he is not a member of Bristol, but he is a member of Parliament. If the local constituent should have an interest, or should
form a hasty opinion, evidently opposite to the real good of the
rest of the community, the member for that place ought to be as
far as any other from any endeavor to give it effect.[6]

Britain and the Future

What the adherence of the British to this Burkean conception indicates is essentially this: that it is, above all, because
British society has been less completely democratic socially and
culturally that it has been able to operate more effectively as a
democracy politically. In considering British democracy's prospects for the future, it is therefore necessary to ask whether this
paradoxical combination of circumstances is likely to continue
to prevail.

What will be the effect on the traditional dignity and self-
discipline of British government and political behavior of the
progressive carrying out of the economic and social objectives of
the democratic welfare state? Will the mass of the British people
maintain their traditional industry, political awareness, and
willingness to accept the democratic leadership of its superior
citizens? Or will their economic incentive slacken, their sense of
political participation wane, and their attitudes toward political
leadership become less reverential?

Drew Middleton, the long-time *New York Times* corre-
spondent in Britain, has speculated that the prospects in this
regard, at least as far as the British working class is concerned,
are not altogether encouraging. According to Middleton:

The new class has money, security, and leisure: this is the promised land. According to theories of some reformers, the worker, freed from the oppression of poverty, should be expanding intellectually, worrying about the future of Nigeria rather than the football fortunes of Arsenal. My opinion is that the opposite is true, that with the coming of the good life the worker has gradually shed his responsibilities (some of these, in fact, have been stripped from him) and has lost the old desperate desire to improve his lot and make himself and his class the paramount political power in the land.

There is no need to save, for the state provides for all eventualities the worker can foresee. There is no compulsion to ensure that the children get an education that will enable them to rise above the circumstances of their parents. For the circumstances are so good, so unimaginably higher than those into which the fathers and mothers of this class were born, that there seems to be nothing further to be sought. . . . One word sums up the New Estate: the word "security." It is security in working-class terms, maintained and enforced by working-class methods. The traditional values of the middle and professional classes form no part of it; among wage-earners these values are meaningless. . . . Among the many men I have talked to in the New Towns, I never met one who was interested in saving enough money to buy his own small business, to strike out for himself. The ideal seemed to be a community of equals protected from economic dangers by full employment and high wages, politically lethargic, unstirred by Socialist or Tory. Everyone earned about the same amount of money, spent it on the same thing, and appeared to think and talk alike.[7]

Perhaps the phenomenon Middleton cites is only a temporary one. It may well be that once the British working class has become accustomed to its new material welfare and security, it will turn its greater means and leisure to activities that will be both individually creative as well as of benefit to the society as a whole. If, on the other hand, the apathy that Middleton notes should continue and extend to other sectors of the society as well, the effect upon the British economy and the country's international position would be most damaging.

Unfortunately, the danger of such a development is heightened by the very seriousness of the international economic and political problems that Britain already confronts. Ideally, these problems could be conceived of as a challenge inviting all of British society to intensify its collective discipline and effort.

Yet, in the case of Britain as of the other Western European powers, is the challenge not perhaps too great? Does the progressive shift of international economic strength and political initiative to other parts of the world not seem too inexorable? Is the response not much more likely to be an increasingly defeatist one? Will not greater and greater numbers of Europeans, including Britons, be tempted to retreat from the ideal of dedicated public-mindedness and resign themselves to the shorter-term adjustment of "Eat, drink, and be merry—for what can we do about it anyway?"

Of all the European nations, the British are likely to succumb to such a weakening of morale the most slowly. Save, possibly, for their abortive invasion of Egypt in 1956, the British have faced their relative decline in international power realistically, as well as without loss of nerve. In transforming the former British Empire into the free association of sovereign nations now called the British Commonwealth, they have created a global organization that not only performs valuable international services but continues to enhance the status and influence of its senior member, Great Britain. Through their timely bequest of political independence and economic and administrative aid to their former Asian and African colonies, they are assuring themselves of future good will as well as long-range economic advantages. Even in the relations between today's preponderant superpowers they are finding a useful and respected role to play. Circumstances such as these, in combination with the strengths of the British political tradition outlined above, may well enable Britain, the first of the world's liberal democratic states, to survive to become the longest-lived.

SELECTED BIBILIOGRAPHY

BAGEHOT, WALTER. *The English Constitution*, New York, Appleton, 1920.
JENNINGS, SIR IVOR. *Parliament*, London, Cambridge University Press, 1957.
LASKI, HAROLD J. *Parliamentary Government in England*, New York, Viking, 1938.
MACKENZIE, KENNETH. *The English Parliament*, London, Pelican, 1950.
MIDDLETON, DREW. *These Are the British*, New York, Knopf, 1957.

« 10 »

France:
The Problem of Authority

THE POLITICAL EXPERIENCE of modern France has been one of continuing governmental instability. The principal reason for this has been the absence in France of the measure of underlying agreement on political ends and means that the effective functioning of a liberal democratic governmental system requires. From this insufficiency of political consensus in France have followed two main consequences. One has been a militant emphasis on political liberty. The other has been a more or less chronic condition of governmental impotence. It was in the hope of remedying this nationally debilitating political ineffectualness that the French in May of 1958 repudiated their Fourth Republic (dating from the end of World War II) and embarked upon their fifth experiment in liberal democratic government.

Whereas the defunct Fourth French Republic was dominated by an all-powerful legislature, the Fifth, set up and headed by General Charles de Gaulle, assigns greatest initiative to the office of President. Whether or not this new governmental formula can come to grips with France's underlying problems, and whether or not it represents a *permanent* move in the direction of a more authoritarian type of republican government, is still too soon to predict.

The Political and Social Heritage

Modern France's political difficulties have stemmed largely from the greatest event in the country's history—the French Revolution of 1789. Before the Revolution, France had for several centuries been the West's leading power. Centralized and developed by its succession of absolute monarchs, it had served as the very model of Western civilization at its finest. In spite of all that has happened since, the image of France as it was in that pre-Revolutionary period, the image of *La Grande Nation,* continues to arouse in France the one sentiment in which all its citizens have remained united.

If the absolute monarchy that built up the France of this image had gradually permitted its sovereignty to be transferred to a parliament, as happened in England, the subsequent political history of France would certainly have been very different. But the French kings refused to make the necessary concessions. As a result, both those who defended the old order and those who attacked it were driven to extremes and the French political consensus was deeply and permanently fractured. Before the Revolution, as one historian has put it,

> the people were able to accept a common ideal: One God, One Law, One King, over a society organized in social hierarchies that assured to each the privileges of his class and the economic status appropriate to the station in life to which God had called him. [After the Revolution, in contrast] the first thing that attracts our notice is the fragmentation that appears in the national will. The old myth, One God, One King, One Law, no longer compels loyalty; in its place we find slogans that proclaim programs: "Liberty, Equality, Fraternity"; "Equality, Order, Obedience"; "Social Justice"; "Property is theft"; "Workers of the world unite." The Revolution of 1789 shifted the axis of political life from the organic conception of the state to an atomistic one, and at the same time expanded the number of political wills to include all members of society. This sharp break with traditions opened wide the possibility of divergent political and social mythology, and granted to every group, indeed to every individual, the right to proclaim a program and to elevate it to the status of a political absolute.[1]

In addition to preventing the French from achieving sufficient unity of concept and purpose to solve their country's internal and international problems, the experience of this fragmentation created a historical accumulation of sensibilities and fears that impaired even further the possibility of rational political adjustment. Having lived under two French empires and five republics since the Revolution, Frenchmen have alternated between too little authority and too much. As a result, the French attitude to authority and liberty has often tended to be a matter of passionate assertion of ideology rather than of sober-minded consideration of the country's actual circumstances and needs.

France's ideological fragmentation has been strongly reinforced by the nature of the country's traditional social structure and economic patterns. Having consistently lagged behind the other major Western powers in large-scale industrialization, French society has in effect been living in three different and in many ways conflicting ages. Part of France has continued to live with the goals and dreams of the pre-Revolutionary monarchical and feudal age. Another part has adhered to the way of life of the fiercely individualistic republican middle class which dominated the Revolution and has been politically identified with it ever since. And a third part is the France of the workers and managers engaged in the urban and industrial sector of the nation's life. The adherents of these three patterns of existence have been characterized by different world views, different aspirations, and often incompatible interests. There has been no one governmental institution (such as Parliament in Britain) to which all of them have been willing to look for the assertion of their respective interests and views. And none of them— nor any combination of the three—has been strong enough to assume leadership over the others. As a result, each has adopted an unyielding defensiveness which, when projected into politics, has produced France's characteristic condition of governmental stalemate.

An example of the effects of these unreconciled patterns of life in France may be seen in the criteria by which Frenchmen still tend to rank one another socially. In spite of the strength

of the middle- and working-class sectors of French society, the
dominant criteria of social stratification have continued in large
measure to be those of the monarchical and feudal *ancien
régime*. In the eyes of most Frenchmen, those deemed to rank
highest—and therefore to be most emulated—have not, as in
the more advanced industrial nations, been the people who are
most outstanding in the areas of economic productivity and
technology. Instead, top position in the social hierarchy has
tended to be accorded to those able to afford the aristocratic life
of leisured, cultured, and landed elegance.

What this carry-over from the pre-industrial age has meant
for France's economic development has been summed up by
one American observer as follows:

> These attitudes, wherever they linger, clearly restrict the growth
> of new institutions. They operate against social mobility, they
> discourage efforts to push ahead rapidly. In sociological terms, they
> act against the distribution of rewards and status according to
> occupational achievement; in economic terms, against the bold and
> aggressive innovator. . . .
>
> Further than this, these traditionalistic attitudes in France
> have operated in general against engaging in business activity. . . .
> If the successful businessman does not himself divert capital into
> a château, he is likely to see his sons do so and to see the most
> talented of them move off into the bureaucracy or the professions.
> The result has been, beyond question, to affect the recruitment and
> motivation of the entrepreneurial class in ways that have seriously
> retarded the development of the economic order on which French
> prosperity in this century depends.[2]

A further impediment to French economic development
has been the tendency of the French to prefer the small-scale
entrepreneurship dominant in the early nineteenth century, what
the French call *le petit commerce*. The typical motivation among
French businessmen has not been to build up large-scale industry
aiming for a small profit on the largest possible turnover. Rather,
the unit most characteristically striven for has been the moder-
ate-sized family concern content to settle for the largest possible
margin of profit on a *limited* volume of production or sale. This
has inevitably discouraged improvements in productive efficiency

and has made the French businessman less willing and able to
yield concessions to the country's laboring groups—a fact that
in turn helps to account for the high degree of political aliena-
tion of the French working class.

Another expression of the coexistence of economic and
social patterns belonging to different historical periods may be
seen in the distribution of the French population. For one thing,
the growth of urbanization in France has been much slower than
that in the other major Western countries. As late as 1950,
for example, almost 50 per cent of France's population still
lived in rural areas; another 20 per cent lived in communities of
less than 20,000; and, apart from Paris, only 2.5 million were
residents of cities with a population of more than 100,000.
Among the inhabitants of rural areas, moreover, the same pattern of small-scale operations has predominated as in urban
business enterprise. Again as of the year 1950, some 62 per cent of
French peasant holdings were between 2½ and 25 acres; 34 per
cent were from 25 to 125 acres. Only 2 per cent of French farms
were larger than 200 acres, that is, suitable for large-scale,
mechanized farming. According to experts, more than one
quarter of French land under cultivation is divided into holdings that, even with the most intensive effort, are too small to
afford the peasants working them a subsistence livelihood.

Social and economic circumstances such as these have long
sustained French political instability and impotence. Their
remedy has long been known to be a drastic modernization and
rationalization of the entire French economy and social order.
Yet until the Fourth Republic's demise, no French government
proved able to undertake such major economic and social re-
construction. The reason for this was the fact that each of the
country's successive sovereign legislatures was dominated by the
very interests whose determination it has been to maintain the
anachronistic *status quo*. As one French observer has put it:
"Since the traditional political parties wanted to win elections,
they were always ready to penalize financially all big industrial
and commercial firms, in favor of artisans, small business and
family enterprises. The inventive, innovating elements of the
economy have thus been at the mercy of its backward sector." [3]

Traditional Political Parties

The most characteristic expression of France's unsettled political and social situation has been the country's traditional multiple-party system. The political parties in question have gravitated around three distinct positions, each corresponding to one of the coexisting French ways of life outlined above. The nucleus of the Right has been made up of the advocates of aristocracy, paternalistic authoritarianism, and reverent Catholicism. The Center is dominated by the politically liberal but economically conservative middle classes. And the Left is the pole of those who stand in sharp protest against the republican order because of its failure to remedy what are felt to be long-neglected social and economic injustices. Each of these three political poles has traditionally been represented by various parties and groupings. During the Fourth Republic the most important of these, from extreme Left to far Right, have been the Communists, the Socialists, the Radicals, the Catholics, the republican conservatives, and the antirepublican reactionaries.

The fundamental issue that has divided French political groupings and parties has been the question of commitment to the liberal democratic Republic. The Center, which has been the traditional political embodiment of this commitment, extends to the Left to include the Socialists and to the Right as far as the conservatives but short of the antidemocratic reactionaries. The extreme Left and the reactionary Right, on the other hand, have been consistently negative in their attitudes toward liberal democratic institutions. Since more than one third of the French electorate have regularly chosen to be represented by the parties of the extreme Left and Right, the Republic has rested on the slimmest of popular majorities.

On the far Left have been the approximately five million Frenchmen who have cast their votes for the Communist party. The leadership of this party has used its mass support not only to discredit republican institutions but, wherever possible, actively to undermine them. As a result, the liberal democratic parties have felt it advisable to exclude the Communist party from all governmental power and responsibility.

It has, of course, been well known that the vast majority of Communist voters have been less interested in Communist ideology and subservience to Moscow than in politically registering its social and economic grievances. As one American student of French politics has characterized them, "They are an army of . . . malcontents who are fed up with the failures and broken promises of weak governments, bitter at being gouged by profiteering speculators and shopkeepers, wary of hot, cold and colonial wars." [4] Yet even though the possibility of reclaiming these millions of voters for the Republic has thus been recognized, the fact has remained that as long as they have continued to vote Communist the remedying of their grievances has been made next to impossible. This point was emphasized by Herbert Leuthy, speaking of events during the Fourth Republic:

> Since 1948 the Communist Party has counted in the political life of France only as a dead weight which has had to be taken into account as a negative quantity in all political calculation and has sterilized the votes, wishes, demands, and dissatisfactions of five million Frenchmen. . . . The weight of their votes, which in a healthy democracy might have turned the scales in favor of economic and social reform, henceforth counted as little as if they had left their voting papers unmarked or had stayed away from the polls.[5]

The loss of the constructive participation of the Communist sector of the electorate has been the more debilitating for French government because of the additional two million or so votes that have regularly gone to the parties of the antirepublican Right. With a small minority of these Rightists, rejection of liberal democratic institutions has been a matter of principle. A somewhat larger group—typified during the Fourth Republic by General de Gaulle—opposed the Republic from a conviction that it could not muster sufficient authority to solve France's internal problems and maintain its international power position. But for the largest group of extreme Rightists, including the hundreds of thousands of shopkeepers and artisans who in the election of 1956 supported the antitax campaign of rabble-rousing Pierre Poujade, hostility toward the Republic has had nothing to do with political principle at all. As is true of the mass of Communist supporters, these people have been motivated by regional, social, and economic grievances for which the Republic had for generations failed to find remedies.

As much of a political hindrance as the dead weight of the Leftist and Rightist opponents of the Republic have been the sharp differences that have traditionally prevented unity of action among the members of the prorepublican Center. The chief parties comprising the French political Center have been the Socialists, the Radicals (meaning Liberals in the nineteenth-century, free enterprise sense), and the republican Catholics. Effective political unity among these parties has been prevented because of their differences on two major issues: the state's responsibility for economic management and social welfare, and the state's relations with the Church, particularly in matters pertaining to education. The Socialists and a large section of the republican Catholics are in general agreement on social and economic questions but are kept from stable co-operation by their differences on the privileges that should be accorded the Church. The Socialists and Radicals see eye to eye on Church issues but differ sharply in regard to economic and social policies. And the Radicals and republican Catholics are opposed in their views not only on Church-state matters but on the role of the state in economic and social affairs.

Because of these differences, what parliamentary co-operation has existed among France's prorepublican parties—thanks largely to the threat from the far Left and the far Right—has served merely to maintain the *status quo*. The undertaking of any major reforms has proved impossible. Whatever the measures proposed, one or the other of the liberal democratic parties has objected and withdrawn its parliamentary support. The result has been the fall of one cabinet after another and, hence, permanent governmental impotence.

Government of the Fourth Republic

The central feature of modern French governmental organization has been the almost unlimited sovereignty of the lower house of the legislature, during the Fourth Republic called the National Assembly. As in Britain, this lower house has operated under the leadership of a cabinet. Headed by its Premier, called the President of the Council of Ministers, the Cabinet has proposed bills for the legislature to vote upon and has been responsible for the administration of the law.

The great difference between the British and French parliamentary systems has lain in the relationship between the Cabinet and the lower house. The British House of Commons is empowered at any time to call the executive (the Cabinet) to account by demanding a vote of no confidence. And the Cabinet, for its part, has the right at any time to dissolve the House of Commons and call for a new election. The executive and the legislature thus stand and fall together; if the legislature refuses to support the executive and decides to force it to resign, it thereby also ends its own existence.

In France, the executive's power of dissolution has been virtually nonexistent. Under the Fourth Republic, the Prime Minister was forbidden to dissolve a National Assembly unless at least eighteen months had passed since the previous general election; and unless two cabinets had been overthrown by a formal vote of no confidence during a consecutive eighteen-month period. This meant that the legislature was able to withdraw its support from the executive with impunity and that the executive, for its part, was powerless to enforce legislative discipline.

Legislative supremacy over the executive was exercised during the Fourth Republic within an institutional framework that did little to limit the National Assembly's power. It is true that the Assembly's legislative prerogative had in some small measure to be shared with the indirectly elected French upper house, the Council of the Republic. Certain functions, too, were constitutionally assigned to the formal head of the Fourth Republic, the President, whose election, for a seven-year term, was by joint session of the two houses of the legislature. However, the upper house's role in legislation was so minor and circumscribed as to be negligible. And the functions of the President—in decreeing parliamentary dissolutions, accepting the resignations of prime ministers, and proposing candidates to be considered for the premiership—were largely formal and ceremonial. In practice, the power of the National Assembly was unchallengeable.

Even in a country with the high degree of unity and political

self-discipline of Great Britain, such one-sided dependence of the
executive on the legislature would be dangerous. During the
Fourth Republic (1947–1958), the system resulted in an average
life span for French Cabinets of barely six months. The immediate political reason for this was that French Cabinets had to be
staffed by the leaders of the country's prorepublican parties which
for purposes of Cabinet formation had to enter into parliamentary
coalitions. Yet since the forces upholding the Republic were themselves badly divided, their coalitions were inevitably unstable. In
order not to offend at least one of the partners in the coalition,
every Cabinet found it necessary to keep its program limited and
to content itself largely with administering the country as it was.
If it planned any major initiative it was certain to violate the
narrow and tentative mandate of one or another of the parliamentary groups in the coalition. The latter would then withdraw
from the coalition, causing the particular Cabinet to fall.

     An important contributing factor in the National Assembly's
lack of discipline and stability during the Fourth Republic was
the employment of an only slightly modified system of proportional representation. This system of election contrasts with the
one-member, plurality representation that is the custom in Britain
and the United States. In these countries, whichever of two or
more candidates gains the largest number of votes is thereby
elected. The other candidate or candidates lose; and those who
voted for them in effect remain unrepresented—even though, in a
two-candidate election, for example, they may constitute as high
as 49.9 per cent of the electorate. The reason these unrepresented
voters accept the verdict of the majority is, of course, that they
trust the general consensus, which they know will require even
candidates not of their choosing to support policies not too far at
variance from those they themselves would prefer.

     In the Fourth Republic, party differences were felt to be too
great and uncompromising to permit the acceptance of such
denial of direct representation to constituents who voted for
candidates other than the one who gained the highest number of
votes. Under the system of proportional representation each party
that had entered candidates was accorded approximately the same
percentage of the total number of seats in the National Assembly
as the percentage of the total popular vote it received from the

electorate. Its representation in the Assembly was thus roughly proportionate to the size of the vote it received from the country at large.

This highly democratic system of proportional representation very faithfully projected into the National Assembly the divisions among French electors as a whole. This fact, combined with the Assembly's unchallengeable supremacy, gave all fragments of French society maximum opportunity to work for the maintenance of the *status quo* and, in the process, to impede the exercise of executive authority in the interests of the nation at large.

The Fifth Republic and De Gaulle

The French Fourth Republic died from the malady that had so seriously afflicted it from its beginnings—political impotence. The immediate crisis with which it proved unable to cope was the uprising of Algerian colonial extremists in alliance with officers of the French army in Algeria. Protesting against the Fourth Republic's inability to bring the long war against Algerian independence to a successful conclusion, these dissident elements on May 13, 1958, seized the General Goverment building in Algiers, set up an emergency Committee of Public Safety, and threatened to invade the French mainland. Rather than bring the Algerian civilian and military insurgents to heel, the Government in Paris in effect capitulated to them by alleging an imminent danger of civil war. To head off such a turn of events it announced the necessity of adopting the only solution that both the rebels and everyone concerned seemed willing to accept: its resignation in favor of the emergency premiership of General Charles de Gaulle.

Having first voted for a constitutional reform, the National Assembly of the Fourth Republic then undertook its final act before dissolving itself: it invested General de Gaulle as premier and gave him six months in which to clear up the crisis, present a new constitution, and arrange for new general elections. The new constitution—marking the beginning of the Fifth French Republic—was submitted to the French citizenry and the peoples of France's overseas territories on September 28, 1958. It received the endorsement of approximately four fifths of the electorate. The first elections under the new constitution were concluded on November 30 and gave an overwhelming majority to the parties supporting the person and policies of General de Gaulle. And on December 21 occurred the third and final step in France's political renovation: the election of General de Gaulle as President of the Fifth Republic.

What made this major political transition so easily possible was the fact that the majority of the French people had come to regard the governmental procedures of their Fourth Republic as hopelessly unworkable. Although the initiative came from the dissidents of the Right, the hesitant conduct of even the prorepublicans in the last Cabinet of the Fourth Republic indicates that they too felt the urgent necessity of a basic political overhauling and reorientation. It was thus that despite the various protagonists' sharp differences in political and economic views, all of them were able to compromise in handing power over to De Gaulle. In representing the interests of France above and beyond differences of political party, De Gaulle, the great Resistance leader of World War II, offered the one symbol under which France seemed able to unite—at least for the time being—in at last attending to its fundamental national problems.

The motivation of De Gaulle himself has been thus described by the eminent French scholar and political figure, André Philip:

> De Gaulle conceives himself basically as the arbiter and rallier of the nation—that is to say, as an uncrowned king rather than a Premier expressing the will of the majority party or the traditional President of the Republic, supervising the functioning of institutions. For him, all antagonisms and conflicts of interest notwithstanding, there exists a general interest which touches all basic questions. He thinks this "essential" interest, independent of political beliefs and passions, can be objectively ascertained by all nonpartisan people who are sufficiently competent. Since he is linked to no social class, neither the bourgeoisie nor the peasants nor the workers, De Gaulle believes that the technicians, top civil servants and experts are capable of determining this general interest and of providing for the welfare of the incompetent and ignorant people. . . .
>
> This "essential," which can be objectively ascertained, is for De Gaulle the *national* interest. *Notre Dame la France,* something different from *Frenchmen,* is his supreme value, conceived in Platonic fashion. His entire career has been devoted to his belief in

the world mission of the "French idea." His nationalism is very different from that of the petty bourgeoisie with their patriotic ribbons; it is based neither on sheer force nor on transient interest but on this sense of France's mission. . . .

Finally, De Gaulle feels that he himself can personify that "essential" national interest, captivating the masses in the service of a grand design which lifts them above their daily lives. This was the case on June 18, 1940; then he, in effect, *was* France when the French people weren't. He now thinks he can re-establish the authority of the state, reconcile France and Islam, place the country on the road to prosperity, and realize around his own person the unity of the people—even if it should prove necessary to use certain esthetic manipulations to rouse a unanimous enthusiasm.[6]

The Fifth Republic's Constitution was designed very largely with the leadership role of De Gaulle in mind. Its basic innovation consists of a drastic strengthening of the independent authority of the executive over the legislature as well as over the nation as a whole. It does this primarily through vast new powers conferred upon the President. Whereas under the Fourth Republic the chief executive was largely a figurehead, he is now the key center of power. He is no longer required to submit his choice of Premier and Cabinet to the National Assembly for formal endorsement. In a dispute between the Assembly and the Cabinet, he can avoid a governmental overthrow by appealing directly to the electorate in a popular referendum. He holds the power to dissolve the Assembly and call for new elections. And, under the new Constitution's Article 16, he is given vast and very general powers in the event of circumstances that he himself may decide amount to a national emergency.

The Fifth Republic's first general elections constituted a sweeping popular endorsement of General de Gaulle and the new political order. Parties that were closely associated with the Fourth Republic, or opposed De Gaulle in the pre-election campaigning, lost heavily; those that favored De Gaulle and canvassed in his name won handsomely. After the final tabulation, the number of Communist deputies had been cut down from 144 to 10; the number of Socialists had been reduced from 91 to 40; and the legislative representation of the Radical party had shrunk from 42 to 13. The greatest gain, in contrast, went to the Gaullists. These in the previous Assembly had had only 13 deputies, whereas now their number jumped to 188. Moreover, another pro–De Gaulle party, the Independent Conservatives, raised its membership from 107 to 132; hence the new Assembly was certain to provide De Gaulle with whatever legislative support he might ask.

It must be noted that, at least in part, this Gaullist triumph was due to the substitution of a majority system of election for the former method of proportional representation. That is, the number of votes cast was not as overwhelmingly pro–De Gaulle as the rostrum of the elected candidates seemed to indicate. Under the proportional system, votes for candidates who did not win majorities would have counted in computing the final representation. Under the new majority system, only the votes cast for candidates who gained a majority were effective. As has been the practice in the Anglo-Saxon countries, votes cast for candidates who lost won no political recognition at all. It was thus that the Communists, for example, who had 20.1 per cent of the popular vote, elected only 2.1 per cent of the membership of the legislature. Their misfortune, in other words, was that while they secured a large and widespread measure of electoral support, their candidates in only 2.1 per cent of the electoral contests were able to lead with actual majorities. The Union of the New Republic, in contrast, benefited from the fact that it had a high percentage of front-running candidates and so, with only 26.3 per cent of the popular vote was able to win 40 per cent of the seats in the Assembly.

In spite of this mechanical qualification, however, it was clear that more than 60 per cent of the voters of France actively favored the new French political orientation. Since the transition from the Fourth Republic had occurred over a six-month period, their decision could not be construed as a hasty or impulsive one. Although they could not be sure what the new regime would turn out to represent substantively, they seemed resigned to one important point: that effective government demanded greater and more sustained executive authority than the French people for three quarters of a century had been willing to admit.

The Future of the Fifth Republic

It seems likely that as long as General de Gaulle remains its central figure, the Fifth Republic will survive, will provide the

French with considerably more statesmanlike leadership than what they have received in the recent past, and will assure them of continued enjoyment of their basic political liberties. Whatever De Gaulle's policies and successes, his constitutional powers and his standing with the nation at large seem strong enough to enable him to cope with all opposition, whether it comes from his political adversaries or from among the rather motley amalgam of his own supporters in the Union of the New Republic.

About what will happen *after* De Gaulle, on the other hand, both French and foreign observers are much more apprehensive. The membership of the Union of the New Republic is known to be predominantly right wing and to have considerably less regard for democratic procedures and liberties than does General de Gaulle. What if such a parliamentary majority were supporting—or, worse, dominating—a less self-respecting and reliable man in the Presidency? Would not the provisions of the new Constitution enable such a political combination to convert France into a veritable presidential dictatorship?

Although such an eventuality is by no means impossible, a more likely development after De Gaulle's departure from the scene would be the rapid reappearance of something like the old political divisiveness. For, though the traditional republican parties are temporarily weakened, they remain very much alive. And no less important, without the unifying figure of De Gaulle, the currently dominant Union of the Republic is likely to fall apart quickly into the divergent elements of which it has in fact all the while been composed. When and if this occurs, the mandate and power of the President will in practice, even though not in constitutional theory, be greatly reduced.

What responsible Frenchmen of all political leanings appear to hope for is that the period of De Gaulle's leadership may see sufficient changes in the French economy and social structure to create more permanent foundations for liberal democratic governmental institutions. Above all, it is felt, the French economy must be made productive enough to furnish the French people as a whole a higher standard of welfare. To the extent that this is achieved, it is pointed out, France will at last acquire the kind of economically progressive and politically moderate entrepreneurial and working classes that elsewhere have proved to be the very backbone of liberal democratic government. Since indications are that such changes in the French economy and social structure have for some time been under way, a more stable popular basis for free government in France may soon be in existence. To the extent that it is, France's alternation between too much authority and too little will probably be progressively overcome—regardless of *what* the formal constitutional structure may be.

Such a development, however, is generally agreed to depend upon two preconditions: the winning away of the mass of French workers from the politically obstructive leadership of the Communist party, and the ending of the war in Algeria—whether it be through some form of social and economic integration of Algeria with the French mainland or, as the Moslem rebels demand, through a program of progressive evolution of Algeria to independence. If De Gaulle's leadership proves instrumental in solving these two central problems of French politics, the survival of stable liberal democratic government in France seems assured.

SELECTED BIBLIOGRAPHY

EARLE, EDWARD MEAD, ed. *Modern France,* Princeton, N.J., Princeton University Press, 1950.

LUETHY, HERBERT. *France against Herself,* New York, Praeger, 1955.

ROMAINS, JULES. *A Frenchman Examines His Conscience,* London, André Deutsch, 1955.

SCHOENBRUN, DAVID. *As France Goes,* New York, Harper, 1957.

WILLIAMS, PHILIP. *Politics in Post-War France,* London, Longmans, 1954.

« 11 »

Germany:
Democracy versus Nationalism

THE PEOPLE OF GERMANY have never succeeded in establishing for themselves either a clearly defined international role or a stably evolving political idiom. Their internal politics have ranged from extreme liberalism to totalitarian regimentation; and their behavior as a nation has alternated between resignation to fragmented powerlessness and limitless nationalistic aggression. They were the last of the numerically and culturally major European peoples to achieve big-power national status; and they have been the first to lose it again. They have incorporated Western civilization's values in some of its most inspired music, philosophy, and science; yet at the same time, as a nation, they have violated Western man's ideals more ruthlessly and on a larger scale than has any other people.

The explanation of these paradoxes of the German record lies above all in the nature of the obstacles the Germans have had to contend with in the establishment and maintenance of their status as a major nation. When they have bowed to these obstacles and resigned themselves to the impossibility of such status—as they did before 1871, during the Weimar Republic, and again after World War II—their dedication to the ideals of Western civilization has been unsurpassed in both its sincerity and its productiveness. When, in contrast, they have insisted upon a major role as a nation—as they did between 1871 and World War I, and again after 1933 under Hitler—they have become involved in

199

problems whose solution has seemed possible, if at all, only by their unquestioning acceptance of what have appeared to be the dictates of power.

The Price of Nationhood

The obstacles that so long impeded the achievement of German national statehood were geographic, political, cultural, and economic. Perhaps the most important lay in the fact that, unlike nations such as Britain and the United States, the Germans never enjoyed the advantages of natural geographic boundaries. This posed for the Germans an ever-present fundamental question: where did Germany begin and end?

The answer that came to be given to this question was the claim that Germany was wherever German culture and language prevailed. But a demarcation of Germany in terms such as these created almost impossible political problems. Since German culture and language extended into contiguous areas in France, the Alps, Poland, and the Baltic States, what was to be the relationship of Germans to the peoples with whom they were intermingled? Where were the political boundaries of Germany to be drawn? How could they be secured recognition, defended, and administered? For more than four centuries after both Britain and France had established their power and limits as major national states these problems for Germany continued to prove unsolvable. And in the resulting absence of national *political* expression, the Germans' desire to assert their collective identity appeared to have only one recourse: to rely instead upon exhortations to solidarity in terms of German language and German *Kultur.*

The geographic obstacles to successful German nation-state development were related to another unfortunate fact for the Germans: their centuries-long political fragmentation into several hundred petty and despotically governed principalities. Even after 1803, when Napoleon had imposed a measure of political consolidation on the Germans, the number of their miniature states remained at more than thirty. As before, rivalry among these political units made foreign intervention in German affairs a permanent fact of life. As before, the majority of the rulers of

these German states could look no further than to the maintenance of the political *status quo*. And as before, having no meaningful political process in which to participate, the German
citizenry continued absorbed in its traditional way of life, accepting the government of authoritarian officialdom, shunning politics as something too vulgar to be concerned with, and devoting
its intellectual energies to various cultural pursuits instead.

The effects of these geographic and political circumstances
were further aggravated by Germany's lack of religious homogeneity. The fact that western and southeastern Germany are
predominantly Catholic, while the central, northern, and eastern
areas are strongholds of Lutheranism continues to the present day
to introduce disruptive differences into German politics. That
such differences constituted even more serious obstacles to the
development of a national consensus when they were identified
with a host of separate political units goes without saying.

If, finally, there had emerged in the prenational German
states a powerful middle class such as those which were responsible for national strength and liberal democratic development
elsewhere, the effects of many of the impediments to German
national unification might have been successfully counteracted.
But this did not occur. Until well into the nineteenth century the
German area was overwhelmingly rural and agricultural; such
manufacturing as existed continued to be of the small-scale handi-
craft variety. The German middle class therefore remained economically weak, culturally parochial, politically conservative, and
socially subservient to the traditional, feudal type of aristocracy.[1]
Even when, in the 1840's, many of the German states acquired
formal constitutional government, the middle-class groups who
led in parliamentary activities were unable to muster enough determination to use the new constitutional instruments in more
than an advisory capacity.

In spite of these obstacles, however, the desire among Germans to establish their nation-state grew steadily as the nineteenth
century progressed. It finally culminated, in the years 1848–1849,
in the assumption of national initiative by Germany's liberal intellectuals. What these professors and writers of the various German states hoped to accomplish, moreover, was not merely to
bring about national unification; their simultaneous objective was

to establish for the new nation a government of constitutional democracy. At one stroke, that is, they intended to bring Germany's stage of political development up to date with that which in a country like Britain had evolved over a period of centuries.

In the view of these German liberal intellectuals, national unification and constitutional democracy could be realized by two possible courses of action: either they would have to foment revolts throughout the country to compel the traditional dynasts to accept subordination to a national constitutional regime in response to popular pressure *from below;* or they could attempt to persuade the king of the most powerful of the German states, Prussia, to become the champion of the liberals' national and constitutional objectives and to use his prestige and power to impose them *from above.* The former of these strategies, however, was rejected. On one hand, the Germans seemed politically too fragmented and passive to make large-scale revolt possible; on the other, it was feared that if a major revolt actually broke out, popular violence and radicalism might get out of hand altogether. The campaign upon which the national liberal German intellectuals therefore embarked was to persuade the king of Prussia to espouse their cause. Even when, in 1848, widespread popular uprisings offered them the opportunity of using force to achieve their ends, they refused to swerve from their adopted plan. Instead, they assembled from all over the country in Frankfurt's *Paulskirche* to draft a national constitution. When, after months of debate, an acceptable version had finally been agreed upon, the convention voted 290 to 248 to invite King Frederick William IV of Prussia to make himself united Germany's first constitutional monarch.

But the Prussian King refused to accede to the liberals' moderate demands. His reply was curt and indignant: the only crown to which he could give serious consideration would be one conferred by his peers, the other German princes; a crown offered by what he termed a revolutionary assembly was an affront. And therewith, at one stroke, the liberals' long-planned and conciliatory bid to create a liberal democratic German state was reduced to naught.

Although tragic enough in itself, this failure of the years 1848–1849 became all the more unfortunate through the events that followed. Whereas the liberals and their methods had proven powerless in the creation of the much-wanted national state, the strategy of force and authoritarian manipulation employed a generation later by the Prussian Chancellor Bismarck brought spectacular success. After a series of brilliant political and military coups Germany finally became a nation-state—even though, unfortunately for the country's subsequent cultural composition, at the price of the exclusion of the Austrian Germans from the Prussian-led Reich. Yet because of the way it had been established, the new German state was a very different one from the liberal constitutional monarchy envisaged in 1848–1849. It was, instead, an imposed federation of authoritarian principalities, brought together not of and by the people, but merely for them.

What had in effect happened was that nationhood and liberal democracy had after 1848–1849 seemed mutually exclusive and that in accepting the Bismarckian Reich the Germans had decided for the former. Because of the nature of this decision the German nation began its life with several basic handicaps. In the first place, it was not based upon a free political consensus; its major premise was not popular sovereignty but the admission by the society's various groups and classes that they depended for their continued collective life upon submission to the management of an authoritarian chancellor. Second, because of the circumstances of the nation's establishment, Germans tended thenceforth to associate national fulfillment and greatness not with liberal democracy but with the strong hand of an inspired political leader. And finally, at least during the decades immediately following, the political elite that Germans most frequently identified with highest national decision making was not that of civilian politicians but of military-minded aristocrats.

As long as the statesmanlike Bismarck continued at the helm of the new German nation the price of the way it had been hammered together and of the system of executive leadership by which it was operated did not become apparent. However, when in 1890 the management of German internal and foreign affairs was assumed by the inexperienced and arrogant Kaiser William II, the nation's historical debt became increasingly apparent, yet could in no way be evaded. What had in the meantime become the most populous, industrially developed, and militarily powerful nation in continental Europe found itself at the mercy of a supreme decision maker whose image of politics dated back to the days of the Divine Right of Kings.

The dilemma was not, moreover, merely a matter of governmental structure. That the Emperor's executive dominance was a grave source of national political vulnerabilities became evident enough. But the question remained: how, save through common submission to the authority and symbol of the Emperor, could the German nation be held together? If executive power were in the hands of responsible politicians, would not the lack of free political consensus among Germany's regions, economic interests, classes, and cultural groups make stable and coherent government impossible?

Even German liberals long remained of the opinion that these considerations made the maintenance of the Kaiser's position essential. As many of them saw it, the task was therefore to accept supreme royal power and to seek to improve it by liberalizing its administration. This, for example, was the purpose of the liberal-minded social scientists who in 1872 banded together to form the famous *Verein für Sozialpolitik* (Association for Social Policy), Germany's approximate equivalent of the British Fabian Society. In the words of Gustav Schmoller, one of the founders of this association of scholars:

> We in Germany today [the early 1900's] have a stronger monarchical power than any other country, a monarchical power which, thank God, actually still rules in basic matters. In the last century and this we have effected great and beneficial reforms. . . . But for this work the precondition is that the economy and the ultimate power of decision be reserved for the elements of government which stand above the partisan struggle.
>
> The practical job which the political and social sciences of our *Verein für Sozialpolitik* face today seems to me to be to supply the intellectual tools and techniques to strengthen these elements. Our task is to maintain control on behalf of our collective interest of the self-interest of the various classes.[2]

Whether or not such reasoning was justified remains a matter of speculation. What is clear is that by the time the German liberal intellectuals finally concluded that the benefits of authoritarian rule were far outweighed by its disadvantages, it had become

too late to do anything about it. Having for more than a generation abdicated its political responsibilities, German society was
simply not able to furnish itself with effective leadership of a
more democratic kind. In the agonized words of the German so-
ciologist Max Weber, written after the Kaiser had blundered Germany into World War I:

> Bismarck left behind as a political heritage a nation without
> any political education, far below the level which, in this respect, it
> had reached twenty years earlier. Above all, he left behind a nation
> without any political will, accustomed to allow the great statesman
> at its head to look after its policy for it. . . . He left a nation ac-
> customed to submit, under the label of constitutional democracy,
> to anything that was decided for it without criticizing the political
> qualifications of those who . . . took the reins of power into their
> hands. . . . Not a shot would I fire, not a penny war loan would
> I subscribe to if this were not a national war. If it were only con-
> cerned with the maintenance of our state structure, or that we
> should keep this incapable dynasty and our unpolitical civil service,
> I would not support it.[3]

In addition to its lack of experience in democratic leadership,
imperial Germany suffered from an even more fundamental weakness. That was the fact that, unlike other nations that had evolved
popularly and around unifying and directing philosophical ideals,
the Germans had acquired a nation that could claim to stand for
nothing save its own power and survival. To Americans, the
United States represents a historical commitment to the notion of
the inalienable rights of man and the ideal of government of, by,
and for the people. The British can interpret the course of events
in terms of their traditional dedication to the cause of human
freedom and dignity. To the French, their nation represents the
universal inspirations of liberty, equality, and fraternity. The
Germans, in contrast, possess no nationally meaningful and universally relevant philosophical direction whatsoever. Herein, as
one of their most perceptive political thinkers noted as early as
1915, lay their gravest collective shortcoming:

> . . . the absence, in both our national and international political
> development, of a great and clear sense of purpose which might
> have inspired, oriented and united our public opinion. After the

establishment of the German Empire this basic deficiency was at first not felt because of the momentousness of the national events themselves, and then concealed by general preoccupation with all manner of incidental developments. But for some time now, this lack of goals has resulted in an oppressively sterile sense of emptiness. Self-preservation and maintenance of what has been achieved is the precondition, but cannot be the sole content of the international and domestic political life of a creative people.[4]

This lack of a sense of a larger national politico-philosophical significance has beset the German nation throughout its history. It has been expressed in the Germans' perennial uncertainty as to their proper role in world affairs; in their constant emphasis on "the state" (instead of, as elsewhere, on the ideals that the state purports to represent); in their need in times of war to resort excessively to the unifying inspiration of various kinds of cultural bravado; in their lack of success in appealing for the support of foreign peoples; and, perhaps most unfortunate of all, in the absence in German collective life of the optimistic sense of progress that has contributed so constructively to making citizen and society feel "on top of" historical developments in the Anglo-Saxon countries.

Not, of course, that the Germans have been less philosophically minded, more chauvinistic, or less forward-looking as individuals. The problem, simply, has been that these aspects of life in Germany have remained private. The German state, having once been established as "above" the people, has tended to remain so permanently. And being "above" the people rather than "of" or "by" them, it has never become a successful embodiment of its constituent individuals' and classes' values and feelings of moral responsibility.

The Weimar Republic

When, after World War I, the Germans finally acquired a liberal democratic governmental system, the event did not mark a high point of national fulfillment but a nadir of military and political collapse. Despite a series of minor military mutinies and a wild bid by the Communists to use the confusion following military defeat to organize the country as a Russian type of soviet system, the Weimar Republic was in no sense the triumph of a groundswell of sudden popular political will. It was, rather, a system devised in response to the old imperial order's failures and was intended to come to grips with Germany's unsolved problems.

The gravest of the problems inherited by the Weimar Republic was the politically unintegrated condition of German society. After World War I this condition was much aggravated because of the disappearance of the monarchy, the one symbolic and operative institution in terms of which the German state had from its beginnings been united. In addition to this inherited burden, moreover, the new democratic system was soon compelled to cope with a host of serious current problems. Among these were the psychological and economic consequences of the lost war, the destruction of the population's cash holdings through a runaway inflation, and, by the end of the twenties, the impoverishment and demoralization of a world-wide depression.

The governmental apparatus that was to attempt to deal with these problems consisted of a two-house legislature, a cabinet, a prime minister (chancellor), and the institution of a presidency. The functions of the upper or federal house, the Reichsrat (*Rat* means "council"), were largely advisory and administrative. The real source of legislative power lay in the Reichstag, whose members were elected by proportional representation. The President, elected on a direct popular basis, was to be considerably more than a figurehead.

Indeed, effective political power soon came in practice to stretch between the two poles of the Reichstag and the Presidency. The Reichstag could overthrow the Cabinet and the Chancellor by a simple vote of nonconfidence. And with the President, on the other hand, rested the power to select the Chancellor and the Cabinet, with the proviso, of course, that those selected be endorsed by the majority in the Reichstag. The parliamentary executive—the Chancellor and Cabinet—were thus in effect compelled to serve two masters and tended, as a result, to operate under more or less permanent strain. According to the Weimar Constitution's controversial Article 48, moreover, the President could, "if the public safety and order in the German *Reich* are considerably disturbed or in danger, take such measures as are necessary to restore public safety and order." In situations which he chose to interpret as emergencies, the President was thus empowered to assume all legislative initiative himself.

The Weimar system of government survived for fourteen years. In origin it had been largely the work of a coalition of three parties, the Social Democrats, the economically liberal German Democratic party, and the Catholic democratic Center party. As long as this coalition maintained its strength, until the mid-twenties, the Weimar government continued reasonably stable and effective. As the twenties drew to a close, however, this coalition of moderates gradually lost its dominant parliamentary hold. Greater and greater electoral support shifted to the parties and movements of the antiparliamentary Left and Right. By the election of July, 1932, the Reichstag included members of eight different groups, with the National Socialists having polled 37.1 per cent of the popular vote and the Communists 14.3 per cent.

As this melting away of the liberal democratic center progressed, and as the economic crisis facing the nation worsened, the need for stable and resolute government became more urgent than ever; yet the workable parliamentary majorities that effective government required became steadily more difficult to secure. By 1930 the Reichstag had become so sharply divided and stalemated that it was compelled, in effect, to abdicate its legislative power in favor of what soon became the "constitutional dictatorship" of the President, exercising his rights under Article 48. This, in turn, led to a rapid increase in the activities of the country's extra-parliamentary forces, the organized vested interests of industry, agriculture, the bureaucracy, and the army. The strategy of these interests came to be a twofold one: lobbying directly with the President (the politically reactionary octogenarian General von Hindenburg); and negotiating with the leader of the "safe" anti-Communist movement who seemed most likely in the long run to gain power—Adolf Hitler.

Hitler's advent to power was not long delayed. On January 30, 1933, President von Hindenburg appointed him Chancellor. Hitler, with an eye to the election scheduled for March, immediately set his party's propaganda apparatus and private army of storm troopers to work to create a situation of general confusion and panic. On the night of February 27, 1933, the Reichstag building was set on fire, the deed being attributed to the Communists. Large sectors of the public became convinced that the country was on the eve of a Communist revolution. And Hitler, acting through the President, responded by proclaiming a state of emergency and, under Article 48, assuming what in effect were dictatorial powers.

Not surprisingly, the elections of March, 1933, gave the Nazis 44.2 per cent of the popular vote (as against 14 per cent for the Center party, 18.4 per cent for the Social Democrats, and 12 per cent for the Communists). Shortly thereafter Hitler introduced into the Reichstag a measure designed to enable laws to "be enacted by the Reich cabinet as well as according to the procedure in the Constitution." As a result of Nazi intimidations and the forcible exclusion of more than a hundred members from the session altogether, the measure easily secured the necessary two-thirds majority. Four months later a decree was proclaimed banning all political parties other than the National Socialists. Another decree of December, 1933, legally united the German State and the Nazi party. Finally, upon the death of President von Hindenburg in August, 1934, Hitler merged the former offices of chancellor and president into the new office of *Reichskanzler und Führer,* which he immediately assumed himself. From then until 1945—with all the tragedy that the fact was to mean for the Germans and the rest of the world—Germany was to be Hitler, and Hitler, along with his supporters and his police-state apparatus, was to be Germany.

The Third Reich

How had it all been possible? In part, certainly, the fault lay in the structural deficiences of the Weimar Constitution itself. The ultrademocratic provision for proportional representation inevitably increased parliamentary fragmentation and the difficulty of maintaining stable governmental coalitions. The lower house's power to overthrow cabinets by a simple vote of nonconfidence, and without first having to assure itself of a workable majority for an alternative cabinet, clearly weakened the effectiveness of the parliamentary executive. Most obvious of all, the President's powers, especially under Article 48, enabled him in a parliamentary crisis to hand total effective control to anyone he might choose to select as chancellor. If that person turned out to

possess the extraparliamentary support and political ruthlessness
of a Hitler, there were no further insurmountable obstacles to
prevent temporary and constitutional dictatorial powers from
being transformed into permanent and total dictatorship.

Important as these structural deficiencies were, however,
what ultimately killed the Weimar Republic and brought to
power the nationalistic totalitarianism of Hitler was the same
type of circumstances that had caused the failure of the liberals
of 1848–1849 and had made it appear necessary to accept national
unification under the authoritarian leadership of Bismarck. It
became Bismarck's mission to overcome the many obstacles that
for so long had prevented the establishment of a united Germany
as a major world power. And it was the German people's mandate
to Hitler (whether given enthusiastically or in reluctant acquiescence) to combat the same kind of circumstances—the country's
lack of internal unity and its precarious international position—
so as to assure Germany's survival as a major power.

Undoubtedly, the many irrational brutalities of Nazi policies
are explicable only as the doings of sick and evil men. Recognition
of this should not, however, obscure the further undeniable circumstance that the internal and international situation in response to which Hitler secured initial acceptance by the Germans
was in fact a most critical one. This is attested to by the analyses
of German and foreign scholars alike. In 1931, for example, in his
book *Incertitudes Allemandes*, the French professor and writer,
Pierre Vienot, summed up his view of the German internal situation as follows:

> One witnesses in Germany the collapse of a certain material,
> social and moral equilibrium, the end of the bourgeois way of life.
> How does Germany itself react in the midst of this crisis? . . .
> Above all by a vast uncertainty; the intellectuals haunted by the
> cultural crisis and the masses disoriented by realities which are too
> new. . . .
>
> Uncertainty is a permanent fact of German life. The problems
> of Germany are inexhaustible. While the intellectual is overcome
> by the complete relativization of traditional values . . . the average
> German has become hesitant and confused. The spontaneity of his
> reactions and his judgment, at times, even the simple intervention
> of practical common sense, are half paralyzed. Even in ordinary,

every-day life, the imitation of what is foreign, especially American
—or, with others, the desire "to be German"—betray, by the way
they are expressed, the absence of a simple, intuitive and natural
sense of balance.

That this anxiety could easily become desperation and violence
goes without saying. . . .

The average German of today says to himself: "This condition
of instability and contradictions, this world without laws and forms
surely cannot last. We are witnessing the dying of the past in order
that the future may be reborn; the present moment is only an
historical exception."

Every German imagines a tomorrow that will be different. . . .
They are waiting for it; they want it; they love it in advance. . . .
But from now until then, how to live? [5]

Internationally, too, the German situation lent plausibleness
to the Nazis' claims that Germany's survival as a major world
power was in increasing jeopardy. For one thing, the Treaty of
Versailles had stripped the country of very sizable territories and
populations, had imposed heavy reparations payments, and had
left the Germans compulsorily demilitarized. For the time being,
moreover, the system of collective security represented by the
League of Nations made it seem impossible for the Germans to
reverse this weakening of their international position.

In addition, the Nazis were able to exploit the alleged long-
range threat of the Soviet Union. With a population and birth
rate more than twice those of Germany—not to speak of its vast
continental size and rapid industrialization—Russia seemed to
German political geographers to be at once their country's most
dangerous adversary and the most likely area into which Germany
could expand. This logic was taken up after 1941 by Nazi propa-
gandists with the stated objective of conquering and dismember-
ing the Soviet Union and of settling its most fertile Western
territories with Germans. The over-all reasoning of this propaganda was summarized in the slogan *Weltmacht oder Untergang*
—first-rate world power or decline.

To point out these facts and interpretations of Germany's
situation at the time of Hitler's rise to power is not to defend
either the Nazis' objectives or the means they employed. It is
merely to show that *if* the Germans' purpose was to maintain the

bases for a role as a first-rate world power, the domestic and international problems they faced were grave and were bound to require the most intensive efforts. Apart, therefore, from the Nazis' many irrational and wanton brutalities, the essentials of their domestic and international strategies were logically inherent in what they were attempting to accomplish: the restoration and maintenance of Germany as a major world power. Once again, as at the time of Germany's establishment as a nation, the choice seemed to be *either* liberal democracy *or* nationalism. And once again the Germans decided for the latter at the cost of sacrificing the former.

The West German Federal Republic

Four years after the total defeat of the Nazis' desperate bid for German international hegemony a German parliamentary council, on May 8, 1949, promulgated the so-called Basic Law or constitution that prescribed the system of government for the amalgamated British, American, and French zones of occupation that were thenceforth to be known as the Federal Republic of Germany. The drafters of the new 146-article Constitution were for the most part seasoned survivors of the Weimar period and strongly determined to avoid the former republic's fateful structural weaknesses.

The basic difference between the Weimar and the Bonn republican systems is the latter's greater limitation of the powers of both the President and the legislature in favor of the increased freedom of action of the Chancellor. The presidental office has undergone several significant changes. For one thing, the President is no longer elected on a popular basis but indirectly by a special convention consisting of the members of the lower house of the German parliament plus an equal number of persons elected by the parliaments of the eleven federal states or Länder. The purpose of this change was to deny the President the possibility of claiming to be the German people's most directly representative collective spokesman. And even more important, the Bonn Constitution contains no equivalent of Weimar's notorious Article 48. That is, there is no provision authorizing the President to declare a state of emergency and compel parliament to become a mere collaborator with constitutional executive dictatorship. Indeed, the role that remains to the Bonn President is largely that of a ceremonial figurehead whose various functions are chiefly designed to give formal significance to otherwise self-operating governmental processes.

The Bonn Constitution has also circumscribed the powers exercised by the new German legislature. As before, predominant legislative power is vested in the lower house, the Bundestag. Yet compared with the functions of the Weimar Republic's Reichstag, those of the present lower house have been altered in at least three significant respects. First, the election of the members of the Bundestag is no longer exclusively on the basis of proportional representation. It is now only in part by proportional representation and in part on the basis of the Anglo-Saxon type of single-member constituency.

Second, the Bundestag has been compelled to share somewhat more of its power with the federal upper house, the Bundesrat. The members of the Bundesrat are members of their respective state governments and must vote at the instructions of their states. In order to help protect the interests of the states, the new Constitution distinguishes between federal laws and general laws. In the passage of federal laws—laws in which the federal subdivisions or Länder have a direct interest—the Bundesrat's consent is essential for enactment. When deadlocks occur between the two houses over such laws a joint arbitration committee proposes a compromise which both houses must then vote upon and accept. In the passage of general laws, in contrast, the Bundesrat's power is merely suspensive. It may reject a bill within a week after receiving it from the Bundestag. If its rejection is by an ordinary majority, the Bundestag may set aside the veto by an ordinary majority; if it is by a two-thirds majority, then the Bundestag must also override by a two-thirds majority.

Another important change under the Bonn system has occurred in the relations prescribed between the Bundestag and the Chancellor. No longer, as in the Weimar period, is it possible for a majority of the lower house to turn a government out of office by simply refusing to vote confidence in it. To eliminate this source of legislative irresponsibility the present Constitution has introduced the principle of what is known as the "constructive vote of no confidence," whereby the exercise of the Bundestag's non-confidence right depends upon its ability to suggest an alternative government to carry on immediately. In other words, if a majority of the Bundestag wishes to overthrow the Chancellor and his Cabinet it must first elect a chancellor and a cabinet to succeed the government it has decided to overthrow. Only then can it request the President to dismiss the defeated government and officially appoint the new one it has agreed to support.

As a result of these and other provisions, the Bonn Constitution's dominant office is, very clearly, that of the Chancellor. Not only has it become very difficult for the Bundestag to dislodge him: the Chancellor for his part has been provided with the powerful threat of dissolution. That is, if the Chancellor himself asks for a vote of confidence and does not receive it, he has the right to ask the President to dissolve the Bundestag. The President must comply within two weeks. If within that interval the Bundestag can agree upon and suggest to the President a successor for the Chancellorship, the right of dissolution lapses and the Chancellor must step down. If it cannot agree upon a successor, it must submit to the Chancellor's exercise of his power of dissolution and, along with him, seek re-election.

This constitutional strengthening of the Chancellorship and enforcement of responsibility upon the Bundestag has contributed substantially to making possible the Federal Republic's first decade of exemplary governmental stability. A second important factor has been the domination of the post–World War II political scene by two major democratically dedicated parties, the Christian Democratic Union and the Social Democratic party. The former, the party of Chancellor Adenauer, is the heir to the Weimar Republic's Center party. Catholic, solidly middle class and oriented toward the West rather than nationalist at core, the CDU's support has come from all classes, regions, and religious affiliations. In the first ten years of the Republic's life it has polled between one third and one half of the total electoral vote—enough to enable it to furnish every successive government and to sustain the uninterrupted tenure of its leader, Conrad Adenauer.

The other major party, the Social Democrats (SPD), with popular strength varying from some 25 to 30 per cent of the total electoral vote, has come to occupy the role of the Federal Republic's permanent Opposition. More disciplined and coherent in its

membership than the CDU, it is primarily the party of the workingman and the intellectual. In basic ideology it is secularist and
welfare-statist with a tradition of non-Communist Marxism. In
order to prevent the appropriation of nationalistic appeals by less
genuinely democratic groups, it has hewn to a moderately nationalist position, urged the exploration of possibilities for negotiating with the Russians concerning German reunification, and
opposed West German rearmament and too close political and
military ties with the United States.

Although there are a number of other West German parties
—including principally the Free Democratic party—the Bonn
Republic has been blessed by the absence of any substantial
groupings on the far Right or far Left. By Article 9 of the Basic
Law, "Associations . . . which are directed against the constitutional order or the concept of international understanding are
prohibited." Thus far this provision has seldom been used. The
feared revival of neo-Nazism failed to materialize. And the Communists—whose handiwork is to be seen immediately across the
eastern borders—have had no success whatsoever.

In addition to its fortunate party situation and its improved
Constitution, the Bonn Republic's govermental stability has
rested upon one additional important circumstance: the long-
continued leadership of Chancellor Adenauer. Though neither
a colorful nor a brilliant man, his stolid bureaucratic poise appears to have offered the defeated Germans a moral reassurance
they badly needed. Moreover, in having headed the Bonn Republic during its rapid postwar economic and political recovery,
he soon came to represent to the Germans a symbol of internal
rebirth and international reacceptance that even his political
enemies have not slighted. With him, indeed, the Germans appeared to have become what they were so long reputed to be
before they first entered upon their fateful national road: individually hard-working, collectively docile, cosmopolitan in their
political ideals, and provincial in their political practice.

Prospects for German Liberal Democracy

In attempting to assess the Federal Republic's chances for
continued success one must, above all, consider its prospects in
the light of the challenges that have determined the outcome of

similar experiments in the past. For, once again, as before 1870 and during the Weimar years, the enjoyment of liberal democracy coincides for the Germans with a condition of national weakness and fragmentation. Are they resigned to the permanence and inevitability of this condition? If they are, judging by historical precedent, German liberal democracy is secure. If they are not, again by historical example, German liberal democracy seems destined to undergo the most difficult trials.

It is true that internal German social and political unity has come a long way since the Weimar period. The strength of the reactionary Right appears to have been permanently destroyed. Many of its members lost their lives in World War II and their survivors appear to have learned the wisdom of economic concession and political compromise. This has been made easier for them by the fact that the rule of communism in the neighboring Soviet satellites appears also to have permanently destroyed the appeal of the radical Left. Assuming the maintenance of even a modest level of economic prosperity, the bitter economic and social animosities that helped destroy German liberal democracy in the past would therefore seem to have been overcome once and for all.

Yet against this internal progress must be balanced the fact of Germany's continued internationally imposed political division. Approximately one quarter of Germany's pre–World War II area has been annexed by Poland and Russia, some twelve million of the original German inhabitants having been compelled to emigrate to the West. More than another quarter of the pre-1937 German territory constitutes an entirely separate Russian-occupied state. In the midst of that artifically maintained Soviet satellite state lies, isolated, Germany's largest city and traditional capital, Berlin, itself in turn divided into two sealed-off parts.

Whether or not one judges the Germans morally to deserve this divided condition of their country is irrelevant. What matters is that from a German point of view the present Federal German Republic is not necessarily the Germany—territorially and otherwise—that could and should be. This fact, indeed, is recognized in the Bonn Republic's Constitution. According to the preamble of that document, "The entire German people is called upon to achieve, by free self-determination, the unity and freedom of

Germany." And according to its concluding Article 146, "This Basic Law shall become invalid on the day when a Constitution adopted by the German people by means of a free decision becomes effective."

During the first decade of the Federal Republic's life the strategy employed to bring about this goal of reunification has been one of close alliance with the West, through NATO and various other supranational arrangements. As stated repeatedly by Dr. Adenauer, the assumption underlying this strategy has been that a prosperous, rearmed, and Western-allied Bonn Republic would ultimately succeed in *intimidating* the Russians into permitting German reunification. Even though this assumption has shown no tangible signs of being borne out, the Germans' electoral support of Adenauer and his strategy has not in the least diminished. Judging therefore from their behavior and reactions during the past decade, the Germans would appear to have more or less permanently resigned themselves to their country's politically disunited condition.

But will this situation continue? It very well may not. For one thing, the assumption that the Soviet Union can be intimidated into releasing its sector of Germany has become less and less plausible. As a result, the Adenauer strategy in question has come under increasingly widespread attack. This mounting dissatisfaction with the Adenauer record in regard to reunification, moreover, has been nourished by a second circumstance: the growing prosperity and sense of political importance of the Germans. As long as they continued preoccupied with the anxieties of physically maintaining themselves, their concern with such larger matters as reunification was bound to be less acute. Once having re-established their economic and political base, they are, not surprisingly, looking ever further beyond their immediate situation.

As long as the figure of Adenauer remains on the German political scene this growing preoccupation with reunification will undoubtedly be safely contained. With his retirement, however, West German liberal democracy will almost certainly be severely tested. The temptation to explore alternative strategies to bring about German reunification will be irresistible. Whatever politicians and parties espouse these alternative strategies are certain to meet with a large-scale response. It is not impossible, indeed, that the dynamic of democracy will result in the reunification issue's becoming a slogan for some entirely new national political movement.

The potential danger to West German liberal democracy of such possible developments arises from the fact that whatever alternative strategies for reunification may be advanced, one premise will, in the nature of the situation, undoubtedly be common to all of them. That premise will be the unavoidable necessity of negotiating with the Soviet Union. Both on their own initiative as well as through French, American, and British encouragement, however, a considerable number of Germans may be expected to oppose direct Russian-German negotiations. The question therefore arises: How would a majority in favor of reunification, conceivably with its own leader in the Chancellorship, react to such opposition? Would it permit its opponents to use the liberal democratic machinery and its freedoms to resist the acceptance of whatever terms the Soviet Union might ask? Or would it—in re-encountering the historically traditional German dilemma of liberal democracy versus nationalism—so alter the existing system as to suppress those in opposition to the politics of reunification? Upon the answer given to this question, if and when it should be posed, the prospects of German liberal democracy would once again depend.

SELECTED BIBILIOGRAPHY

BUTZ, OTTO. *Germany: Dilemma For American Foreign Policy*, New York, Doubleday, Doubleday Short Studies in Political Science, 1954.

GOERLITZ, WALTER. *The German General Staff*, Introduction by Walter Millis, New York, Praeger, 1953.

HABE, HANS. *Our Love Affair with Germany*, New York, Putnam, 1953.

TAYLOR, A. J. P. *The Course of German History*, New York, Coward-McCann, 1946.

THAYER, CHARLES W. *The Unquiet Germans*, New York, Harper, 1957.

« 12 »

Soviet Russia:
Government from Revolution

THE TRADITIONAL RUSSIAN GOVERNMENTAL PATTERN has been one of imperialistic despotism. Communism, though claiming to repudiate this tradition, has merely continued it in different form and with a different justification. In the name of various adaptations of the ideas of Karl Marx, it has organized the transformation of Russian society into an industrialized welfare state. Its purpose in this has been to make Russian imperialism (under the guise of the Marxian ideal of world communism) more efficient and to make Russian governmental autocracy (as operated by the leaders of the Communist party) more secure.

In remaking Russia into an industrialized welfare state, however, communism has generated accompanying social and cultural developments that may well be transforming not only communism itself but also, at long last, the traditional Russian subservience to political despotism that communism has for so long been able to exploit. That is, in encouraging people to assert their individuality and rationality in the realms of economics and technology, communism may not be able to prevent the extension of these attitudes into the areas of culture and politics as well. .

In the West, the movement for political equality preceded the struggle for social and economic equality by many decades. In the Soviet Union, in contrast, pursuit of the ideal of social and economic equality has come first. How long it will require for progress in the achievement of political equality to follow will depend upon many circumstances. That in fact it has begun, the many liberalizations of Russian life that have occurred since the death of Stalin would seem to indicate. These liberalizations have not been the spontaneous gifts of a benign despot. In its internal competitions for successorship to Stalin, rather, the Communist leadership has found it necessary at last to begin to recognize the demands of Russian public opinion.

This recognition by the Communist leadership of industrialized Russian society's cultural, economic, and political demands has taken two principal forms. The one has been the granting of such concessions as reduction of the arbitrariness and terror of the secret police, higher levels of consumer goods, and greater freedom of cultural and intellectual expression. In addition, since Stalin's death Communist leaders have begun to institute various changes in original Communist economic arrangements. Where ideologically dictated methods of organization have demonstrably impaired productivity—as in the total collectivization of agriculture and the excessive centralization of industrial planning—insistence upon ideological purity and the directness of Communist party control show signs of being increasingly compromised. Here again, the ultimate moving force has not been the generous impulses of Communist leaders but the demands of the Russian peoples for the higher standards of welfare that only ideologically unimpeded efficiency can provide.

In itself, of course, whatever success the Russians may achieve in liberalizing their way of life will not make of the Soviet Union a less formidable adversary internationally. From the point of view of the rest of the world, indeed, Soviet society's involvement in the consequences of the democratic-industrial revolution is only a very qualified blessing. Until the growing consensus among the nations acquires more effective international political expression, a liberalized (and hence more internally secure) Soviet Union will, if anything, prove a more dangerous opponent than before. Its danger, however, will lie less in the Communist ideology itself than in the economic, military, and political capabilities that have been built up in communism's name. The U.S.S.R.'s spectacular achievements in missile development and its expanding foreign aid programs are indications of this impending turn of events.

The Russian Political Tradition

The Russian political tradition to which Soviet communism became heir has been one of uninterrupted despotism. It was this despotism, with the Russian peoples as its passive agents, that first founded the Russian nation, that first introduced into it Western ideas, that for centuries suppressed the development of liberty, and that in its Communist guise finally revolutionized the country into an efficiently organized industrial state.

There have been many reasons for this tradition of more total and long-lived despotism in Russia than elsewhere. For one thing, the territorial and political establishment of this largest country in the world was not a matter of peoples coming and growing together as a free community. Primarily, rather, it was a military operation extending over five centuries, initiated by the dukes of the garrison-duchy of Moscow and involving the subjugation of dozens of ethnically and culturally different peoples over much of the Eurasian continent. Once established, Russian rule over this sprawling, conquered empire could only be maintained through the ruthlessly administered control of an autocratic monarch.

This political origin of Russian despotism was reinforced by the fact that Church and state in imperial Russia were united in one and the same authority, that of the emperor or czar. Beginning in the tenth century the Russian peoples had been converted to Eastern Christianity, with its headquarters in Byzantium (later Constantinople). In 1439, however, the Eastern Church had lost its separate identity through merging again with Roman Catholicism. A few years later, in 1453, Byzantium itself had been captured by the Turks. It had been at this point that the Russian priesthood, rather than subordinate itself to Rome, had proclaimed Moscow as the new center of the Eastern Church and the Russian Czar as "the only faithful and true Christian Prince in the world."

Because this unity of spiritual and secular rule in Russia continued, Russia never came to experience the kind of centuries-long struggle of Church versus state that played such an important part in stripping away nonrational claims to authority in the West.

Russian despotism therefore remained much more entrenched, and the peoples of Russia wholly lacked the religion-inspired utilitarianism that in the West served as such a persistent and powerful force in challenging nonresponsible authority.

At no time, moreover, did the subjects of imperial Russian autocracy enjoy extensive opportunity to acquire inspiration for resistance to absolutism from more liberal lands abroad. For, although the czars were not averse to accepting more advanced Western scientific and organizational techniques, their insistence upon the exclusion from Russia of Western political ideas was as complete as their police-state bureaucracy could make it. Upon returning from a visit to Russia in 1839, a French aristocrat, the Comte de Custine, noted:

> The more I see of Russia, the more I approve of the Emperor forbidding the Russians to travel and rendering access to his country difficult to foreigners. The political regime of Russia could not withstand twenty years of free intercourse with Western Europe. . . . One has to have lived in this prison without leisure that is Russia in order to feel the freedom one enjoys in the other countries of Europe, whatever form of government they may have adopted.[1]

Finally, the very hopelessness of resisting Russia's continent-spanning autocracy operated as a factor aiding in its perpetuation. Even among the system's enemies, the helplessness of the Russian masses eventually came to be romanticized as a phenomenon of epic grandeur. Russian collectivism and pious subservience were held up as morally superior to the allegedly shallow individualism and secularism of the West. Indeed, there developed an almost proud acquiescence in what came to be accepted as the unique Russian way—the way of force, of vast sacrifices, and of tragic disregard for human costs.

Reflecting upon the Russians' probable long-range evaluation of Stalin in terms of this heroic and fatalistic Russian self-image, Edward Crankshaw, the well-known British student of Russian affairs, has written as follows:

> St. Petersburg was founded on the broken bodies of innumerable slaves. Peter the Great is remembered with a shudder for his fearful demon, but with mingled awe and pride for creating Rus-

sia as a European power. Ivan the Terrible strangled his son, the Tsarevitch, with his own hands, scourged his nobles with unspeakable cruelty, and, on his death-bed, tried to rape the wife of his second son. But today in Russia his name is venerated for his unifying mission. Other Russian autocrats committed vile outrages and condemned their subjects to unmeasured suffering, not only in the Middle Ages, but also in the Age of Reason. When Nicholas I had the vast Winter Palace rebuilt within a year of the disastrous fire that destroyed it, thousands of artisans were condemned to work in rooms which were heated like ovens to dry them off while the work was going on. Many died each day. Victoria was on the throne in England.

Stalin will be remembered with a shudder for his atrocities. But all Russian autocrats commit atrocities. And he will also be remembered with Ivan and Catherine for his colossal achievements in a land where nothing material has ever been achieved unless it was colossal, nor without an infinity of human sacrifice. . . .

Peter the Great picked Russia up by the scruff of her neck and thrust her bodily into the lap of an apprehensive Europe. Afterwards there were back-slidings; but the Russians were never the same again. Stalin made Russia into a power strong enough not only to dominate Europe but also to face the only power strong enough to dominate the world. That is not nothing. His methods were the methods of the Russian autocratic tradition carried to their atrocious conclusion with the help of twentieth-century science. Let the Russians judge them, those millions of Russians who, while broken by Stalin, still take a mystic pride in the magnitude of his despotism. Our judgment is irrelevant.[2]

Revolution, Marxism, and Leninism

Three times the Russian peoples rose in large-scale revolt against the autocracy and exploitation of the czarist order. On the first occasion, after the Russian loss of the Crimean War, they gained the generously conceived but inadequately implemented Emancipation Edict of 1861. On the occasion of their second major revolt, in 1905, after Russia's defeat in the Russo-Japanese War, they were granted three successive parliaments, or Dumas. Yet as a result of the influence of the landlord class upon the Czar, the Dumas were severely restricted in their powers and, whenever about to embark upon major reforms, were dissolved. With the outbreak of the third and last large-scale resistance to czarism, in March of 1917, the imperial regime collapsed and the Czar abdicated. For a brief interval power passed to two centers: the parliamentary liberal democrats of the so-called Provisional Government, and the radical councils of workingmen and soldiers, called soviets. But before these two loci of revolutionary power could join forces to establish Russia as a constitutional democracy, the Bolsheviks—only 23,000 strong in March, 1917, but brilliantly and ruthlessly led by Lenin—gained control of the soviets, through the soviets gained control of the revolution, and therewith made themselves the Russian peoples' new masters.

What did the actions and success of the ambitious Lenin and his followers have to do with the ideas of Karl Marx? In a substantive sense—very little. Lenin's prerevolutionary program, his improvisations during the revolution, and his own and his successors' policies to the present day have been the expressions of a political dynamic much older than Marxism: a desire for power, a thorough understanding of the situations to be exploited, and an ability and willingness—in the true Machiavellian sense—to act with unswerving singleness of purpose.

This is not to say that Marxism's role in Russian Communist behavior has not been a vital one. Its importance, however, has pertained less to communism's policies than to its political psychology. For one thing, in committing themselves to the philosophy of Marxism the Communists acquired a sense of self-confidence and self-righteousness without which the sacrifices and brutalities that their struggle for power has entailed would hardly have been possible. Second, Marxism has given the Communists an orthodoxy with reference to which they have been able to maintain continuity and discipline among themselves. Internal Communist conflicts have never had to be admitted to be the naked struggles for power that they have in fact been; it has always been possible to dignify them by explaining them as historically significant incidents in the working out of the true Marxist orthodoxy. And, finally, the identification with Marxism has given the Communists an intellectual and moral appeal that few other dictatorial elites have ever enjoyed. Through this appeal they have been able to gain the loyalty of millions of people both in and outside Russia, not only through the use of force and the manipulations of vested interest but, in a great many cases, on the basis of honest if misguided intellectual and moral conviction.

The Russian Communists have gained these advantages from their commitment to Marxism at the cost of never more than a safe minimum of ideological distortion of their sense of reality and power. In the course of their history, it is true, some of their leading members have been sorely tempted to give precedence to considerations of ideology over those of power. But these have always been overridden and sooner or later destroyed by those who have placed the dictates of power first and have been prepared to reinterpret Marxism in whatever ways power seemed to demand.

The Russian Communists' power-minded reinterpretation of Marx's writings has involved three major ideological turning points. The original and by far the most important of these concerned the vital initial question of whether Marxist theory, as a guide to political action, could be applied to Russian conditions at all.

The fact was that in the sense that Marx had stated his program it very plainly did *not* pertain to the situation that at the time prevailed in Russia. Marx had been concerned in his analyses with the industrialized societies of Western Europe. His prescriptions had been designed for socioeconomic systems where the bourgeois industrializers had already triumphed, where the population consisted predominantly of urbanized workers, where economic control had become highly concentrated, and where, therefore—as he saw it—revolution against the bourgeoisie and socialization of the means of production could be quick and could rapidly be followed by the establishment of democratic freedom and welfare. But prerevolutionary Russia? Here was a land still more than 90 per cent rural, a land where industrialization and the appearance of a bourgeoisie were just beginning. Obviously, in Marxian categories, Russia was still far from ready for a proletarian revolution. It first needed a powerful proletariat. It first required the development of industry as the major sector of the economy to be socialized. It first had to have a dominant liberal democratic bourgeoisie to be overthrown for the cause of communism.

This basic issue of the applicability of Marxism as an immediate guide for action first came up among the exiled Russian revolutionary intellectuals around the turn of the century. One group, the Mensheviks, believed that Marxism was not immediately applicable, that Russia had first to pass through an industrializing bourgeois revolution, and that the first task of the proletarian revolutionaries was to ally themselves with the bourgeoisie in order to make the latter's discharge of their necessary historical function as quick and successful as possible. Only then —in Marxian terms—would Russia be ripe for a proletarian revolution; and only then should the proletarian revolutionaries embark upon their separate Marxian course and overthrow the bourgeoisie.

Lenin, however, disagreed. He and his supporters, the Bolsheviks, maintained that it did not matter that Russia was still industrially underdeveloped and primarily a nation of peasants. This was, indeed, a blessing in disguise. For it meant, they pointed out, that a major danger could be avoided: the danger that a strong bourgeoisie might head off the development of a true proletarian state by gaining leadership of the workers through nothing more than a program of concessions to them. When the revolution in Russia could be brought about, its prospects would therefore be much more favorable than if, as Marx had originally envisaged, there actually were a powerful bourgeoisie to contend with.

The revolutionary strategy that Lenin proposed on the basis of this readaptation of Marxism for Russian conditions was outlined in his treatise of the year 1905, *Two Tactics of Social Democracy in the Democratic Revolution.* As here suggested, the revolution was to involve two stages. The first, which Lenin called the "revolutionary-democratic" revolution, was to be carried out by an alliance of the proletariat and the peasantry and was to secure the Communist seizure and establishment of power. The second, which Lenin called the "socialist" revolution, was to be effected by an alliance of the proletariat and the village poor and was to bring about achievement of the final goal of a society based upon the Marxian ideal of "from each according to his ability, to each according to his needs."

But what would revolution in terms of this Leninist strategy

in effect mean? It would mean that an elite—the Bolsheviks—
controlling a minority—industrially underdeveloped Russia's
proletariat—was committed to building an all-proletarian industrialized society at the expense of the majority, the peasantry. It
would mean, that is, that once power was in Communist hands
the revolution's principal concern would be Communist-enforced
industrialization: the creation of means of production to be socially operated and of a large enough proletariat to operate them.

But how and by whom should this two-stage Leninist revolution be brought about and led? The answer to this important
practical question became the subject of the second major Communist readaptation of original Marxism: Lenin's insistence upon
the necessity of developing a disciplined revolutionary party
based upon a core of professional revolutionaries. Marx himself
had simply exhorted the workers of the world to unite and throw
off their chains. But how, particularly in the conditions prevailing in czarist Russia, was this injunction to be carried out? By
trade-union action and other democratic mass organizations?
Impossible, said Lenin, "because any attempt to practice the
'broad, democratic principles' will simply facilitate the work of
the police in making big raids." The only strategy likely to bring
success, he maintained in his treatise, *What Is to Be Done?*, was to
train qualified experts in revolution who could be counted upon
to prove a match for the Czar's secret police:

> I assert (1) that no revolutionary movement can endure without
> a stable organization of leaders that maintains continuity; (2) that
> the wider the masses spontaneously drawn into the struggle, form-
> ing the basis of the movement and participating in it, the more
> urgent the need of such an organization, and the more solid this
> organization must be . . . (3) that such an organization must con-
> sist chiefly of people professionally engaged in revolutionary ac-
> tivity; (4) that in an autocratic state the more we confine the mem-
> bership of such an organization to people who are professionally
> trained in the art of combating the political police, the more dif-
> ficult will it be to wipe out such an organization, and (5) the
> *greater* will be the number of people of the working class and of
> other classes of society who will be able to join the movement
> and perform active work in it.[3]

Stalin and Enforced Industrialization

The third major power-motivated improvisation upon original Marxism occurred in the mid-twenties. The revolutionary alliance of proletariat and peasantry had triumphed. The Communists were firmly in control. For the first several years after the revolution the vast damage caused to crops and equipment during the revolutionary struggle had led Lenin to permit the reappearance of a large private economic sector. This was intended merely as an emergency concession to be followed as soon as possible by the revolution's second stage—the implementation of "socialism." But at that point Lenin had died. Who would be his successor? How should the final goal of "socialism" be implemented? Once again, in Stalin's formula of "socialism in one country," original Marxism was reinterpreted to justify a course of action that seemed required by the dictates of power.

According to Marxism as well as earlier Bolshevik theory, the precondition for the ultimate success of the proletarian revolution was that it should occur throughout the world. Only thus, it was held, would peoples everywhere come to one another's assistance, refrain from meddling in one another's affairs, and assure one another of safety from aggression and imperialistic exploitation. But the Russian Communists had waited in vain for simultaneous outbreaks of revolution in countries like Germany, France, and Britain. Obviously, Stalin therefore concluded, if there were to be no global revolution, there would also be no global achievement of "socialism." And obviously, too, if the rest of the world remained capitalistic and fearful of the example of Russian communism, every effort would be made to bring about the overthrow of Communist rule. To assure Communist survival, Stalin maintained, there was therefore no alternative but for Russia to proceed unilaterally and independently with the establishment of "socialism," that is, with the creation of an industrial economy and a proletarian society.

In part, undoubtedly, Stalin's determination to embark on the program of "socialism in one country" was motivated by a desire to justify his own and the Communist party's continued dictatorial rule. At the same time, however, his decision was based upon a more objective historical reason: what he held to be the danger of attack upon the Soviet Union from abroad.

During the revolution Western nations had intervened in Russian affairs in an effort to help defeat communism. During the 1920's official as well as public opinion throughout the Western world had continued strongly hostile to the Soviet Union. By 1930, with Hitler on the rise in Germany, eventual attack upon Russia seemed to have become almost a certainty. How deeply Stalin was concerned with preparing the country to meet this danger he indicated in an impassioned speech in 1931, at the very height of his program of collectivization and industrialization:

> No, comrades . . . the pace must not be slackened! On the contrary, we must speed up to the limit of our possibilities. This is dictated to us by our obligations to the workers and the peasants of the U.S.S.R. It is dictated to us by our obligations to the working-class of the whole world. To slacken the pace would be to lag behind; and those who lag behind are beaten. We do not want to be beaten. No, we do not!

One of the most tragic features of the history of pre-Communist Russia, he continued, was that the country was time and time again militarily defeated because of her backwardness:

> She was beaten by the Mongol Khans. She was beaten by the Turkish beys. She was beaten by the Swedish feudal lords. She was beaten by the Polish-Lithuanian *pans*. She was beaten by the Anglo-French capitalists. She was beaten by the Japanese barons. She was beaten by all—for her backwardness. For military backwardness; for cultural backwardness; for political backwardness; for industrial backwardness; for agricultural backwardness. She was beaten because to beat her was profitable and could be done with impunity. You remember the words of the pre-revolutionary poet: "Thou art poor and thou art abounding; thou art mighty, and thou art helpless, Mother Russia." . . . We are fifty or a hundred years behind the advanced countries. We must make good this lag in ten years. Either we do, or they crush us.[4]

The program of industrialization and agricultural collectivization that Stalin carried out in this spirit of "do or die" became the most ambitious and bloody experience in imposed change that the world had ever seen. Between 1927 and the mid-1930's some

25,000,000 independent peasant holdings were forcibly transformed into approximately 240,000 collective farms. Peasant resistance was widespread and desperate. Crop production dropped
sharply and the total number of livestock was reduced by nearly
50 per cent. Millions of people died of famine. Yet Stalin gave no
quarter. Some six million resisting peasants were either killed or
transported to Siberia as slave laborers. And in the end, however
high the cost, the elimination of the politically distrusted peasantry and the freeing of additional labor for industrialization
had been achieved according to plan.

Similar determination and ruthlessness marked Stalin's program of enforced industrialization. The immediate purpose of this
program was not to raise the Russian standard of living but to
provide the Soviet Union with the heavy industries that would
give it economic self-sufficiency. With this objective in mind Stalin
in 1928 instituted his famous series of so-called Five Year Plans.
Successive production goals were set up and publicized; various
psychological techniques were employed to provide worker incentive and to give the mass of the Russian people a sense of personal
involvement in the progress achieved; and, in order to motivate
the development of scientific and managerial skills, a highly dis-
criminatory system of differential economic rewards was set up.
All attempts to interfere either with Stalin's direction of the program or with his unrelenting concentration on expansion in
heavy industry at the cost of rises in consumer goods were brutally
crushed.

Not surprisingly, the results achieved were phenomenal.
Between 1928 and Stalin's death in 1953 the industrial sector of
the Russian economy grew at an average annual rate of approximately 15 per cent. Even when the showing of the inefficient system of collectivized agriculture was added to the computation,
the over-all annual rise in the Russian national product remained
at around 9 per cent, the most rapid expansion on record anywhere and three times the figure achieved in the United States
during the same period. Stalin's objective had been achieved. Not
only was Russia no longer industrially backward; in its total production of such vital materials as iron and steel it stood second
only to the United States. Indeed, if past rates of expansion could

be even partially maintained for another decade, Russia threatened to become the most powerful industrial nation in the world.

Control and Government

The institutions through which the Communist leadership
has enlisted and controlled the participation of the Russian peoples in these ruthlessly achieved accomplishments consist chiefly
of two hierarchies of power: the hierarchy of *actual* power of the
Communist party, and the hierarchy of *formal* power of the system
of soviets (councils). Together, these two hierarchies provide for
the Russian peoples' formal involvement in the Communist state
and, at the same time, constitute the instruments through which
the Communist leaders maintain their hold over the state's operation.

Most directly under the control of Communist leaders and
also most centrally involved in the state's operation is the hierarchy of the Communist party. True to Lenin's theory that revolutions must be led by well-disciplined minorities, membership in
the Russian Communist party has never been permitted to rise to
more than a small fraction of the total Russian population. In
1955, for example, Communist party membership stood at approximately 8,000,000 as against a total Soviet population of some
200,000,000. These 8,000,000 people are the system's political ac-
tivists.

The hierarchy of the Communist party—in which all direction passes from top to bottom, and mere reactions, when solicited,
are relayed from the bottom to the top—consists of five levels. At
the base of the pyramid are the primary party organizations,
formerly called cells. Of these there are some 350,000. Established
in factories, collective farms, units of the armed forces, schools,
and various kinds of cultural organizations, these primary party
units range in membership from a handful to several thousand
people. They constitute the main link between the party leadership and the masses. Each unit is headed by a secretary who must
be approved by and receives his instructions from the highest level
of the party hierarchy in Moscow. The principal function of these
primary party organizations is characterized officially as "agita-

tional and organizational"; they are concerned, that is, with the promotion of maximum economic effort and the mobilization of greatest possible popular support for the party's objectives and activities.

Between these local Communist party units and the party's highest organs in Moscow are three intermediate levels of organization: the district party bodies, numbering about 5,500; the regional party organizations, of which there are some 175; and the territorial and union-republic organizations, which number 21.

The "highest organ" of the party at its top level in Moscow is in theory the national or All-Union Party Congress. The representatives to this national party congress are elected by and from among the members of the regional, territorial, and union-republic party organizations. In theory—though not in fact—the national party congress meets every four years. On the occasions when it meets, the national party congress elects as its permanent executive a central committee. The theoretical function of this Central Committee is to conduct party affairs in the intervals between meetings of the party congress. In actual fact, however, the Central Committee has long been too large and unwieldy for the exercise of this function and has progressively abdicated its power to a still higher body.

This actually operative highest executive organ of the national party organization is the Presidium of the Central Committee, formerly known as the Politburo. Made up of from twelve to fifteen members, the Presidium has been variously called the party's "leading summit," "directing kernel," and "general staff," and in effect serves as the party's equivalent of a cabinet. At the head of this Presidium, and completely dominating its activities, is the party's leader and highest executive officer, the secretary-general. Under Stalin, who occupied the secretary-generalship for nearly three decades, the powers of this office were equivalent to those of absolute dictatorship.

While actual power in Russia is thus concentrated in the personnel and organization of the Communist party, the country's day-to-day government is conducted through the system of soviets or, as the Communists like to represent them, parliamentary councils. Though subjected to constant Communist party control both in its policy making and in its selection of candidates, the soviet system is depicted by the Communists as the purest possible expression of democracy. Despite the fact that elections to its offices always involve only one slate of Communist-approved candidates, the occasions of these elections are celebrated by the Communist party as major national events, with a resulting customary electoral turnout of more than 99 per cent.

The system of soviets operates on three levels. Its lowest tier comprises the district, borough, city, and village soviets on the local level, of which there are some 100,000. Each of these local soviets has its permanent elected executive and operates such standing arrangements for local government and administration as committees for budget-finance, education, health, agriculture, local industry, social insurance, and road building. Yet in carrying out these tasks, the local soviets are by no means independent or democratically responsible. They are directed by departments of the highest level of soviets in Moscow and serve as little more than democratically disguised administrative instruments of the central government.

The intermediate link in the soviet system is at the level of the country's sixteen union republics, the approximate equivalents of the American federal states. Each union republic possesses its own unicameral council or legislature, called its supreme soviet, with its own permanent executive, or presidium. In Soviet constitutional theory the union republics are depicted as entirely self-governing sovereign states. In fact, however, they are almost completely dependent upon the initiative of the central government in Moscow. Candidates for election to the union-republic soviets must be approved by Communist-supervised election commissions; the union republics' administrative departments are for the most part mere subsidiaries of central government departments in Moscow; a number of important national ministries have no counterparts at the union-republic level at all—thereby depriving the union republics of even an administrative role in the matters in question; and, finally, since the union republics have no power to levy their own taxes, they are at the central government's mercy in all fiscal matters.

At the highest level of the soviet system is the bicameral Supreme Soviet of the USSR, in theory the country's supreme legislative organ. One of its chambers, the 700-member Council of the

Union, is elected on a popular basis. The other, the 640-member Council of Nationalities, has a federal representation with a fixed number of deputies elected from each of the country's federal subdivisions. More than 50 per cent of the members of these two chambers are also members of the Communist party.

The theoretically supreme legislative power of the Supreme Soviet is, once again, a constitutional myth. Its function in fact amounts to little more than voting formal (and usually unanimous) approval of measures submitted to it by its permanent executive, the Presidium of the Supreme Soviet. The laws proposed by the Presidium of the Supreme Soviet, moreover, are in turn merely formulations of the decisions of a still higher organ, the national Council of Ministers. The men who occupy the ministries that make up this Council are the executive heads of the Soviet Union's various government departments. They are formally selected by the Chairman of the Council of Ministers (a post sometimes referred to as the premiership) and are confirmed in office by the vote of the Supreme Soviet. Most important of all, it is in the Council of Ministers that the Soviet system and the Communist party hierarchy come together. For the men who head the Council's ministries are none other than the members of the Communist party's highest organ, the Presidium of the party's Central Committee. And these, as has already been pointed out, are in turn subject to the decision making and control of the Communist party's most powerful figure of all, its secretary-general.

The Revolution's Future

Operating through this system of power and control, the leadership of the Communist party has, in effect, sustained for more than four decades the Russian revolution that began in 1917. How much longer can this system of revolutionary and dictatorial direction be continued? And if the system is to change, how can one expect such change to be brought about?

In a formal institutional sense the Communist system must be assumed to be unshakable. If it did not disintegrate during the immense strains and stresses of the 1930's, its disruption in the more stable and prosperous conditions of today must be dismissed

as most improbable. Yet this does not mean that the system cannot and will not change. The change, however, will have to occur
—as indeed it already shows signs of occurring—within the center
of revolutionary direction and control itself, the Communist
party.

At least two major circumstances are contributing to the
changes that the Communist system appears to be undergoing.
The most obvious of these is the Communist party's seeming inability to provide a regularized procedure of selection for the
nation's highest executive office. The dignity that the all-powerful
role of the Communist party's leadership requires can ill afford
the denunciations and protracted jungle battles for supremacy
that have followed the deaths of Lenin and Stalin. In the uncertain years after Lenin's death the revolution was still young
enough to lend the struggle for successorship an air of acceptable
inevitability. In the stable and internationally powerful Soviet
Union of the time of Stalin's passing, on the other hand, the repe-
tition of the same violent process has been an anomaly that can
be presumed to have substantially weakened the basis for continued Communist absolutism. In the first place, it has encouraged
popular doubts as to the Communist leadership's much-vaunted
infallibility and right to unquestioning obedience. And second,
it has compelled the individual competitors for successorship to
rely less on claims to unique political wisdom and virtue and more
upon alliances with various groups outside the Communist hierarchy who might be inclined—in return for concessions—to support them in their quest for highest Communist office. But to the
extent that this has occurred, it has meant that the determination
of top Communist personnel and policy is no longer an exclusively internal Communist party matter. In effect, the freedom of
decision of Communist leadership is thus no longer absolute but,
at least indirectly, is limited by a formerly unknown measure of
larger responsibility. For this larger voice in the selection and
exercise of highest Communist executive leadership to become a
matter of regular institutional procedure would seem—judging
from the course of comparable political evolutions elsewhere—to
be but a matter of time.

It might be countered, of course, that once successorship has
again been firmly established there will be little to prevent the

new incumbent from reimposing the Stalin type of autocracy and simply destroying those to whom he has become politically indebted. It is in this connection, however, that a second major circumstance affecting the Communist dictatorship's future becomes operative: the fact that, in its industrialization of Russia, communism has created and come to depend upon a highly developed class structure which Russian leadership can no longer disregard or wantonly defy.

In order to make possible his economic and military development of the Soviet Union, Stalin was compelled to raise the level of education of the Russian peoples as a whole and, most important, to encourage the formation of a vast intelligentsia of economic administrators, scientists, engineers, military experts, and artists. By today the members of these professions have become the Soviet Union's wealthiest and most prestigious citizens and the most essential contributors to its continued stability and progress. Not surprisingly, therefore, it has been to the support of these people that the would-be successors of Stalin have had to look. Will it be possible, once the succession is finally established, to shift to a policy of ignoring or persecuting these economically vital and culturally dominant Soviet citizens? If this were attempted, would they not retaliate by offering their endorsement to a competing leader who would be prepared to allow political expression to the Soviet Union's changing economic, social, and cultural realities? That such a dilemma is indeed building up for Russia's Communist leadership is the opinion of the majority of our best-informed observers of the current Russian scene. For example, the former American Ambassador to the Soviet Union, George Kennan, has analyzed the considerations in question as follows:

> The situation in the senior echelons of the regime is characterized at this time by the fact that the Communist party has been, in recent years, by no means the only channel of advancement to personal power and influence within the Soviet system. Industrial management, the armed services, and, to some extent, science and engineering have provided careers in many ways more attractive than that of the regular apparatus of the party. Those external professional empires have been only loosely linked to the party through the membership of a few of their senior figures in

the top policy-making bodies, the Presidium or the Central Committee.

In the period immediately following Stalin's death Khrushchev had no choice but to share power extensively with these outside entities as a means both of consolidating his personal ambition and of enabling the system to survive the shock occasioned by Stalin's death. More recently he has been trying to divest himself of this somewhat cloying partnership, to reassert the clear predominance of the party over all these professional elements and, at the same time, to strengthen his own position within the party. Were he to succeed in all this the result would, of course, be in many ways the re-establishment of a form of Stalinism, only minus, thus far at least, the terrorism of the secret police. Khrushchev has now been formally successful in a number of these efforts; the expulsion of Zhukov was only the last and most important of them. But the success has been purchased at a heavy cost. There is a great deal more talent in Russia today outside the apparatus of the Communist party than inside it. Khrushchev has now offended and estranged from the central political process, one by one, the intelligentsia, the industrial managers and a portion of the officer corps of the armed services. . . . Plainly this is not a very stable situation, and it is hard to see how real stability can be achieved until some regular arrangement is made for representation of these outside professional hierarchies in the key processes of government. But if this is done what becomes then of the traditional role of the party? The Soviet leaders stand here at a parting of the ways. Either they keep up with the times and change the system, or they relapse into the rigidities of Stalinism at an ever-increasing cost to the ultimate soundness of the system itself.[5]

The same dilemma, Kennan continues, has come to characterize the relationship between the Communist regime and the Russian people at large:

Stalin's successors, thinking to undo some of the evil effects of his ruthless repression of intellectual and artistic activity, at first made moderate concessions to the feelings of the intellectuals, but the effect of these concessions was mainly to reveal the full depth of the unhappiness of these people and the startling degree to which the Marxist-Leninist ideology had lost its power over their minds and their creative impulses. Frightened at what they saw, the leaders have recently drawn back and have made a fumbling effort to reimpose something like the old Stalinist controls over cultural life. But surely this is no adequate response. It is already too late to recapture minds which have once begun to ask troubled and penetrating questions. If the leaders attempt to go further along the road of repression they are only going to alienate the intelligentsia entirely and lose its indispensable co-operation in maintaining the morale and the enthusiasm of the people at large. If, on the other hand, they go further in the attempt to meet the real needs of the educated strata of the people—and in increasing measure these are the needs of the people at large—then I am sure they will find no stopping point short of complete cultural freedom, and whether this is compatible with Communist rule is something to which the Communists themselves have, on many occasions, given a negative answer.[6]

If this analysis of the growing crisis of the Communist dictatorship is correct, it would seem that the most profitable American policy toward the Soviet Union would be to permit Russian internal developments to run their course with the least possibility of external diversion. For, to the extent that Communist leaders should be able to point to external threat or victory for the Soviet Union, their justification for their continued dictatorship will be strengthened. To the extent, in contrast, that Communist leadership can be denied major international successes and grounds for charges of threats to the Soviet Union, its ability to resist an internal showdown—and thus to survive as a revolutionary dictatorship—will be weakened.

But what does such an American posture toward Soviet developments require? It requires, above all, that Americans accept Communist Russia as an unalterable fact and be prepared—however reluctantly—to deal with it as it is. It is true that from a human point of view the long decades of Communist revolutionary dictatorship have been a great tragedy. Nevertheless, now that that tragedy has occurred, there is nothing to be done save to attempt to make the most of what has been accomplished in return for the immense price that has been paid. Among the more significant of these accomplishments for which the Communist dictatorship must be given historical (though not moral) credit are these: First, it has succeeded in bringing the mass of the Russian peoples (who in 1917 were 80 per cent illiterate) economically, technically, and culturally into the main stream of twentieth-century civilization. Second, it has created the basis for a social, economic, and cultural consensus among the many diverse peoples of Russia that holds very considerable promise for a stable and increasingly liberal Russian political evolution. And finally, in accomplishing these things, the Communist dictatorship has brought about the paradoxical situation in which it itself has become the increasingly obvious principal obstacle to the Russian peoples' further fulfillment in the future.

SELECTED BIBLIOGRAPHY

CRANKSHAW, EDWARD. *Russia without Stalin,* New York, Viking, 1956.

FAINSOD, MERLE. *How Russia Is Ruled,* Cambridge, Mass., Harvard University Press, 1955.

GUNTHER, JOHN. *Inside Russia,* New York, Harper, 1957.

KENNAN, GEORGE F. *Russia, the Atom and the West,* New York, Harper, 1958.

KOHN, HANS, ed. *The Mind of Modern Russia,* New Brunswick, N.J., Rutgers University Press, 1955.

MCNEAL, ROBERT H. *The Russian Revolution,* New York, Rinehart, Source Problems in World Civilization, 1959.

RAYMOND, ELLSWORTH. *Soviet Economic Progress,* New York, Rinehart, Source Problems in World Civilization, 1957.

ROBERTS, HENRY L. *Russia and America,* New York, Mentor, 1956.

SCOTT, DEREK J. R. *Russian Political Institutions,* New York, Rinehart, 1958.

« 13 »

Politics
of Underdeveloped Countries

WHAT DO WE MEAN by a "developed" as contrasted with an "underdeveloped" nation? A developed nation means, by agreement of the peoples of developed and underdeveloped countries alike, a nation with the collective goal of maximizing its citizens' this-worldly welfare and with the prerequisites—economic, cultural, and political—for implementing this goal.

That this distinction between "developed" and "underdeveloped" is today universally accepted is one of the most hopeful facts of contemporary civilization. It means that for the first time in history, men the world over have achieved a basic agreement: inasmuch as they all aspire to be "developed"—in the originally Western sense—they share the same basic goals and faith in the same basic way of life. For the first time, that is, through universal commitment to the ideals and organizational techniques of the democratic-industrial revolution, the socio-economic foundations are being laid for a truly one-world community.

The promise of global participation in the ends and means of the democratic-industrial revolution has, however, been achieved at a high price. That price is the sum of the circumstances in which the peoples of the non-Western world first became involved in international economic and political relationships. For one thing, this involvement began almost exclusively at the initiative of the West. From the beginning of the age of

exploration at the end of the fifteenth century until the period
of League of Nations mandates after World War I, the Western
powers planted colonies and established areas of influence
throughout the world. Western imperialism had the primary
objective of exploiting, on behalf of the mother countries, sources
of raw materials and markets for manufactured goods, although
this aim was rationalized or disguised in terms of slogans such as
"manifest destiny," "civilizing mission," or the cruder "white
man's burden." The sincerity and the good intentions of many
colonial administrators, as well as the missionaries who often
preceded or accompanied them, have been recognized gratefully
even by rebel leaders of the colonial peoples themselves. Especially in retrospect, the West's contributions to health, education,
economic progress, administrative efficiency, and the dispensation
of justice are a valuable legacy in much of the non-Western
world. Nevertheless, it is fair to say that in most cases Westernization was inflicted upon the underdeveloped peoples not in a
spirit of neighborliness but with greed and arrogance. Where
the native peoples were politically disorganized and numerically
weak, as in North and South America, they were conquered and
either assimilated or destroyed altogether. Elsewhere they served
a period of tutelage, ranging from decades to centuries, as
victims of Western subjugation and exploitation. It was largely
incidental to this experience and with the intention of defending themselves against it that the non-Western peoples came to
adopt their Western masters' cultural purposes and organizational methods. Taking advantage of the victors' weakened condition after World War II and the avowed ideals of the United
Nations, native leaders have used lessons learned from their one-
time masters in a world-wide national independence movement.

Were it not for this historical legacy, the implementation
of the non-Western peoples' desires to be "developed" would
pose much less difficult problems. As it is, however, a number of
the Western nations believe still that the maintenance of their
"developed" condition requires a measure of exploitation of
non-Western peoples (however this conviction may be rationalized and disguised); and among many of the non-Western peoples
the memory of exploitation in times past—even where it long
since has ceased—has left such a residue of bitterness that they

too are impaired in the rational pursuit of their objectives.

The resulting paradox of increased international agreement in terms of the ends and means of the democratic-industrial revolution and, at the same time, of increased hostility between already developed and would-be developed nations is being affected by two other key circumstances. The one, operating to aggravate the conflict, is the struggle between the Communist nations and the liberal democratic West. The other, making for a reduction of tensions and irrationalities, is the inescapable fact of the world's growing interdependence and its increasing need for international co-operation. Precisely how each of these circumstances will affect the integration of the developing nations into world society will depend at least in part upon how well the West understands their problems and how generously and intelligently it can aid in dealing with them.

The Objectives

What does the new goal of maximized this-worldly welfare mean to the peoples of the underdeveloped nations? In committing themselves to this goal, what objectives are they setting for themselves? The answer, in the most general terms, is: freedom and equality—political, cultural, and economic. It has been in the achievement of these objectives that they see the strength and dignity of the Western nations; it is to the same kind of achievement that they look in contemplating their own future.

Political freedom and equality are understood in the underdeveloped countries in the same sense as they have been in the West: as the people's right and power to govern themselves, that is, to live for whatever collective purposes, in terms of whatever institutions, and guided by whatever leaders that they themselves may choose. This objective of sovereign self-government is usually first formulated among the non-Western peoples in reaction against the fact or threat of some imposed foreign colonialism or occupation. It is what has motivated the struggles of men like India's Nehru and Ghana's Nkrumah against British rule and what drives the Algerian Moslems in their fight against being administered as part of the metropolitan area of France.

Underlying the quest of self-government and serving as a refuge when it is frustrated is usually the further objective of *cultural* freedom and equality. Every people possesses its own identity and idiom, its own history, symbols, language, and way of life. When it sees these native traditions threatened, either through their suppression or their gradual replacement by the traditions of another culture, it becomes acutely and jealously aware of them. It seeks a political expression and defense of them through self-government and international political recognition. And if this political way is blocked, it retreats to the assertion of its cultural solidarity and identity with ever greater vehemence and magnification of its alleged differentness.

It was, as we have seen, as a compensation for their centuries-long failure to achieve national political expression that the Germans turned to an invidious emphasis on the alleged uniqueness and superiority of their German *Kultur*. It was in the same sense that the Kikuyu people of Kenya, thwarted in their efforts to achieve independent political assertion, in 1954 reacted with the violently tribalistic expression of their cultural identity in the so-called Mau Mau revolt. Had the achievement of self-government seemed even remotely possible, the Kikuyu's Western-educated intellectual leader, Jomo Kenyatta, would undoubtedly have become a responsible politician and statesman (as did his counterparts in British West Africa). With such prospects of sovereign political expression denied to the Kikuyu by the presence of the European settlers of Kenya's White Highlands, Kenyatta, as did his people a few years later, turned instead to impassioned cultural protest. Thus, Kenyatta's book, *Facing Mount Kenya,* is dedicated "to . . . all the dispossessed youth of Africa; for perpetuation of communion with ancestral spirits through the fight for African Freedom, and in the firm faith that the dead, the living, and the unborn will unite to rebuild the destroyed shrines." [1]

Finally, in addition to the objectives of independent political and cultural expression, the peoples of the underdeveloped countries are, of course, committed to the achievement of *economic* freedom and equality. For, to the extent that their economic freedom and equality are once secured, their achievement of political and cultural independence becomes very much easier;

and conversely, even if their political and cultural independence be formally acknowledged, unless they possess freedom of action in their economic life they remain vulnerable to outside domination culturally and politically as well.

Much has been made of the nationalism of today's impatient and restless underdeveloped peoples. Yet all that this phenomenon fundamentally involves is the assertion of these peoples' objectives of political, cultural, and economic freedom and equality: their statement of these objectives; their emotional and organizational mobilization for the earliest possible achievement of these objectives; and their protest when that achievement seems rendered difficult or impossible.

Economic Problems

The most difficult of all the problems confronted in the non-Western world are raised by the underdeveloped peoples' objective of economic development, usually understood to mean industrialization. The reason for this difficulty is essentially that, whereas industrialization in Western Europe and the United States was not originally a planned development but a gradually ripening outgrowth of a large number of accidentally converging circumstances, industrialization in today's underdeveloped nations is sought as something to be imported and achieved full-blown and almost overnight. As a result, since a good many of the circumstances that underlay the West's spontaneous industrialization are not natively present among non-Western peoples, these preconditions must be either artificially created or artificially compensated for.

Among the more important preconditions required for industrialization is, for example, the availability of capital and credit. But how does an underdeveloped, predominantly agricultural people accumulate such capital and credit? Consumption is by tradition at a bare subsistence level. Emergency situations in the lives of the citizens are provided for not through individual financial reserves but within a collectivistic family structure. Where there is a surplus it is invested in such fixed goods as cattle; and when it is liquidated it is not turned into cash but reinvested in terms of the traditional barter system. Who is there to save and lend in such a situation? Who, indeed, feels the needs for the goods that industry can produce? Clearly, patterns and levels of consumption must first be altered; traditional self-sufficient family structures broken down; the barter system replaced by a money economy; and the habit of saving and borrowing introduced. But how? Through changed experiences and changed education. But how does government, assuming that it exists and is strong enough for the purpose, secure the necessary revenues and skills to implement such changes?

Related to the difficulty of the underdeveloped countries in accumulating the capital required for the financing of an industrial base is their problem of securing an aggressive enough entrepreneurship and a sufficiently stable labor force. Here again, non-Western social and cultural patterns operate to the serious disadvantage of the underdeveloped societies. On the subject of the motivation of labor, for example, one eminent anthropologist and student of underdeveloped peoples has this to say:

> It is a commonplace that one of the greatest difficulties faced in the development of enterprises of any sort in underdeveloped areas, whether extractive, agricultural or industrial, is that of holding workers on the job. Typically, what occurs is that men will take employment for a period of time and then, when money to meet specific wants is in hand, leave. . . . A man will work long enough to meet the limited goal set by the needs of his family unit. When he has earned enough for this, he leaves, to return to a mode of life that is in harmony with an economic system that existed before industrialization was introduced into the area, whereby subsistence and prestige wants are satisfied without reference to pecuniary considerations.[2]

A further related obstacle to rapid industrialization throughout the non-Western world lies in the generally low level of education, at least of the empirical and rationalistic variety that successful participation in an industrialized society is known to require. In the first instance, of course, this is a question of generally low literacy rates and of scarcities of technical and administrative skills. Beyond that, however, it is often a matter of culturally and historically conditioned basic beliefs. As has been noted by an official of the American Point IV program, there tends to be a great deal of resistance to changes incident to

industrialization "if they contravene the folklore, religion, super-
stition, magic or other beliefs . . . which serve in ordinary living
to release the anxiety feelings of the individual, for conflicts
with such beliefs threaten the security of the individual." [3]
The problem of modifying or replacing such beliefs, moreover,
is at times rendered especially difficult by the fact that there
are those with a decided vested interest in the way of life of the
pre-industrial order. Thus, "obviously, the medicine man will
resist hospitals and clinics that have no place for him and
tend to drive him out of business." [4]

Difficult as these problems of traditional attitudes are, they
are overshadowed by another and much more ominous question:
Can the underdeveloped peoples modernize and industrialize
rapidly enough to prevent population increases that will wipe
out the significance for their standard of living of whatever economic development they may achieve? That is, as the improvements which they institute in public health and welfare bear
fruit in quickly falling death rates, can they simultaneously—
through changes in family patterns, man-woman relations, and
more effective methods of birth control—also bring down the
birth rates of their societies?

What is involved in this vital question is the well-known
demographic pattern that has historically characterized periods
of modernization and industrialization. The way of life of non-
industrial peoples tends to be characterized by social systems
conducive to high birth rates and poor sanitary and health
conditions that result in correspondingly high death rates. In
such societies, at least over long periods, births and deaths therefore tend to remain in equilibrium. A similar equilibrium tends
to characterize industrialized societies, though for different
reasons. Here sanitary conditions and available medical care are
such as to reduce death rates far below those of underdeveloped
countries; yet at the same time, changed family patterns, more
individualistic attitudes to life, and birth control tend to result
in a corresponding drop in birth rates.

During the transitions from a stage of underdevelopment
to an industrialized socioeconomic order, however, the combinations of circumstances that normally make for such demographic equilibriums tend for a time to be disrupted. For, while

the improvements in sanitation, medical care, and basic education that accompany even the initial steps toward industrialization bring about an immediate reduction in the death rate, the changes in social and cultural patterns that eventually also produce a lowering of the birth rate tend to require several generations to become fully operative. The results, of course, are a large excess of births over deaths lasting for several generations and consequent massive increases in total population. During its most intensive period of industrialization (covering the seventy years from 1821 to 1891), Great Britain, for example, despite exceptionally high emigration, increased its population by 79 per cent. And the period of similar socioeconomic transition in Japan, coming between 1870 and 1940, resulted in a total population growth of 120 per cent.

What will this seemingly inescapable demographic logic of the transition to industrialization mean for that two thirds of the world's 2.5 billion people who live in today's underdeveloped areas? Even as they embark upon industrialization their population densities are formidably high. Given their non-Western cultural backgrounds, moreover, their increases in productivity and adoption of social patterns making for lower birth rates is likely to prove much slower than was true where industrialization evolved indigenously. Nor will they be likely to enjoy any significant opportunities for emigration. Yet disregarding these added handicaps, even if their population increases should be only of the magnitude of those experienced in the West, the economic problems confronting them will be staggering. China, for example, with a present population of some 600 million, by the year 2000 will have reached a figure of approximately 1.2 billion; India, within the span of a lifetime, will have doubled its present population of some 400 million to the vicinity of 800 million; and comparable rises are projected for most of the other nations now embarked on the road of modernization and industrialization.[5]

How can modernization and industrialization be made to proceed quickly enough to cope with the threat of these vast anticipated population rises? Behind the distracting flow of day-to-day events, this is the question upon which the future of today's underdeveloped lands ultimately depends. It is, by the same token, the question upon which our own and the entire world's future rests. We need only remind ourselves of the havoc that European nations wrought upon one another and the rest of mankind during *their* industrial development and demographic expansion. Will not the Asians and Africans too feel driven to embark upon quests for additional resources, markets, living space, and psychological release from their internal tensions? And if and when they do, will it not be we, the citizens of the world's wealthier and less densely populated countries, who will be the most natural victims of their aggressions?

Cultural Problems

Unfortunately as well as fortunately, man does not live by bread alone: fortunately, because if he did he would be nothing more than a physical being, a mere animal; unfortunately, because if he did he would probably come by his bread much more easily. In one sense, for example, the economic problems of the underdeveloped areas are of such magnitude and urgency that their solution would demand a putting aside of all complicating considerations of culture. In another sense, however, man being man, the solution of economic problems—at least above a certain minimum subsistence level—is meaningful only because men do see the world in terms of a culture and because their ultimate purpose in economically improving themselves is to assert themselves more richly and creatively as cultural beings.

It is a characteristic expression of this dilemma of human nature that the cultural aspects of the industrialization of underdeveloped peoples almost everywhere involve one very fundamental ambivalence. That ambivalence consists in the fact that in order more successfully to assert their native identity culturally, in the process of industrializing, these peoples are having to abandon their native identity socially and economically in favor of the ways and methods of the very nations against whom their cultural assertion is primarily directed. In order the better to resist Westernization culturally, they have committed themselves to Westernize their societies economically and socially.

The question raised by this ambivalence is, of course, whether this desire to have one's cake and eat it too will prove possible, and if so, at what price. Will not cultural nativism, however it is asserted, tend to interfere with successful socioeconomic Westernization? And similarly, will not the introduction of Westernization economically and socially tend gradually also to undermine original native cultural identity?

This question was raised with reference to the future of Africa at a Congress of Negro Artists and Writers held in 1956 in Paris, under the auspices of the French-African institute, *Présence Africaine.* Among the assembled intellectuals from all over sub-Sahara Africa and other lands with large Negro populations there emerged two basic and contrary points of view. On one side were the Africanophiles, the proponents of African nativism or "Negritude"; on the other, the Westernizers, who were prepared to concede that most of traditional African culture would prove an impediment to successful modernization and should therefore be sacrificed willingly. Significantly, the most determined spokesmen for the nativist position were representatives from French West Africa, a colonial area where the long-established French policy of attempting culturally to make Frenchmen of Africans has aroused an impassioned desire on the part of the Africans to maintain and assert their native cultural identity.

The central thesis of the Africanophile position was "the need for Negro writers to return to their sources, to the African classics, where they can find as rich a variety of myth and story, poetry and drama, sculpture and decoration, as any man could desire—based on a kind of grasp of man's essential nature that Europe has lost. . . . We are very old, and all our future achievement depends upon grasping and using this ancient African inheritance." [6] The Westernizers' answer to this thesis, formulated most prominently by the American-African writer, Richard Wright, was unromantic and matter-of-fact:

> These traditional cultures . . . might they not simply be, in the contemporary context, a beautiful dream? Had they any relevance, really, to the needs of contemporary African man? The ancestor-cult religion . . . with all of its manifold poetic richness, that created a sense of self-sufficiency—did not that religion, when the

European guns came in, act as sort of an aid to those guns? Did that religion help people to resist fiercely and hardily and hurl the Europeans out? . . . We are very young; and while we can admire this ancient culture, we must recognize that, wherever it survives, it is the reflection of a moribund medieval metaphysic: the ideas which we can use are secular, scientific, Western.[7]

In itself, cultural nativism, in the sense of identification with pre-industrial values and traditions, can lend itself to useful as well as destructive purposes. If it most often and noisily operates with the latter consequence, the reason is that it tends most naturally to become appropriated by reactionaries who endeavor to employ its appeal to masquerade their own vested interests. When expressed honestly, on the other hand, it may serve ends of a most worth-while nature. In already industrialized and democratized societies, for example, it may provide the individual with precious inner convictions and strength to resist the many pressures upon him merely to live a life of acquiescent adjustment and conformity. Among underdeveloped peoples, still lacking established national institutional patterns, it may constitute a most effective inspiration for common effort, discipline, and sacrifice.

An example of such enlightened cultural nativism among underdeveloped peoples is the jealously African but politically responsible Pan-African movement. Whether, in view of African internal diversities, anything tangible ever comes of this movement's efforts seems doubtful. Its value for the present lies in its exhortation, in the name of the native cultural ideal of Africanism, to intra-African understanding and co-operation for the most rational and creative possible development of Africa by and for Africans. The movement's approach to the problems of Africa's political future, for example, has been set forth as follows:

> Black Africa as a whole has not reached the stage to achieve a democratic system. Even among old nations few have reached near that ideal. If the greater Africa is to be, we of this generation, the initiators of this Pan-African movement, must be altogether tolerant to all forms of government practices by the Africans. . . .
> Furthermore, the case before our generation is not whether we are going to choose between the western philosophy of democracy, the Stalinist philosophy of democracy, Hitlerism or Fascism,

Christianity or Islamism. Our duty is to lay the foundations of an
African ideology suited to our race, our history, our traditions, our
geographical position, our destiny, and to set an ideal toward which
our offspring will work.[8]

Undoubtedly, the cultural tensions between nativism and
modernization will long play a considerable part in the development of the non-Western world, especially because industrialism
is so thoroughly alien to the indigenous ways of life of these
societies. Yet while the presence of these tensions will certainly
affect the progress that can be made in the solution of economic
and political problems, the measure of progress achieved in this
latter regard will in turn strongly affect the significance of the
cultural tensions. As we know from the history of the older
West, it is principally in situations of economic and political
stress and strain that societies suffer from cultural ambivalence
and conflict. In conditions of stability and harmony, in contrast,
pre-industrial traditions and the ways of democracy and industrialism not only can harmlessly coexist, but can even
mutually support each other to a people's over-all enrichment.
One need only recall the fortunate experience of the British in
combining age-old historical traditions and symbols with the
contemporary processes of democratic and industrial society.

Political Problems

The evolution that the underdeveloped peoples are undergoing in pursuit of their objective of political freedom and
equality is in its essentials the same as that which was experienced earlier by the nations of the West. Indeed, the West has
never understood the dynamic of its own political development
as fully as during the past decade when, with the perspective of
an observer, it has witnessed the establishment of the nations
and governments of the non-Western world.

What differences there have been between earlier Western
and contemporary non-Western political developments have
chiefly been those of timing. Britain as a nation, and liberal
parliamentary democracy as its form of government, evolved
and matured over a period of centuries. Nations like India,
Ghana, and the Republic of Indonesia were created almost over-

night. That these new nations and their governments should require further years and decades of crisis, experiment, and consolidation to transform legally established institutions into effectively operating political realities is therefore not surprising.

The fundamental political problem confronting the under-developed peoples is that of achieving a politically workable national consensus. This, as it has been in the West, is a matter of overcoming age-old linguistic, religious, social, economic, and political divisions in order to make possible general acceptance of the decision making of a common government, representing an acknowledged common collective interest. As has been noted with reference to the nations of the West, it is above all the measure of success achieved in the development of such a free national consensus that determines a people's potential for political stability and freedom and, in times of crisis, survival.

Among the newly established or about-to-be-established non-Western nations the achievement of such a politically work-able national consensus is raising the most difficult problems. The central government of the new state of Ghana, the former British Gold Coast, has had to cope with the trying task of integrating into its national life the proud and regionally minded chiefs of the interior Ashanti people. The Republic of Indonesia, comprised of dozens of East Indian islands, has been torn by civil war among hostile religious, regional, and socioeconomic groups. The small nation of Ceylon has experienced repeated and bloody clashes between religious and linguistic interests. Even India, more than a decade after independence, continues to be seriously handicapped by its deep-rooted traditional divisions. In fact, as one Western student of Indian affairs has pointed out, in a number of respects the country's prenational fragmentation has even been aggravated by its establishment as a liberal democratic nation-state:

> The problem of national unity is an old one in India. . . .
> Most of the current divisions—language, caste, religion, and re-gionalism—have long histories, but the more recent agitation has been compounded by a number of new elements. For one thing, formation of a democratic independent state has opened up new possibilities for the achievement of objectives by subnational groups; the possibility of change is greater than ever before, and

access to means for effecting change is easier. A national democratic government, by its very nature, must be more responsive to popular demands than a foreign authoritarian government. Secondly, and perhaps most important of all, the Western impact has intensified existing divisions and created others not only as a result of the imperial "divide and rule" policy, but by the divergent effect of the West on different groups within Indian society. For example . . . the West has raised the expectations of tribal, untouchable and other underprivileged groups by making them aware of their status in society; the result is the rise of new self-conscious interest groups expressing demands not only for special legislation, but frequently for direct political power as a means of asserting their cultural identity. The demands of many of the tribal groups for states of their own is one illustration of this.

A third element in the growth of subnational allegiances, or what one might call "particularism," is the threat which a number of minority groups feel as a result of the growing inroads of the Hindu religion. . . . A fourth element . . . has been the modern development of mass communication. A century ago, the absence of easy methods of transportation and communication put severe limitations on the size of a group, whereas it is now possible for national or subnational allegiances to cover large areas. . . . Were India not already divided by linguistic and other cultural barriers, then mass communication might have served solely as a means of reinforcing nationalism; but given the divisions which were there historically, existing ties in language and culture could be intensified by easier methods of communication.

Many Indian, as well as foreign observers, have been very much concerned lest the growth of these subnational loyalties interfere with the development of a strong national unity. Many have come to feel that the problem of achieving national unity is even more pressing than the problem of economic development, since the latter is hardly possible without the former.[9]

Upon such precarious internal unity, in India as in most other new non-Western nations, have been imposed various versions of the Western type of representative parliamentary institutions. In the first flush of independence, the formal establishment of these institutions has been acclaimed with overwhelming support and enthusiasm: independence has meant, at long last, the achievement of self-government and the attainment of equality of status and dignity with the former occupy-

ing colonial powers. Yet once this initial sense of national
fulfillment has been enjoyed, there has remained the much less
glamorous challenge of effecting day-to-day national political
expression in terms of the new institutions. If the first political
problem of the new underdeveloped peoples be described as that
of achieving a national consensus, their second and hardly less
basic problem is the related one of mobilizing such national consensus as exists in terms of political parties that are able to staff
and operate the new governmental machinery.

Almost everywhere, the initial postindependence national
life of underdeveloped peoples has been dominated by the
political parties and movements under whose leadership national
status and self-government were achieved. In India, for example,
it has been Nehru's Congress party that has supplied postindependence government, and in Ghana this function has been
performed by Nkrumah's Convention People's party. For the
longer run, however, the problem of political parties in these new
nations appears far from solved. There is, in the first place, the
question whether the heterogeneous independence parties can
maintain themselves, both internally and in their relations with
the electorate. As long as they retain as their central figures the
original heroes of the fight for independence, men of the political appeal and statesmanship of a Nehru or an Nkrumah, their
hold on government seems assured. Thereafter, most experts
agree, the formation of majorities to operate stable representative government may be expected to pose serious and prolonged
problems. The danger of this development is all the greater
because of a second important circumstance characterizing the
political life of most of the new non-Western nations: the
general absence of any strong opposition parties capable of
forming an alternative government in the event of the disintegration or electoral defeat of the originally dominant independence
parties. To quote again from Professor Wiener on the situation
in India:

> In virtually every state [India's federal divisions] in which
> there is the possibility of a Congress [party] defeat, no one party
> by itself is in a position to assume power. This feature of instability
> is further complicated by the fact that the opposition parties them-
> selves are badly split, sometimes by personality differences but often

on fundamental ideological questions. There is little agreement among the oppositional groups as to the nature of the Indian state. There are some, including the Communist and the Marxist left groups, who reject the democratic framework; others, like the Hindu communal parties, reject the secular framework; and still others, such as linguistic and other provincial groups, reject the present national framework. Without a basic consensus on the value of democracy, secularism, and nationalism, it is hardly possible for opposition groups to work together for long periods of time.[10]

These problems of governmental operation and political consensus involve another important long-range challenge: the question of ultimate political direction and leadership. During the first generation in the lives of these new nations their course is being determined largely by the pre-independence captaincy of Western-trained statesmen. Politically and culturally, Nehru and the Indian leaders in his age group are as much Englishmen as they are Indians. The leaders of African independence, too, are almost without exception men who received their early schooling in European-run public or mission schools and who attended universities in Britain, the United States, or continental Europe. With the present generation of leaders the direction of the new underdeveloped nations thus remains in the hands of men who politically and culturally are still in large measure Westerners. The reason that this is significant is that though their goal is to serve their own nations, and though—like everyone else—they are prepared to compromise with necessities, they have shown themselves deeply committed not only to Western civilization's techniques and amenities but to its underlying philosophical ideals as well.

Can this Western philosophical direction of the new non-Western nations be sustained after the present Western-trained leaders, and perhaps their sons, have passed from the scene? Or, as would prove equally satisfactory, can it be replaced by a similar direction of native origin? To pose these questions is not to suggest any new justification for Western cultural imperialism or for "the white man's burden." In its practical operations, one must admit, Western civilization has engaged in brutalities unrivaled by any other. Yet what throughout so many ages has repeatedly enabled Western civilization to save itself from self-corruption has been the fact that it has possessed its Greco-Roman and Judaeo-Christian ideal intellectual and normal standards. For these, regardless of how many follies and crimes have been committed in their names, have provided concepts and values in terms of which man possessed both dignity *in* himself and significance *beyond* himself. How many times these intellectual and spiritual standards have been disregarded and compromised, our history painfully records; yet they have always been there to return to and, through readaptation, to derive redirection from.

Even in our contemporary Western civilization where these ideals are the native heritage, they today seem in danger of being relativized and rationalized out of existence by democratic-industrial society's logic of conformity in return for economic success and social approval. How much greater will be the danger of ultimately valueless abdication to socioeconomic fulfillment on the part of the non-Western world. There our Western civilization's more transcendental values are established only very tenuously; such native cultural direction as exists tends to be so incompatible with industrialization that it is likely to remain powerless; above all, since the need for socioeconomic improvement is so much greater, it may also prove much more costly in terms of individual human dignity.

Challenge to the West

The West's interest in the future of the underdeveloped nations is both altruistic and selfish. It is selfish in the sense that we know that we will increasingly need these peoples' resources and good will to maintain our own prosperity and security. It is altruistic in the sense that we wish that they too may be enabled to enjoy the inspiration of our Western civilization's basic values and the benefits of its more efficient technology and organizational methods.

From the point of view of the underdeveloped peoples, Western civilization seems today to offer itself in two versions: the liberal democratic version represented internationally by the Atlantic alliance under the leadership of the United States;

and the Communist version typified and internationally supported by the Soviet Union. On what bases, it is therefore vital for us to consider, will the underdeveloped nations make their choice? What are the advantages and prospects they see in our version of Western civilization and in international alignment with us? What are the appeals for them of communism and of international liaison with the Soviet Union?

Fortunately, the appeal of communism among today's underdeveloped peoples is not a matter of intrinsic preference for Russia over the United States or for the theories of Karl Marx over the governmental philosophy of the West. Such appeal as communism exercises for these peoples is primarily a matter of practical national interest. Their concern is the solution of their economic, cultural, and political problems. The question they ask is essentially this: What principle of political and economic organization and what international relationships promise to help solve our problems the more rapidly and effectively? The method of politico-economic development of liberal democracy they see as one of immediate freedom, immediate reliance upon the economic and political initiative of the people, and dependence for industrial capitalization upon funds borrowed from more economically advanced nations abroad. Communism, in contrast, they see as the method of regimentation, financial self-sufficiency, and centralized planning by a dictatorial native political elite.

Unfortunately, in competing with the appeal of communism as a guide for the political consolidation and economic development of the new non-Western nations, we begin with a serious initial disadvantage. This disadvantage lies in the fact that we in the West are at a much more advanced stage of political and economic development than are the underdeveloped nations looking for guidance. Our recommendation to them to rely for their development upon the humanitarian ways of liberal democracy as we now practice them is the recommendation of people who have long since passed through and solved the problems that these non-Western nations still have before them. Politically and economically, that is, we are rather like successful self-made men giving advice to younger men who must still travel the road to success. We tell them not to drive themselves too hard, not to compete with each other too fiercely, and to show proper regard for their own and other men's dignity. But this humanitarian prescription is not the one that in fact guided us in our own earlier pursuit of success. It is the wisdom of success achieved: if followed, the younger men listening to us may fear, it might well make impossible the achievement of success.

As has been shown earlier in these pages, the establishment of the nation-states of Western Europe was accomplished not by the humanitarian methods of liberal democracy but through the agency of a succession of authoritarian monarchs prepared to employ every known stratagem of treachery, violence, and suppression. The reduction of the power of royal absolutism, in turn, was by no means what we today would call a civilized achievement; even in England, it required a cruel civil war, the public execution of a king, and an aftermath of nearly a decade of dictatorship. The institutional implementation of the ideal of liberal democracy that followed was itself a long and tortuous process; for centuries the British Parliament was not the affair of the British people as a whole but of a small oligarchical elite; it was not until after the middle of the last century that the majority of Britons were accorded even the formal right to vote. Nor was the economic system that accumulated the capital for the decisive initial steps toward industrialization the humane and egalitarian welfare-capitalism that we enjoy today. Rather, for several economically crucial generations, the order of the day was ruthless production-minded discipline, subsistence-level wages, and eighty-hour workweeks.

Steps and stages such as these—hardly less harsh than the method of political and economic development today represented by communism—went into the making of our present efficient and humanitarian Western order of things. Yet what we are in effect asking of the underdeveloped peoples is that they achieve these same high levels of efficiency and humanity without passing through such a painful and protracted process. Indications are, indeed, that most of the underdeveloped nations would be most happy to comply with our request. The question they ask, and that we must answer, is how they can do this and at the same time solve their gigantic and pressing problems.

The answer is obvious: we must assist these peoples in all

the ways necessary to enable them to avoid the necessity of regimentation and coercion and, hence, the temptation to look to communism for guidance and inspiration. In a sense, we are concerned with two interdependent variables—coercion and aid. To minimize the measure of coercion required (for such purposes as capital formation, land reform, industrial construction, and education), the underdeveloped countries are in need of our financial and technical aid. The more of such aid we provide (assuming that it is intelligently and responsibly applied), the less need they will have to resort to coercion and the methods of communism. The less of such aid from us, the greater will be their temptation to reject liberal democratic methods and to fall back upon the Russian type of politico-economic development.

Nor should we refuse to recognize this logic because of the inclination of the underdeveloped nations to neutralism and their willingness to accept aid from the Soviet Union. The hard fact is that in their present circumstances these nations cannot afford to reject aid of any kind, whatever the source. Nor would it be rational for many of them to make unconditional commitments in international politics. To understand their situation one need only recall the similar reasoning of American leaders during a comparable period of early United States history. In 1792, for example, Austria, Prussia, Sardinia, Great Britain, and the United Netherlands were ranged in the so-called War of the First Coalition against Revolutionary France, which was tied to the United States by a treaty of alliance. Should the United States honor its obligation to France in her fight for liberty? George Washington's decision, given in a proclamation of neutrality in April, 1793, was in the negative. Why? Alexander Hamilton, in a series of articles defending Washington's stand, summed up the answer: "The obligation to assist the cause of liberty must be deduced from the merits of the cause *and from the interest we have in its support.*" [11]

It is this same ultimate reasoning, under comparable circumstances, which guides the international policies of today's new and underdeveloped nations: the reasoning of their national self-interest as they see it. We have no alternative but to respect that reasoning. And if we wish to see it operate to the advantage of our ideological satisfaction and national self-interest, we have no alternative but to make what we have to offer—by way of understanding, assistance, and international leadership—seem more attractive than what is being offered by the Russians in the name of communism. Had the United States not followed a course of opportunistic neutrality while it was in its interest to do so, the result might well have been to prejudice America's ability to fulfill itself in the longer run. Perhaps in the future the same will be said of the neutralism being practiced by some of today's new and underdeveloped nations.

SELECTED BIBLIOGRAPHY

BOWLES, CHESTER. *Africa's Challenge to America,* Los Angeles, University of California Press, 1956.

DEAN, VERA MICHELES. *The Nature of the Non-Western World,* New York, Mentor, 1957.

EMERSON, RUPERT. *Representative Government in Southeast Asia,* Cambridge, Mass., Harvard University Press, 1955.

GOLDBERG, HARVEY. *French Colonialism: Progress or Poverty?* (Source Problems in World Civilization), New York, Rinehart, 1959.

GUNTHER, JOHN. *Inside Africa,* New York, Harper, 1953.

HOLLAND, WILLIAM L., ed. *Asian Nationalism and the West,* New York, Macmillan, 1953.

VILLARD, HENRY H. *Economic Development,* New York, Rinehart, 1959.

Politics
as International Relations

« 14 »

The United States
and World Politics

TWENTIETH-CENTURY WORLD POLITICS has been dominated by the working out of two contrary processes. On the one hand, the nations have attempted ever more desperately to maximize their power and to achieve for themselves the greatest possible economic and military self-sufficiency; on the other, the measure of power and self-sufficiency that the nations have managed to achieve has proved less and less effective in providing the standards of welfare and the assurance of security that their citizens have demanded.

The hopelessness of the resulting dilemma is generally recognized. The growing inadequacy and irrationality of the nation-state as the legally and morally ultimate unit of political organization is widely admitted. And the need for political organization and moral loyalty on a world scale is urged almost universally. But how to translate this global agreement into global political reality? How to make the shift from the anarchical interaction of national interests and sovereignties to the order of a universal political and moral community? That is the challenge with which the international political events and crises of our times are confronting us. It is a challenge that will continue to confront our children and our children's children.

The development of the nation-state out of chaotic post-feudal particularism required several centuries. The evolution of a global political community out of the disorder of dozens of very different and competing nation-states is not, in its turn, likely to occur any more quickly. Yet that it will occur is almost a certainty; the logic of the globally triumphant democratic-industrial revolution demands it. It demands it on grounds of economic efficiency and universal welfare. And it demands it, above all, to save mankind from the danger of global self-destruction through international nuclear war.

The Balance of Power

The anarchical competition of national states seeking to maximize their power and security has not, despite its tragic cost, been an expression either of human folly or evil. It has resulted, rather, from combinations of cultural, social, and economic circumstances that men have not had it in their power to evade or quickly to alter. International differences in cultural and socioeconomic patterns and interests have been such that a politically workable consensus simply could not be organized on any more inclusive basis than that of the nation-state. The limited boundaries of the nations have merely expressed the fact that mankind's ability to communicate and to live and work as a member of a social team has been confined to geographically limited areas and numerically limited groups.

Until very recently there were lacking both enough motivation and sufficiently advanced technology to overcome the circumstances impeding the world's political organization into larger than national units. In pre-industrial and predemocratic times the vast majority of men's social and economic expectations were modest enough to be adequately met by the resources available to their individual nations. Nor did the citizens of the traditional nation-states feel reason to rebel against the existing order of things on grounds of inadequate security. On the one hand, available military means were such that with recourse to an occasional limited war external threats could be kept in check or removed. And, on the other, the undertaking of more ambitious politico-military operations, such as would have been required to supplant the national with a larger political order, remained militarily beyond the realm of technological possibility.

The most characteristic international expression of these circumstances of the nation-states, and at the same time a factor that heavily contributed to enabling nation-state politics to survive so long, was the success of the strategy of balance of power. Evolved even as the nation-states were being established, this strategy of keeping power in balance by means of alliances, diplomatic maneuverings, and limited wars was first described in English in the following passage of an essay, *Of Empire,* by the Elizabethan philosopher, Francis Bacon. The dynamics of international politics, Bacon here observed, could not be summed up in any general rule

> save one which ever holdeth—which is, that princes do keep due sentinel, that none of their neighbors do overgrow so (by increase of territory, by embracing of trade, by approaches, or the like), as they become more able to annoy them than they were. . . . During that triumvirate of kings, King Henry VIII of England, Francis I, King of France, and Charles V, emperor, there was such a watch kept that none of the three could win a palm of ground, but the other two would straightways balance it, either by confederation, or, if need were, by a war. . . .[1]

Until the outbreak of World War I, international politics in terms of this principle of balance of power remained supreme and unquestioned. Then, in one sudden and tragic event, the old logic failed. For, instead of becoming involved in a limited conflict of adjustment as in the past, the European nations between 1914 and 1918 fell victim to a total war in which they not only permanently crippled one another but also permanently undermined their collective European power and influence vis-à-vis the rest of the world.

Underlying this tragic failure of the strategy of balance of power was the fact that, during the nineteenth century, Europe had been transformed by the democratic-industrial revolution into a very different civilization from that which in the fourteenth and fifteenth centuries had originally found its political expression in the nation-state system. This transformation was reflected most obviously in two circumstances. In the first place, the military weapons that the science and technology of the new industrial systems had made available were of a much more formidable kind than any that had ever been known before. Traditionally, the nation-state and its strategy had been based upon the musket, the cannon ball, and the horse; and, except in cases of enemy occupation, the only sector of the population involved in hostilities comprised the members of the armed forces. By 1914–1918, in contrast, war had become a matter of massed heavy artillery, grenades, machine guns, armored cars, tanks, and airplanes; and in support of the lethal new in-dustrial war machines entire economies and nations had to be mobilized. Before, casualties had been counted in the thousands and tens of thousands; now, the lists of dead ran into the millions. Before, wars had been safely and rationally employable means of statecraft; now, once a war was begun, its own tech-nological and psychological logic threatened to consume not only those against whom it was fought but the fighters themselves.

Related to this revolutionary change in the costliness and destructiveness of the nation-states' instruments of war, resulting from industrialization, was the hardly less significant change in their decision-making processes that resulted from political de-mocratization. From the nation-states' establishment until well into the nineteenth century, Europe's foreign-policy makers had not been the people as a whole but, in each nation, a king or a small circle of aristocrats. These, as one political historian has characterized them,

> were in constant, intimate contact with the princes and the aristo-cratic rulers of other nations. They were joined together by family ties, a common language (French), common cultural values, a com-mon style of life, and common moral convictions about what a gentleman was and was not allowed to do in his relations with an-other gentleman, whether of his own or of a foreign nation. The princes competing for power considered themselves competitors in a game whose rules were accepted by all the other competitors.[2]

Such international competition within gentlemanly limits could exist as long as those in control required for the execution of their policies nothing more than the obedience of their soldiers and the passive acquiescence of their general citizenry. As war became a more total process, however, this precondition for the maintenance of aristocratic foreign-policy making, and of the moderating benefits thereof, rapidly ceased to prevail. Because the general public's participation in the course of World War I had steadily to be increased, it was inevitable that, in return, the direction of the war had also progressively to be democratized and surrendered from the hands of the traditional policy makers to those of the citizenry as a whole. By 1917, as Walter Lippmann has put it,

> The existing governments had exhausted their imperium—their authority to bind and their power to command. With their traditional means they were no longer able to carry on the hyperbolic war; yet they were unable to negotiate peace. They had, therefore, to turn to the people. They had to ask still greater exertions and sacrifices. They obtained them by "democratizing" the conduct and the aim of the war: by pursuing total victory and by promising total peace. In substance they ceded the executive power of decision over the strategical and the political conditions for concluding the war. In effect they lost control of the war.[3]

In the long run, this involvement of the people in the making and carrying out of foreign-policy decisions was undeniably a progressive step. International political community—assuming that that is our ultimate objective—is possible only as an expression of a prior international cultural, social, and economic community. For centuries the foreign-policy monopoly of the traditional European elites served as a compensation for the absence of such a community. It performed the vital function of making possible more or less orderly relations among peoples in spite of their cultural and socioeconomic differences. Yet in so doing it also deprived the world's peoples of the necessity and opportunity of undergoing the only kind of common experience from which community can develop: that is, the overcoming of differences of interest and identity through a process of direct contact, conflict, and mutually imposed suffering leading to the eventual discovery and acknowledgment of a higher and transcending *common* interest and identity.

In the shorter run, however, until such time as international differences among peoples could be transcended, the projection of these differences into international relations through the democratization of foreign policy was bound to prove most disruptive. It made national policy a much more easily manipulable instrument of whatever domestic vested interests—whether responsible or not—happened to succeed in winning the electorate's backing. It emotionalized the making and carrying out of foreign-policy decisions by encouraging the individual citizen to identify his own personal psychological impulses with the international policies and experiences of his country. And, perhaps most serious of all, it tended to make international relations much more rigid and uncompromising. It did this because of the peoples' insistence upon ascribing to the international policies of nations the moral standards of right and wrong that prevailed in private relationships. And since the natural inclination in international conflicts was to claim right and justice for one's own nation's position and impute wrong and evil to the other nation, relations between states tended to become much more easily stalemated and embittered than had been true during the amoral chess-game diplomacy of the cosmopolitan nation-state aristocracies.

Even today, four decades after World War I, we have not yet succeeded in devising and implementing forms of political organization to make the rational most of our civilization's economic, technological, and psychological potentialities. On the surface, indeed, world politics appears to be much as it has been for centuries: we have our sovereign nations—more numerous, in fact, than ever before—and we have a constant rivalry and balancing of power among them. Yet such surface appearances are misleading. The old nation-state system may still exist in form; in essence, however, it is undergoing decisive alterations. And although these alterations still fall far short of what is required, they undeniably represent important advances in the direction we must travel.

The most important contemporary alteration in the traditional pattern of world politics has resulted from the development of a small number—at present two—dominant international power blocs, each centering about one of the world's superpowers. It has been the most significant consequence of this development that the course of world politics is no longer, as it was in the past, determined by one single type of relationship— that among individual sovereign states. Today, rather, decisions as to what shall and shall not happen in world affairs are the outcome of the interaction of no less than three types of relationships: first, as before, the relationships of sovereign nations *with* other sovereign nations; second, the relationships of superpowers and their associated nations *within* the world's power blocs; and third, the relationships *between* power blocs.

The significance of this development is that it serves to make the decisions taken in world politics at once more internationally responsive as well as responsible. The reason for this is that in terms of whichever of the three relationships a decision is contemplated, it must take into consideration the two further relationships in which the decision makers are simultaneously involved.

In 1954, for example, during the Communist victories in French Indo-China, the United States was confronted with the question whether or not actively to intervene. A half century earlier the issue could have been decided unilaterally and with reference to no other considerations than a narrowly national understanding of the country's national interest and the anticipated reactions of the American electorate. By 1954 there were two additional sets of questions to be weighed. What was the thinking on the matter of the various members of the power bloc with whose collective interest the more immediate American national interest was identified? And what would be the effects of the decision upon relations between the American-led power bloc as a whole and the system of hegemony of the Soviet Union?

The same diffusion and limitation of international initiative through enlargement of the framework in terms of which decisions must be made can be assumed to be operative within the orbit of the Soviet Union. Before World War I, for example, the decision of two Balkan nations to make war upon each other was in law as well as in fact wholly their own affair (regardless of how many other nations might later be involved in the war and compelled to suffer its damages). Today such a unilateral and internationally nonresponsible decision would be most unlikely. The two nations in conflict would be compelled to consider not only their immediate nation-to-nation relationship but, no less, their relationship to the Soviet leadership of their power bloc and, beyond that, the relationship of the Soviet power bloc as a whole to the American-led power bloc of the West. Should the two nations in question ignore these large interdependencies and responsibilities of their national decisions, their actions— as happened within the American power bloc when the United States halted the unilateral British-French invasion of Egypt in 1956—would undoubtedly bring quick intervention by the Soviet Union.

What this increasing responsiveness and responsibility of international decision making above all reflects is the nations' and peoples' growing need of one another's co-operation. The cost and destructiveness of present-day weapons, the rising standards of living of the democratic welfare state, and the resulting increase in international economic interdependence are creating problems with which neither large nations nor small can any longer cope independently. Ideally, these problems could most rationally and happily be solved through organization on a global basis. Until the achievement of such global organization becomes possible, however, the usefulness and significance of the currently evolving pattern of informal international accommodation through politics within and between power blocs should not be overlooked.

Temporarily disruptive reassertions of the former type of nonresponsible nation-to-nation relations will no doubt continue for decades. But both within and between power blocs they are likely to become steadily less frequent and less far-reaching. Even between power blocs there is, if nothing more, the common and disciplining interest in avoiding mutual nuclear annihilation. And within power blocs even the superpowers cannot afford too frequently or wantonly to defy the moderating complexity and weight of the larger patchwork of common interests. What happens when they do, the course of such nations as Yugoslavia, Egypt, and India indicates: the alienated nations defect from the existing power blocs and move to fashion blocs of their own. And while such third-force blocs may not enjoy the actual military strength of the two dominant ones, rivalry between the latter assures them—as the positions of both Yugoslavia and Egypt demonstrate—of survival and considerable bargaining power to boot.

International Organization

A further major factor which has contributed to the changing relationships among nations has been the development of systems of international organization for collective security: the League of Nations, and, after World War II, the United Nations. The stated purpose of both these arrangements has been to provide for the settlement of international disputes without resort to war and, if such peaceful settlement fails, to array the collective international might of all the nations against the aggressor. In the Charter of the League of Nations, this purpose was put most succinctly in Article 10, according to which the "Members of the League undertake to respect and preserve as against external aggression the territorial integrity and existing political independence of all Members of the League. In case of any such aggression or in any threat or danger of such aggression the Council shall advise upon the means by which this obligation shall be fulfilled." In the United Nations Charter this similar central purpose is summarized at the beginning of Article 1: "To maintain international peace and security, and to that end: to take effective collective measures for the prevention and removal of threats to the peace, and for the suppression of acts of aggression or other breaches of the peace, and to bring about by peaceful means, and in conformity with the principles of justice and international law, adjustment or settlement of international disputes or situations which might lead to a breach of the peace. . . ." In addition, the United Nations is described in the same introductory article as intended to serve such larger and less exclusively political purposes as "to develop friendly relations among nations . . . to strengthen universal peace; to achieve international cooperation in solving international problems of an economic, social, cultural, or humanitarian character, and . . . to be a center for harmonizing the actions of nations in the attainment of these common ends."

In over-all appearance the League of Nations, and even more so the United Nations, would thus seem to have provided for a supranational government in effect supplanting the in-

dividual nations' ultimate sovereignty and need to engage in
the politics of balance of power. In actual fact, however, this
has not been so. In the case of both the League and the United
Nations, traditional nation-state realities have continued to be
recognized fully. Each member nation, regardless of size and
power, has, following the custom first formulated by Grotius in
1625, been acknowledged as sovereign and equal in its rights with
all the others. In the United Nations Charter, moreover, the most
determining of all the traditional nation-state realities has been
frankly faced: the dominant role of the major world powers in
international politics and their desire—and ability—to fashion
and carry out their policies without externally imposed restraints.

Recognition of this reality is, in fact, central to the entire
United Nations structure. According to the Charter, Article 24,
the organization's members, "confer on the Security Council
primary responsibility for the maintenance of international
peace and security, and agree that in carrying out its duties
under this responsibility the Security Council acts on their
behalf." Since the five permanent members of the Security
Council (in contrast to its six elected nonpermanent members)
are the United States, the Soviet Union, Britain, France, and
China (representing, since the Communist take-over, Chiang
Kai-shek's Formosa), this means that the United Nations' management of world affairs is in the hands of the same powers
that would be globally dominant even if the United Nations did
not exist. By Article 27, moreover, insisted upon at the time of
the Charter's framing by both the Soviet Union and the United
States, limitations upon the freedom of action of the major
powers, that is, the Security Council's five permanent members,
are recognized to be possible on a voluntary basis only. All
substantive decisions of the Security Council, even in regard to
threats to peace and collective security in which one or more
of its members may be directly or indirectly involved, must be
taken "by an affirmative vote of seven members, including the
concurring votes of the permanent members . . ."

Features such as these, as well as the record of the operations
of the United Nations, show that the organization is certainly
not, in any meaningful sense of the term, a supranational
government. It is, in fact, little more than a permanent inter-

national conference institutionalized in the name of the ideal of world government but expressing in its actual operations, as all conferences do, the objectives and power relationships of its members. Yet it is precisely in this more modest respect that the United Nations has made its valuable contribution. In affording the opportunity for public discussion of the moral and political complexities of international differences—whether within power blocs or between them—it has operated as a subtle but important deterrent to disruptive unilateral national behavior and, thereby, has combined with the circumstances already cited to increase the nations' sense of international interdependence and responsibility. Once again, defiances of the larger consensus represented by the nations' adherence to the United Nations and its ideals will probably occur for many years to come. Yet these too can be expected to become less and less frequent and internationally disruptive. The only danger of a contrary development would be if either of the present superpowers should succeed in making the United Nations its own national instrument or should withdraw from the organization altogether. In view, however, of even the superpowers' economic and military interdependence with other nations within and outside their power blocs, their complete domination of the United Nations is not likely to prove possible; and their withdrawal—even should they be so tempted—is likely to seem too costly in necessary international good will to be consummated.

The American Approach

Every nation approaches the definition and carrying out of its role in international relations in its own idiom, conditioned by its own political and cultural past and by what it believes to be the requirements of its present situation. In the case of the twentieth-century United States, both the theory and the practice of foreign policy have been the expression of one dominant image: that of a powerful and secure nation championing for mankind the cause of international morality and legality. It was this image that inspired in Woodrow Wilson the vision of the League of Nations; that has manifested itself in the American inclination to set great store by formal international treaties; that has caused Americans to react with severe indignation to the conduct of other nations seemingly less mindful of the dictates of international morality and legality; and that has expressed itself since World War II in the tendency to explain American international objectives and policies primarily in terms of liberal democratic ideology.

The appropriateness and usefulness of this dominant American foreign-policy image has been challenged on three principal grounds. On a most general level it has been objected that the application of standards of legality and morality to international relations is, in effect, a case of putting the cart before the horse. Law and morality, this view holds, can have meaning and be considered binding only if they are the expression of a prior agreement as to what shall be considered legal and moral and what shall not. Where such a prior consensus is lacking—as it still is in international politics—the characterization of any specific behavior as legal and moral (or illegal and immoral) must, it is maintained, be rejected for one of two reasons: either because it is a self-deception obscuring the fact that the consensus of interest and view of which international law and morality *could* be a meaningful and commonly acknowledged expression still remains to be created; or because it is a conscious or unconscious cloak for a power-motivated interest in the maintenance of the international *status quo*.

The writer who has been most severe in his attacks upon the premature application of concepts of morality and legality in the relations of nations with one another has been the well-known British historian, E. H. Carr. Whether one agrees with his conclusions or not, Carr's book, *The Twenty Years Crisis,* must be rated as one of the most penetrating studies of the dynamics of world politics ever written. In it, on the subject of the affinity for internationally moralizing and legalizing of the Western democracies in general, he summarizes his thesis as follows:

> Just as the ruling class in a community prays for domestic peace, which guarantees its own security and predominance, and denounces class-war, which might threaten them, so international peace becomes a special vested interest of predominant Powers. In

the past, Roman and British imperialism were commended to the
world in the guise of the *pax Romana* and the *pax Britannica*. Today, when no single Power is strong enough to dominate the world,
and supremacy is vested in a group of nations, slogans like "collective security" and "resistance to aggression" serve the same purpose of proclaiming an identity of interest between the dominant
group and the world as a whole in the maintenance of peace. . . .
There is a sense in which peace and co-operation between nations
or classes or individuals is a common and universal end irrespec-
tive of conflicting interests and politics. There is a sense in which
a common interest exists in the maintenance of order, whether it
be international order or "law and order" within the nation. But
as soon as the attempt is made to apply these supposedly abstract
principles to a concrete political situation, they are revealed as
the transparent disguises of selfish vested interests. The bankruptcy
of utopianism resides not in its failure to live up to its principles,
but in the exposure of its inability to provide any absolute and dis-
interested standard for the conduct of international affairs.[4]

A second and closely related objection to the tendency
to conceive of international relationships in terms of legality
and morality has been voiced by Charles Burton Marshall, a
former member of the Policy Planning Staff of the United States
Department of State. What Marshall deplores in the inclination
to aim for and rely upon international legal and moral commitments is, as he sees it, that it lulls the democratic citizenry
into a false sense of security, diverts attention from underlying
power realities, and so discourages preparedness for effectively
dealing with the issues to which these power realities in the long
run inevitably give rise. For example, on the subject of the
long-held American premise that disruptive world political conflicts could be eliminated by the establishment of "a great network of international engagements to resort to arbitration of
differences," Marshall offers the following observation:

> In a period of about thirty-five years, the United States entered
> into ninety-seven international arbitrational and conciliative con-
> tracts. To what practical effect? The permanent engagements for ar-
> bitrations so elaborately worked out with great public éclat have
> proved relevant in a few claim adjudications of no moment what-
> soever and, if memory serves, in the settlement between ourselves
> and other states of two issues of substance. One case, adjudicated

about forty-five years ago, involved the interpretation of a treaty between the United States and Great Britain with respect to fishing rights in the North Atlantic. The other, adjudicated about twenty-five years ago, related to a dispute with the Netherlands over title to an unimportant island. Not by even the widest stretch of the imagination would either issue be considered to have involved danger of hostilities. . . . One may ask whether harm was done by all this effort so meager of measurable good results. Only the harm—a considerable one, I believe—of encouraging and protracting an illusion. This illusion sees great world political issues as susceptible of being translated into questions solvable by legal and judicial means. It entertains the futile belief in strengthening peace by pretending that the factor of force in the image which nations cast on the consciousness of other nations is not really present.[5]

A final related basic objection to the inclination to conduct the international role of the United States with primary emphasis on international legal arrangements and moral commitments concerns itself with what is held to be the frequent and politically costly rigidity of American policy. According to this objection, the legalism and moralism of the American approach tends to make United States policy too uncritically trusting of those who at the moment appear to be acting legally and morally (as the Soviet Union in World War II); too unconditionally destructive toward those (as the Germans and Japanese at the end of World War II) who at the moment have been acting illegally and immorally; and too unpolitically adamant in rejecting opportunities for diplomatic bargaining with nations which, though uncongenial to the United States ideologically, represent power that must be reckoned with.

Although this criticism of the legalistic and moralistic rigidity of American policy has been raised in many circles in the United States as well as abroad, it has been put most thoughtfully and eloquently by the eminent American diplomat and historian, George F. Kennan, in his brilliant study entitled *American Diplomacy, 1900–1950*:

> History has shown that the will and the capacity of individual peoples to contribute to their world environment is constantly changing. It is only logical that the organizational forms (and what

else are such things as borders and governments?) should change with them. The function of a system of international relationships is not to inhibit this process of change by imposing a legal strait jacket upon it but rather to facilitate it: to ease its transitions, to temper the asperities to which it often leads, to isolate and moderate the conflicts to which it gives rise, and to see that these conflicts do not assume forms too unsettling for international life in general. But this is a task for diplomacy, in the most old-fashioned sense of the term. For this, law is too abstract, too inflexible, too hard to adjust to the demands of the unpredictable and the unexpected. . . . Whoever says there is a law must of course be indignant against the lawbreaker and feel a moral superiority to him. And when such indignation spills over into military contest, it knows no bounds short of the reduction of the lawbreaker to the point of complete submissiveness—namely, unconditional surrender. It is a curious thing, but it is true, that the legalistic approach to world affairs, rooted as it unquestionably is in a desire to do away with war and violence, makes violence more enduring, more terrible, and more destructive to political stability than did the older motives of national interest. A war fought in the name of high moral principle finds no early end short of some form of total domination.[6]

International Leadership

If the above critique of the appropriateness and usefulness of America's self-image as the champion of international legality and morality is accepted, the question arises as to what alternative approach might more effectively serve as the inspiration for the role of the United States in world affairs. In considering this question one must begin with the assumption that international leadership is for the United States not only a unique historical opportunity but an inescapable political necessity. It is a unique opportunity in that it offers the United States a momentous possibility: the possibility of aiding the world's peoples in their democratic-industrial evolution and of leaving upon them the imprint not only of American technology and socioeconomic standards but, above all, of the great values of Western civilization that the United States aspires to incorporate and represent.

It is by the same token, however, that international leadership is also for the United States a vital necessity. Only to the extent that America proves successful in exercising international leadership (that is, in influencing the present and future behavior of other peoples) can the United States assure its present and future security and the success and survival of the values and way of life it represents. Failure to exercise its leadership as fully and effectively as possible therefore amounts to nothing less than a betrayal, a betrayal not only of the future of America and its potentialities but also of the future and the potentialities of Western civilization of which the United States is the last remaining first-rate international power.

Within less than a century predominant demographic, industrial, and political power will almost certainly rest in the hands of the world's non-Western peoples. Only by winning these peoples' admiration and gratitude now while they still need us, and only by implanting in them our values while we still enjoy the possibility of influencing them, can we prepare for the day when it is no longer *we* who can aspire to international political leadership, but *they*.

To criticize the American inclination to international legalism and moralism is not to maintain that in order the better to protect its own and the West's future the United States need sacrifice its values today. It means only that if American values are to be meaningful to the peoples whom it is necessary and still possible to lead, these values—whether they concern interstate relations, economic institutions, or political processes—must not be interpreted too literally or narrowly.

In terms of the future of the United States and, indeed, that of the entire world, the highest morality today is not insistence upon this or that institution or type of relationship that in the historical experience of Americans or any other nation happens to have the connotation of being legal or moral. The task, rather, is the building of an international harmony of interests, as a precondition for a global political community, in which, in the future, there finally can be a universally accepted version of what is and what is not legal and moral.

Universal industrialization and democratization are creating both an increasingly felt need for such a universal community as well as the technological, psychological, and cultural means whereby it may be achieved. Yet there is required for the gradual consummation of this development (as there was on a smaller scale in the consolidation of the nation-state) one further factor: the agency of a participating power that can supply the stature, understanding, and resources to help resolve transitional conflicts and to infuse the over-all course of events with a sense of common direction and historical significance. As E. H. Carr has put it, "A new international harmony can be built up only on the basis of an ascendency which is generally accepted as tolerant and unoppressive or, at any rate, as preferable to any practical alternative. To create these conditions is the moral task of the ascendent Power or Powers." [7]

Which of the present superpowers will achieve the greater success in meeting this central challenge of contemporary international politics and morality only the future can tell. Yet Americans owe it to themselves, to the West, and to the entire world to make every necessary adjustment in the theory as well as the practice of their international role to assure that success will be theirs. Not only is the achievement of this success by the United States dictated by American and Western self-interest; it would, in addition, be no more than historically appropriate and just. What the task essentially involves is global direction of the working out of the new universally operative democratic-industrial revolution which originated in the West and which, to date, has achieved its most complete fulfillment in the United States.

The Test of Liberal Democracy

Ironically, however, it is the very completeness of American fulfillment of the social, economic, and political logic of the democratic-industrial revolution that imposes the greatest handicap on Americans in their competition for international leadership. In the Soviet Union only industrialization is approaching a comparable level of success; the development of sovereign popular democracy is still in its earliest infancy. The Soviet government therefore remains free to allocate its resources as it believes the long-range national interest demands; in the United States such allocation must for the most part be left to the short-range operation of the free democratic market. The Soviet government can decree sacrifices in effort and wealth; in the United States such sacrifices must first receive the consent of the freely elected representatives of the people. And in the Soviet Union public opinion in regard to foreign policy can be either ignored or molded to fit whatever decisions government may deem necessary or advisable; in the United States, in contrast, even the most vitally important foreign-policy decisions are ultimately dependent upon the support of free public opinion.

In view of these democratically imposed limitations upon government policy, is the American handicap in the international competition with the much less democratized Soviet Union perhaps an insurmountable one? Are not—at least in the present situation—democracy and the ability to formulate and carry out decisions required for successful international leadership in effect mutually exclusive?

Unfortunately, there is a considerable body of responsible opinion in the United States today which holds that this is indeed the case. According to the conclusion of Walter Lippmann, for example:

> The rule to which there are few exceptions—the acceptance of the Marshall Plan is one of them—is that at the critical junctures, when the stakes are high, the prevailing mass opinion will impose what amounts to a veto upon changing the course on which the government is at the time proceeding. Prepare for war in time of peace? No. It is bad to raise taxes, to unbalance the budget, to take men away from their schools or their jobs, to provoke the enemy. Intervene in a developing conflict? No. Avoid the risk of war. Withdraw from the area of conflict? No. The adversary must not be appeased. Reduce your claims on the area? No. Righteousness cannot be compromised. Negotiate a compromise peace as soon as the opportunity presents itself? No. The aggressor must be punished. Remain armed to enforce the dictated settlement? No. The war is over. . . . Mass opinion has acquired mounting power in this century. It has shown itself to be a dangerous master of decision when the stakes are life and death.[8]

Assuming the correctness of this verdict of Lippmann's, does this then mean that the democratically imposed obstacles to the development of farsighted and flexible American international leadership are insurmountable? It does not. What it does mean is that in foreign as well as domestic affairs, liberal democracy must be recognized to be a much more difficult principle of governmental operation than traditional liberal political philosophy has assumed. Neither individual nor collective man, it is shown once again, possesses within himself the knowledge, understanding, and willingness to sacrifice that those policies capable of assuring his fullest development and survival may in difficult times require. Yet this does not mean that the individual or the mass of the electorate cannot be induced to acquire the concern and knowledge necessary for responsible democratic political participation. It means, simply, that the electorate must be taught and convinced of the facts of public life and of their significance for the nation's and the world's future.

As in regard to liberal democracy's internal problems, however, such teaching and convincing must be publicly responsible. It must not be permitted to fall by default to the representatives of partisan or vested interests. It is the function of liberal democracy's intellectual and cultural leaders, of individuals who are aware of what is at stake, who deeply care about it, and who possess the independence of intellect and the cultural integrity to enable them to resist the lure of mere economic reward and social approval.

To the extent that such liberal democratic leadership is forthcoming, America's internal democratic and industrial progress can be sustained and the momentous challenge of guiding the further working out of the global democratic-industrial revolution successfully met. To the extent that such liberal democratic leadership is not forthcoming, American democracy will fall victim to the same phenomenon—though for different reasons—that twenty-four centuries ago brought about the ruin of Athenian democracy and the squandering of ancient Greece's political potential: the failure of individual and collective public-mindedness and self-discipline.

Wealth, military power, or law cannot substitute for the liberal democratic leadership upon which America's and so much of the rest of the world's future thus depends. It is a matter of nothing less than dedication and will power on the part of individual thinking Americans.

SELECTED BIBLIOGRAPHY

CARR, E. H. *The Twenty Years Crisis*, London, Macmillan, 1946.
KENNAN, GEORGE F. *American Diplomacy, 1900–1950*, Chicago, University of
　　Chicago Press, 1951.
LARSON, ARTHUR. *What We Are For*, New York, Harper, 1959.
LIPPMANN, WALTER. *The Public Philosophy*, Boston, Little, Brown, 1955.
MORGENTHAU, HANS J. *Politics among Nations*, New York, Knopf, 1954.

Notes

CHAPTER 1   The Challenge of Man's Freedom

[1] For a further discussion of the roots of human as contrasted with animal behavior see Felix M. Keesing, *Cultural Anthropology* (New York: Rinehart & Company, 1958), p. 58. See also George Gaylord Simpson, Colin S. Pittendrigh, and Lewis H. Tiffany, *Life: An Introduction to Biology* (New York: Harcourt, Brace and Company, 1957), pp. 241 and 248.

[2] An excellent theoretical consideration of the bases of society may be found in Talcott Parsons and Edward A. Shils, ed., *Toward a General Theory of Action* (Cambridge, Mass.: Harvard University Press, 1951), pp. 3-27.

[3] For a fuller exposition of the functional approach to the nature of society see Marion J. Levy, Jr., *The Structure of Society* (Princeton, N.J.: Princeton University Press, 1952), especially Chap. 4, "The Functional Requisites of Any Society," pp. 149-197.

[4] One of the most respected of recent efforts to come to grips with the problems of methodology in political science may be found in David Easton, *The Political System* (New York: Alfred A. Knopf, Inc., 1953).

[5] For one of the more thought-provoking yet balanced recent discussions of this question see Russell W. Davenport, *The Dignity of Man* (New York: Harper & Brothers, 1955).

CHAPTER 2   The Legacy of the Greek City-State

[1] Quoted in W. G. De Burgh, *The Legacy of the Ancient World* (London: Pelican Books, 1955), I, 142-143.

[2] Quoted in C. E. Robinson, *Hellas: A Short History of Ancient Greece* (Boston: Beacon Press, 1955), pp. 119-120.

[3] Quoted in Edith Hamilton, *The Echo of Greece* (New York: W. W. Norton & Company, 1957), pp. 64-75.

[4] Robinson, *op. cit.*, pp. 139-140.

[5] Plato's *The Republic*, Jowett translation (New York: Random House, Modern Library Paperback), p. 203.

[6] *Ibid.*, Book VI, pp. 227-228.

[7] *Ibid.*, Book VIII, p. 321.

[8] *The Politics of Aristotle*, translated with an introduction by Ernest Barker (New York: Oxford University Press, 1958), Book I, pp. 5 and 6.

[9] *Ibid.*, p. 7.

[10] *Ibid.*, pp. 3 and 12.

[11] *Ibid.*, Book IV, pp. 181-182.

[12] *Ibid.*, Book VII, p. 296.

[13] This is urged most forcefully in *The Republic*, cited above, Book V, pp. 197-199.

CHAPTER 3   The Western Political Orientation

[1] Quoted in William Ebenstein, *Great Political Thinkers* (New York: Rinehart & Company, 1956), p. 159.

[2] W. G. De Burgh, *The Legacy of the Ancient World* (London: Pelican Books, 1955), I, 219.

[3] Quoted in George H. Sabine, *A History of Political Theory* (New York: Henry Holt and Company, 1955), p. 164.

[4] *Ibid.*, pp. 170–171.

[5] Isaiah 49:6.

[6] See the analysis of Jesus' personality and works in C. J. Cadoux, *The Life of Jesus* (London: Pelican Books, 1948).

[7] Quoted in Sabine, *op. cit.*, p. 195.

[8] Romans 13: 1–7.

[9] Martinus Versfeld, *A Guide to the City of God* (New York: Sheed & Ward, 1958), pp. 5–6.

[10] *The City of God by St. Augustine*, translated and edited by Marcus Dods (New York: Hafner Publishing Company, 1948), II, 326–329.

CHAPTER 4   Political Thought of the Middle Ages

[1] Quoted in George H. Sabine, *A History of Political Theory* (New York: Henry Holt and Company, 1955), p. 206.

[2] Ewart Lewis, *Medieval Political Ideas* (New York: Alfred A. Knopf, Inc., 1954), I, 141.

[3] *Ibid.*, pp. 141–142.

[4] Quoted in Lewis, *op. cit.*, pp. 50–51.

[5] Quoted in Robert K. Merton, *Social Theory and Social Structure* (Glencoe, Ill.: The Free Press, 1949), Chap. 14, "Puritanism, Pietism and Science."

[6] See the evaluation of the Thomistic system in John Herman Randall, Jr., *The Role of Knowledge in Western Religion* (Boston: Starr King Press, 1958), pp. 50–59.

[7] Quoted in A. J. Carlyle, *A History of Medieval Theory in the West* (London: William Blackwood & Sons, 1916), III, 94.

[8] *Ibid.*, IV (1922), 201.

[9] *The Statesman's Book of John of Salisbury*, translated with an introduction by John Dickinson (New York: Alfred A. Knopf, Inc., 1927), p. 3.

[10] Quoted in Sabine, *op. cit.*, p. 274.

[11] *Ibid.*, p. 319.

CHAPTER 5   The Reformation and the Nation-State

[1] Ernst Troeltsch, *The Social Teaching of the Christian Churches* (London: George Allen & Unwin, 1931), II, 547.

[2] Quoted in George L. Mosse, *Calvinism—Authoritarian or Democratic?* (New York: Rinehart & Company, 1957), p. 7.

[3] *Ibid.*, p. 3.

[4] *Ibid.*, p. 7.

[5] R. H. Tawney, *Religion and the Rise of Capitalism* (New York: Mentor Books, 1955), p. 98.

[6] *Machiavelli's "The Prince,"* introduction by Christian Gauss (New York: Mentor Books, 1952), p. 138.

[7] *Ibid.*, pp. 101–103.

[8] Quoted in J. L. Brierly, *The Law of Nations* (4th ed.; Oxford: Clarendon Press, 1949), p. 29.

CHAPTER 6   The Philosophy of Liberal Democracy

[1] Quoted in George H. Sabine, *A History of Political Theory* (New York: Henry Holt and Company, 1955), p. 396.

[2] Quoted in Alpheus T. Mason, *Free Government in the Making* (New York: Oxford University Press, 1949), p. 12.

[3] *Ibid.*, p. 13.

[4] *Leviathan*, by Thomas Hobbes, edited with an introduction by Michael Oakeshott (Oxford: Basil Blackwell, Ltd., 1946), p. 112.

[5] *Ibid.*, p. 82.

[6] *The Second Treatise of Civil Government*, by John Locke, edited with an introduction by J. W. Gough (Oxford: Basil Blackwell, Ltd., 1946), p. 5.

[7] *Ibid.*, p. 63.

[8] *Ibid.*, pp. 71–72.

[9] *Ibid.*, pp. 107–108.

[10] See Talcott Parsons, *The Structure of Social Action* (Glencoe, Ill.: The Free Press, 1949), pp. 89–102.

[11] *The Spirit of the Laws*, by Baron de Montesquieu, translated by Thomas Nugent, revised by J. V. Prichard (New York: D. Appleton & Co., 1900), Vol. I, Book XI, Chap. 5, p. 182.

[12] *Rousseau's Social Contract*, translated with an introduction by Henry J. Tozer (London: George Allen & Unwin, 1920), p. 110.

[13] *Ibid.*, p. 123.

[14] *Ibid.*, p. 113.

[15] Quoted in William Ebenstein, *Great Political Thinkers* (New York: Rinehart & Company, 1956), pp. 484–485.

[16] For a somewhat more extensive summary of the ideas of Adam Smith see Robert L. Heilbroner, *The Worldly Philosophers* (New York: Simon and Schuster, 1953), Chap. 3, pp. 33–66.

[17] Ebenstein, *op. cit.*, pp. 670–672.

CHAPTER 7   Political Consequences of Industrialization
             and Democratization

[1] Quoted in William Ebenstein, *Modern Political Thought* (New York: Rinehart & Company, 1954), p. 286.

[2] Quoted in William Ebenstein, *Great Political Thinkers* (New York: Rinehart & Company, 1956), pp. 515–516.

[3] *Ibid.*, pp. 538 and 557–558.

[4] Karl Marx, *Capital*, revised by Ernest Untermann (Chicago: Charles H. Kerr Co., 1909), III, 954–955. For a more extensive analysis and critique of Marxist theory see Alfred G. Meyer, *Marxism: The Unity of Theory and Practice* (Cambridge, Mass.: Harvard University Press, 1954).

[5] See by way of illustration of this point Milovan Djilas, *The New Class* (New York: Frederick A. Praeger, Inc., 1957).

[6] For a fuller discussion of fascism in the perspective of German intellectual and political history see Otto Butz, *Modern German Political Theory* (New York: Doubleday & Company, Doubleday Short Studies in Political Science, 1955).

[7] See above, pp. 96–100.

[8] Adolf Hitler, *Mein Kampf* (Munich: Franz Eher Nachfolger, 1931), p. 501. My translation and italics.

[9] Quoted in Ebenstein, *Modern Political Thought*, p. 525.

[10] John Kenneth Galbraith, *The Affluent Society* (Boston: Houghton Mifflin Company, 1958), pp. 352–356. Reprinted by permission of Houghton Mifflin Company.

[11] Thomas Griffith, *The Waist-High Culture* (New York: Harper & Brothers, 1959), pp. 262–263. Reprinted by permission of Harper & Brothers.

[12] See Lynn White, Jr., ed., *Frontiers of Knowledge* (New York: Harper & Brothers, 1956), Chap. 7, Peter H. Odegard, "Politics—A New Look at *Leviathan*," pp. 94–115.

[13] For a penetrating consideration of the religious ingredient in modern Western individuality see Ernst Troeltsch, *Protestantism and Progress* (Boston: Beacon Press, 1958).

[14] See, for example, Reinhold Niebuhr, *The Self and the Dramas of History* (New York: Charles Scribner's Sons, 1955); David Riesman, *The Lonely Crowd* (New Haven: Yale University Press, 1953); and William H. Whyte, Jr., *The Organization Man* (New York: Simon and Schuster, 1956).

CHAPTER 8   Liberal Democracy in the United States

[1] Robert A. Dahl, *A Preface to Democratic Theory* (Chicago: The University of Chicago Press, 1956), pp. 141–142.

[2] *Ibid.*, p. 145.

[3] Sidney Hyman, *The American President* (New York: Harper & Brothers, 1954), p. 265.

[4] Earl Latham, "The Supreme Court and Civil Liberties," in *American Government Annual, 1958–1959*, Ivan Hinderaker, ed. (New York: Henry Holt and Company, 1958), pp. 23 and 25.

[5] Thomas K. Finletter, *Can Representative Government Do the Job?* (New York: Reynal & Hitchcock, 1945), pp. 2, 7, 8, 9, and 64.

[6] Hyman, *op. cit.*, pp. 307–308.

[7] V. O. Key, *Politics, Parties, and Pressure Groups* (4th ed.; New York: Thomas Y. Crowell and Company, 1958), p. 368.

[8] Stephen K. Bailey, *The Condition of Our Political Parties*. An occasional

paper on the role of the political process in the free society published by
the Fund for the Republic (New York), 1959, p. 4.

[9] *Ibid.*

[10] *Ibid.*

[11] *Ibid.*

[12] *Ibid.*

[13] Robert M. Hutchins, *Is Democracy Possible?* The Fund for the Republic, Bulletin, February, 1959, p. 7.

CHAPTER 9   Great Britain: Parliamentary Democracy

[1] For some stimulating reflections on the relationship between philosophical empiricism and liberal democracy see Bertrand Russell, *Philosophy
and Politics* (London: Cambridge University Press, 1947).

[2] *Independent Labour Party Jubilee Souvenir,* p. 14.

[3] *Ibid.,* p. 17.

[4] See, for example, the pessimistic reflections of Harold J. Laski in his
Parliamentary Government in England (New York: The Viking Press, 1938),
especially pp. 50–52.

[5] Edward R. Pease, *The History of the Fabian Society* (London: The
Fabian Society, 1925), p. 17.

[6] Edmund Burke, "Speech to the Sheriffs of Bristol," *Essays and Orations*
(New York: D. Appleton & Company, 1900), pp. 68–69.

[7] Drew Middleton, *These Are the British* (New York: Alfred A. Knopf,
Inc., 1957), pp. 119–121.

CHAPTER 10   France: The Problem of Authority

[1] John B. Wolf, "The *Élan Vital* of France: A Portrait in Historical
Perspective," in Edward Mead Earle, ed., *Modern France* (Princeton, N.J.:
Princeton University Press, 1951), pp. 21–23.

[2] John E. Sawyer, "Strains in the Social Structure," *ibid.,* p. 302.

[3] André Philip, "France's New Elite," *The New Leader,* June 22, 1959,
p. 13.

[4] David Schoenbrun, *As France Goes* (New York: Harper & Brothers,
1957), p. 89.

[5] Herbert Luethy, *France against Herself* (New York: Frederick A.
Praeger, Inc., 1955), p. 159.

[6] André Philip, "De Gaulle and French Democrats," *The New Leader,*
November 3, 1958, pp. 5–6. Reprinted by permission of *The New Leader.*

CHAPTER 11   Germany: Democracy versus Nationalism

[1] For a fuller consideration of the background of German politics see
A. J. P. Taylor, *The Course of German History* (New York: Coward-McCann,
Inc., 1946).

[2] Quoted in Otto Butz, *Modern German Political Theory* (New York:

Doubleday & Company, Doubleday Short Studies in Political Science, 1955), p. 20.

[3] Quoted in J. P. Mayer, *Max Weber and German Politics* (London: Faber & Faber, Ltd., 1943), pp. 58–59.

[4] Butz, *op. cit.*, p. 32.

[5] Quoted in Butz, *op. cit.*, p. 56.

CHAPTER 12   Soviet Russia: Government from Revolution

[1] Hans Kohn, ed., *The Mind of Modern Russia* (New Brunswick, N.J.: Rutgers University Press, 1955), p. 24.

[2] From *Russia without Stalin* by Edward Crankshaw. Copyright 1956 by Edward Crankshaw. Reprinted by permission of The Viking Press, Inc., New York.

[3] Quoted in Merle Fainsod, *How Russia Is Ruled* (Cambridge, Mass.: Harvard University Press, 1955), p. 40.

[4] Quoted in Crankshaw, *op. cit.*, pp. 143–144. See also Nathan Leites, *The Operational Code of the Politburo* (New York: McGraw-Hill Book Company, 1951), Chap. 18, "Resistance to Attack," pp. 77–81.

[5] George F. Kennan, *Russia, the Atom and the West* (New York: Harper & Brothers, 1958), pp. 5–7. Reprinted by permission of Harper & Brothers and Oxford University Press, London.

[6] *Ibid.*, pp. 7–8.

CHAPTER 13   Politics of Underdeveloped Countries

[1] Quoted in John Gunther, *Inside Africa* (New York: Harper & Brothers, 1955), p. 368.

[2] Melville J. Herkovits, "The Problem of Adapting Societies to New Tasks," in Bert F. Hoselitz, ed., *The Progress of Underdeveloped Areas* (Chicago: The University of Chicago Press, 1952), pp. 91–92.

[3] Samuel P. Hayes, Jr., "Personality and Culture Problems of Point IV," *ibid.*, p. 208.

[4] *Ibid.*

[5] *Ibid.*, p. 210.

[6] Thomas L. Hodgkin, "The African Renaissance," *West African Review*, October, 1957, pp. 941–942.

[7] *Ibid.*

[8] R. N. Duchein, "Different Conceptions of Pan-Africanism," *The African and Colonial World*, January, 1957, pp. 5–6.

[9] Myron Wiener, "India's Political Problems: The Longer View," *The Western Political Quarterly*, June, 1956, pp. 284–285. Reprinted by permission of *The Western Political Quarterly*.

[10] *Ibid.*, p. 291.

[11] Quoted in Hans J. Morgenthau, *In Defense of the National Interest* (New York: Alfred A. Knopf, Inc., 1951), pp. 14–16. (Italics added.)

CHAPTER 14   The United States and World Politics

[1] Quoted in Hans J. Morgenthau, *Politics among Nations* (New York: Alfred A. Knopf, Inc., 1954), pp. 169–170.

[2] *Ibid.*, p. 221.

[3] Walter Lippmann, *The Public Philosophy* (Boston: Little, Brown and Company, 1955), pp. 12–13.

[4] E. H. Carr, *The Twenty Years Crisis* (London: Macmillan & Co., 1946), pp. 82–88.

[5] Charles Burton Marshall, *The Limits of Foreign Policy* (New York: Henry Holt and Company, 1954), pp. 111–112.

[6] George F. Kennan, *American Diplomacy, 1900–1950* (Chicago: The University of Chicago Press, 1951), pp. 98–101.

[7] Carr, *op. cit.*, p. 236.

[8] Lippmann, *op. cit.*, pp. 19–20.

Index